TEACH WRITING WELL

HOW TO ASSESS WRITING
INVIGORATE INSTRUCTION
AND RETHINK REVISION

Ruth Culham

Stenhouse
PUBLISHERS

www.stenhouse.com

Stenhouse Publishers

www.stenhouse.com

Library of Congress Cataloging-in-Publication Data

Names: Culham, Ruth, author.
Title: Teach writing well : how to assess writing, invigorate instruction, and rethink revision / Ruth Culham.
Description: Portland, Maine : Stenhouse Publishers, [2018] | Includes bibliographical references. |
Identifiers: LCCN 2017049035 (print) | LCCN 2018001941 (ebook) | ISBN 9781625311184 (ebook) | ISBN 9781625311177 (pbk. : alk. paper)
Subjects: LCSH: English language--Composition and exercises--Study and teaching (Elementary) | English language--Composition and exercises--Evaluation. | Composition (Language arts)--Study and teaching (Elementary) | Composition (Language arts)--Evaluation.
Classification: LCC LB1576 (ebook) | LCC LB1576 .C8515 2018 (print) | DDC 372.62/3--dc23
LC record available at https://lccn.loc.gov/2017049035

Cover design, interior design, and typesetting by

Beth Ford, Glib Communications & Design

Manufactured in the United States of America

PRINTED ON 30% PCW
RECYCLED PAPER

25 24 23 22 21 20 19   9 8 7 6 5 4 3 2 1

For Sam, always

CONTENTS

PART I: *Read the Writing*

PART II: *Teach the Writer*

Acknowledgments

Writing and sharing ideas with teachers about teaching writing give me joy. Through writing I have built a life with friends and colleagues who sustain me every day. And it is through writing that I survive the passing of my beautiful son, Sam. Maybe knowing firsthand the power that writing brings to my life is what drives me to make sure every student has the ability to write well in order to navigate the streams, rivers, and oceans of what lies ahead, too.

To that end, I want to thank many people who have been key to my writing life. To Terry Cooper and Wendy Murray, who were the first to consider my ideas publishable. To Ray Coutu, who shaped them and then shaped me into a writer and, along the way, became one of the most treasured people in my life. To Laura Robb, who shines a bright light on what matters most every time we speak. To Libby Jachles, who is my sounding board and dearest friend. To Debbie Stewart, who is the best teacher and personal cheerleader—ever. To Bridey Monterossi, who introduces children to writing lives through her music classes—and knows the best happy hours in Portland. To Judy Hood and Marlee Krohn, who listen, make me laugh, and supply the wine and pie. To Dulcy and Prim, my two kitties, who run me and the house—no question.

But most of all, because of *Teach Writing Well*, I want to shower appreciation on Chris Downey, Beth Ford, and Tori Bachman. Chris, taking a book and editing it, line by line, to showcase the ideas and make it read smoothly, is an amazing talent. I couldn't be more grateful for the thoughtful consideration that went into editing every page. Beth, your talent and eye for style and design blow me away—always have, always will. I'm so proud to have your work on the cover and layout of this book. Tori, you are a magnificent editor and friend. You question, support, encourage, and make me a better writer (and person)—and you do it all with grace and consideration for me, the writing process, and your needs as the publisher. No small feat. Thank you and Stenhouse for making sure this book was given the air to breathe.

Introduction

Chances are you picked up this book because you are already teaching writing to your students and want to know how you can do so even more successfully. I want to help you with that. I want to show you how the traits of writing can build your understanding of your students' strengths and challenges as writers, how traits—coupled with revision in the writing process—can add depth and power to your students' writing, and, most important, how you can all come to truly enjoy writing together.

How can you teach writing well? After many, many years of struggling with teaching writing myself, I have learned from students and colleagues what works and how to set up a writing classroom for success without overwhelming students and teachers alike. I've come to believe that the traits and how they work within the writing process are a winning combination.

Everywhere I go, I hear how discouraged teachers feel as they approach the teaching of writing. What makes it so hard? For teachers, often it's assessing students' writing and then finding the words to communicate what needs work; for students, often it's learning how to read their writing and then revise it to show their best thinking. Traits provide a solution to both of these challenges by giving you and your students succinct, clear language that describes specific craft elements. I'm going to show you how to read students' writing with traits in mind so you can get to know them as thinkers and learners. Then I'm going to show you how to teach students how to use traits to produce their best writing. You can teach writing well.

Here you'll get guidance, tools, and ideas.

This book focuses specifically on how to keep adding depth to students' writing through revision—which, believe it or not, begins with formative assessment. Here we pick up once students have generated some writing, because often that's when you and your students need the most support. Here you'll get guidance, tools, and ideas about how to help your students go from drafts to smoother, more polished, and thoughtful writing using the traits and the writing process. And here you'll learn specific strategies with plenty of examples and practice to help you conquer revision. Really. And as a bonus, the ideas here fit within any curriculum, any classroom, any grade, at any time.

The Meeting That Changed Everything

Years ago, when I was still working at Education Northwest as a researcher in the assessment division, I screwed up the courage to contact Donald Graves, the pioneering author, professor, and researcher of writing process instruction, and boldly asked for a face-to-face meeting at the upcoming International Reading Association conference. I desperately wanted to know what he thought of using assessment as a guide to revision—how the work I was committed to might dovetail with his seminal research and practice in writing process. I knew, even then, that revision was the tough nut to crack, and I wanted validation for the direction my work was taking. I don't think I slept the night before our meeting—the prospect of meeting someone I'd considered a mentor in person for a few precious minutes was exhilarating. And humbling. And scary—what if he scoffed at my work? Or didn't see the potential of linking the writing process, especially revision, and the traits?

What you have here is the secret to unlocking revision.

I arrived early, heart in my throat, a huge stack of handouts for workshops that I had created in a big folder. At that time, I didn't have a book to share—just early thinking from workshop materials. Don greeted me warmly, asked a few questions, then took the stack of precious papers from me and thumbed through them. His eyes were intent as he scanned the pages, probing me with thoughtful inquiries such as "How do you see this work fitting into the writing process?" And, "What do teachers say about these traits and how they use them?"

We talked a little about what I thought was powerful about the traits of writing: the shared vocabulary that writers and their teachers can use in the classroom as a guide for revision. After what felt like a minute on one hand but a lifetime on the other, Don gave me a serious look, glanced at his watch, and asked if he could take the papers and review them more thoroughly overnight.

The next meeting was a life changer. Don Graves, the master of writing instruction, summed up his thoughts about the traits very simply. He said (and I wrote this down so I'd never forget), "What you have here is the secret to unlocking revision. This work has the potential to change and enhance how the writing process is taught." I kid you not: I swooned.

This, then, has been my focus and mission ever since: how to use writing assessment to show teachers what to look for in student work so they can teach students how to revise. I wanted to figure out how to move from Don's word, *potential*, to the reality of everyday practice. The book in your hands has been years in the making, a result of sharing and experimenting with ideas and strategies in classrooms across the country and world.

Changing the Way We Teach Writing

Here is what I believe: You have to explore, talk, think, and question to write well. You have to want to find out more, consider different angles, and read what others think on the same topic—because you are curious. Writing is, after all, a process of discovery. It's an intellectual journey of exploration.

It should not be a simple restating of what's already known, which often happens in prompt/response writing in schools. Most often, that prompted response is graded on how much of the teacher-provided information is included and whether it's in the precise form assigned. Students learn to write for the expected outcome, not to communicate their own thinking. They write to show how well they replicate a given format or regurgitate factual knowledge.

It's hard, if not impossible, to motivate students to write under such circumstances. And although there may be a small place for this kind of writing somewhere in the universe of a student's experience, we're moving away from it like it's a fertilizer factory on a hot summer day in today's world of increasingly high expectations.

Writing brings into a student's life an active process of study and scrutiny of something that fascinates them. That's powerful, lifelong learning stuff. I shout with glee if I read a paper where a student has dared to challenge my thinking, come at a familiar topic in a fresh way, or expose his or her thinking by taking risks. If our students are to write more deeply and thoughtfully—digging into the depths of an idea and putting all their energies into discovering something new to say—then we have to ditch the notion that there are only "right," fact-based answers in writing.

George Hillocks Jr. was a brilliant researcher, author, and driving force in the field of writing assessment and instruction. I appreciate his words about how hard it is to teach well:

> The teaching of writing is fraught with difficulties. Teaching well, in my experience and that of my students, can be very time-consuming, demanding, frustrating, and, given institutional constraints, sometimes infuriating. . . . [However,] when students make gains as writers, the gains are likely to affect other educational endeavors. And for teachers, the joy of seeing students create some new part of themselves, and do it well, washes the difficulties to insignificance and provides the impetus to try. (1995, 217)

You have to explore, talk, think, and question to write well.

To teach writing well, we must revolutionize our own thinking about the possibilities of what "good" writing looks like. All the craft knowledge in the world will not make you the writing teacher you yearn to be if you don't begin by thinking big, thinking creatively, thinking resourcefully. What difference does it make, for instance, whether a young writer knows how to use pronouns and their antecedents until he or she has developed a meaty idea that requires grammatical clarification in the first place?

We may offer valid excuses for why students do not excel in writing, but excuses don't help teachers teach or students write better. Consider what happens when we don't make the changes needed to produce positive outcomes. What could provide better evidence than the eighth- and twelfth-grade writing results from the National Center for Educational Statistics (2012), in which just 27 percent of US eighth graders performed at or above the proficient level? And of that group, only 3 percent performed at the advanced level. Even more discouraging (if that's possible), the twelfth graders performed the same: 27 percent at or above proficient, and only 3 percent advanced. In both cases, the bigger number is what looms in our minds: 73 percent of eighth and twelfth graders are not proficient writers. Horrifying.

I know people are working on teaching writing. I see it everywhere I go. But how we are teaching is called into question by results like these. There is a lot of denial going on in the teaching world: *"I use this outdated method, but my kids really like it"*; *"I know the research says otherwise, but I think kids learn grammar best with worksheets. They don't mind them"*; *"Our kids need to be able to write a good five-paragraph essay by the time they hit middle school."* We have to acknowledge that the way we've been doing business for more than a hundred years is not working so we can find the courage to change. Professor Dumbledore told Harry Potter much the same thing: *"You have to make a choice between what is right and what is easy"* (Rowling 2002, 724).

Getting to the place where creativity and imagination are critical parts of teaching and learning, right along with skills development, requires new thinking. This requires latitude and respect for the young writer. We must call upon the fascinations of our students if we are ever going to get them to write beneath the surface of a topic. It's time to abandon

- worksheets;
- canned, formulaic organizational structures that stifle thinking;
- generic, whole-class assignments;
- superficial responses to student writing; and
- obsessive test prep.

Instead, we must develop

- writing classrooms that are joyous and rigorous;
- intentional teaching and a focus on what matters;
- purposeful conversations about writing that lead to revision;
- inspiration for what excites us from what we read, see, hear, and want to know more about;
- and confidence that if students know how to write, they will soar on any test.

When it comes to teaching writing well, *"the teacher has high expectations for herself or himself, and in turn has high expectations for the kids. And nothing stops them,"* explained Donald Graves in an interview based on his observations of exemplary writing classrooms. In other words, if we expect more, both we and our students achieve more.

What are some traditional writing practices that we've outgrown? *Pause and Consider*
Consider where you struggle with your teaching and when it feels most comfortable. What is your favorite teaching strategy that produces results in students of all skill levels in writing?

You have no say in the preparation students receive before they are assigned to your class; your influence begins the day you meet. Yet, by the end of your journey together, your students can be more competent, skilled, and thoughtful writers. There is a certain feeling I get in classrooms where writing is taught as a process and not a destination. It starts with questions: teachers in successful writing classrooms ask a lot of them. They encourage curiosity and the need to find answers. Socrates is credited with saying, *"Wonder is the beginning of wisdom."* Moving forward in writing instruction is a matter of welcoming wonder into your classroom—first through a renewed understanding of what's possible and then by transferring that wonder to your students. In doing so, you empower them to become thoughtful, imaginative writers.

The Power of Choice

Accomplished writing teachers read their students. They ask themselves: *What do my students question? What fascinates them? What do they talk about? What lights them up?* Once they tap into this never-ending wellspring of curiosity, they gain energy, and so do their students. With that energy comes the willingness to learn new skills and strategies to make writing stronger.

It really boils down to this: students must want to write, learn how to write, and explore what to write. In this standards-driven era, we have overlooked the all-important "want to write" part. Most students I know don't get to pick their topics; topics are assigned to the class wholesale. Why don't we give our students enough mental elbow room to learn to write their own sentences, come up with their own ideas, and express them in their own way? I walk into a school that struggles with writing and I see samples of student work posted on the wall that all begin the same way. *"One important thing I learned from Pam Muñoz Ryan's book Echo is:* _____ ." Or, *"I think the Internet is a great invention because:* _____ ." I can sum up this kind of writing in one technical word: *ick.* How can a writer recover from a start like this? If writing is thinking, this approach doesn't move students toward that goal.

We should help students explore ways to begin that grab the reader's interest. Perhaps the writer could share something intriguing that stands out to him or her about a book, or provide an interesting tidbit of information about the Internet before laying out a claim or position. Do we really have such little faith in students that we must begin their sentences for them? Or pick their topics every time? Surely they can do this for themselves if they are shown models, offered support, and given the opportunity to try even if their writing isn't perfect.

I believe the person holding the pen is the one doing the learning. So, when we do too much of the thinking for students, we deprive them of learning how to think for themselves. Sentence starters, canned formulas, whole-class topics—we should not do these things, ever. Here's what Mem Fox has to say on this subject:

> You and I don't engage in meaningless writing exercises in real life——we're far too busy doing the real thing. And by doing the real thing we constantly learn how to do the real thing better. (1993, 4)

Motivating students to write has a great deal to do with giving them real choice. One of our goals, then, is to help them discover what they want to say, what they need to say—so they "ache with caring" (Fox 1993, 5). We want to get them hooked on writing so they can do the difficult, thinking work of revising and editing. Finding the way in through student-selected topics is part of the solution.

Many students don't think they have much to say, but that's just not true. Showing students powerful writing on small, seemingly mundane topics from writers they respect can release that fear: an early morning fishing trip with Dad, as described in *A Different Pond* by Bao Phi; a walk down the street at night to notice neighborhood windows lighting up, one by one, as in *Windows* by Julia Denos; a thoughtful exploration of a house and what it is made of in *This House, Once,* by Deborah Freedman. These simple seeds of ideas became magnificent picture books.

Beware Perfectionism

We must always teach with understanding that students are the key players in this process—they are smart, they want to succeed, and they aren't scared of hard work if it is meaningful. They have to be freed from the notion that their writing will turn out perfectly every time. With this understanding will come the willingness to revise. I believe this.

> They have to be freed from the notion that their writing will turn out perfectly every time.

Bottom line: perfection isn't the goal; learning is the goal. Anne Lamott puts it this way: *"Perfectionism is the voice of the oppressor, the enemy of the people. It will keep you cramped and insane your whole life, and it is the main obstacle between you and a shitty first draft"* (1994, 28). So many times it's getting students to start writing that is such a big hurdle—are they, perhaps, unwittingly intimidated by perfectionism? Lamott continues

> I think perfectionism is based on the obsessive belief that if you run carefully enough, hitting each stepping-stone just right, you won't have to die. The truth is that you will die anyway and that a lot of people who aren't even looking at their feet are going to do a whole lot better than you, and have a lot more fun while they're doing it. (1994, 28)

Kids need time to develop as writers. There's a reason they're in school for so long—every year they are exposed to more, learn more, and accomplish more. But if we are honest, important learning is never finished. I continue to learn about writing and teaching writing to this day. The same is true for you and your students. Perfectionism is not helpful for teaching writing well; it is far more realistic and affirming to think of each day's progress as steps toward significant goals.

Pause and Consider

Read Anne Lamott's quote and talk about "shitty first drafts" and what she is trying to help us understand about the writing process. Replace the word *die* with *revise* in the second quote and you'll get a sense of where students are coming from when they write—or when any writer writes.

Read the Writing to Teach the Writer

Learning to teach writing is a lifelong journey. I'm forty years into this trek—always learning, always listening, always trying to figure out the best way to teach. I've got the writing traits, writing process, writing modes, and writing workshop model by my side—what I've come to call the "4Ws." I know the secrets to teaching writing lie on the shoulders of these giants of highly effective writing practice. I have learned, too, that reading student writing truly unlocks the secrets to revision.

In my lifetime of education, both on the front line and in the professional development bunker, it's become clear that little works for every student in every situation. There is one notable exception, however: I've learned how to read, really read, student writing. It's the secret Portkey that reveals everything about them as writers. Individual students and their words become the priority, and it's easier to understand why teaching writing can't be boiled down to simple, one-size-fits-all methods. Reading the writing provides the formative assessment you need to make instructional decisions that fit each student.

Every time I read a piece by a student, I want to talk to him to find out what he was thinking and why he made certain choices, and nudge him toward the next iteration. I've learned to read the writing for each of the traits—ideas, organization, voice, word choice, sentence fluency, conventions, and presentation—and their key qualities. (See page 18 for details.) I see it all, but over time I've taught myself how to zero in on one quality at a time and dig into it with the student. I learned this from the students themselves. When I become more focused in my feedback and more deliberate in my suggestions, they thrive. Comments such as *"Whatever"* give way to *"I hadn't thought of that"* and *"Okay, I'll try."* And even *"What do you think would happen if I did this?"* Sweet.

> The ultimate goal, however, is not to learn to trait—it's to learn how to write.

The traits play a key role in providing terra firma for writing assessment and instruction. The ultimate goal, however, is not to learn to trait—it's to learn how to write. Never lose sight of that.

 Assessing student writing leads to purposeful revision.

In that spirit, this book is designed to help you look at and respond to your students' writing in a whole new way to help them realize the possibilities for their work. We'll use the traits as a framework, because they work beautifully in this respect, but we'll also consider the different purposes for which we write: to explain (informational), to tell a story (narrative), and to convince using reason and logic (opinion/argument). And, of course, we'll explore the teaching possibilities that come from learning how to read the writing—closing the loop on the teaching, learning, and assessing cycle. Assessing student writing leads to purposeful revision.

I'm also very purposefully drawing research and thinking from the great giants in our field, such as Don Graves, Don Murray, Anne Lamott, George Hillocks Jr., Mem Fox, and others. Many younger teachers have yet to be touched and forever changed by these educators' profound understandings of how children learn to write. I'm honored to feature some of their seminal philosophies here and build on them to reach teachers and students in today's writing classrooms.

To accomplish this, to help you to teach writing well, this book is divided into two parts: 1) Read the Writing and 2) Teach the Writer. In Part 1, we'll explore in depth the traits model as a formative assessment tool to read what students have written, explore their thinking, and make meaningful, productive comments in feedback and conferences that lead to wise revision and editing decisions. The emphasis will be on guiding students to revise since that is, by far, the most challenging area for teachers and students alike. We'll also explore the rhetorical modes for writing and their influence on students' thinking about what they write.

In Part 2, we'll investigate how to take what we've learned from reading the writing and design strategic lessons to teach the writer. We'll tackle the revision beast and help teachers and students find the sweet spot in what historically has been a difficult area to teach and learn. Throughout the book, there will be examples of student writing to show the impact of informed instruction, as well as "Pause and Consider" moments to encourage pivotal content discussions with colleagues.

Before I was a writing teacher, I was a school librarian. I have always known the power of children's books for showing students all that is possible. One of my favorite chapters, Chapter 7, focuses on reading the work of mentor authors to help students learn writing craft—in other words, how to read like a writer. Why not inspire students with the great writers whose words fill our bookcases and brains? Think of these precious resources as a parliament of wise owls standing side by side with you as you take flight teaching writing.

Teach Writing Well allows us to pull best practices together and see writing with new eyes, creating a synergy between knowing what students can do and learning to teach revision in entirely new ways. I believe it's possible to make this shift without overwhelming you or your students, and that's as important to me as it is to you. It begins with reading the writing. I want to help you achieve a lofty goal: to be the teacher who influences students' perception of themselves as writers for the rest of their lives.

It begins with reading the writing !

PART I

Read the Writing

I'm a big believer in researcher and writer Frank Smith's wise thinking, *"A probing [writing] teacher will try to find out what a child does know, and build upon that"* (1975, 45). This is the promise of formative assessment: to ferret out strengths and weaknesses in the developing piece so you can help the writer build on the good and strengthen the rest.

The richest, most mind-blowing professional learning sessions I've ever been part of happen when teachers are given student writing to read, discuss, and come to agreement about using a well-crafted scoring guide. It forces every reader to go deeper into their understanding of the writing—past conventions, past neatness, past topic sentences and supporting details. It's also the least sexy-sounding part of what we do as writing teachers, but I firmly believe this is the secret sauce that makes teaching writing palatable.

Learning how to read the writing

- puts us on the same page—one teacher to the next, one grade to the next;
- establishes why we need a common vocabulary for discussing and teaching writing that both teachers and students can understand and embrace;
- allows us to make meaningful, specific comments to students about what is going well and what can still use some work;
- and provides a road map for instruction.

I firmly believe this is the secret sauce that makes teaching writing palatable.

Imagine teaching in a school where staff and students model themselves after their real conviction—together. It's our responsibility to teach ourselves first and then to share that understanding using concepts that are just right for writers at different ages. Once we "get it," we can put students in a powerful position to know how to read the writing themselves and—through gradual, thoughtful release—develop skills and confidence, take more responsibility for their learning, and own the personas of writers. Frank Smith echoes this sentiment: *"A child does much more than make sense of language, he uses it. As soon as he learns any part of language, that part becomes a tool for his learning more about language and more about everything else"* (1975, 183). What higher standard could we set than independence through shared understanding of how writing works? It's possible, and it all begins with reading the writing.

In Part 1, I'll lead you through the formative assessment process, beginning first with the traits—the language of writers. We'll explore where they come from, how they work, and how to use them. In the next chapter, we'll work through examples of student work—reading them with a writer's eye and examining how to transfer what we've learned to students' writing and learning. From there we'll examine the modes of writing (narrative, expository/informational, and persuasive/opinion-argument) and how these purposes for writing are key components of the writer's world. And finally, we'll explore student self-assessment and conferring and their power to transform how students view the writing process.

1
Thinking Back and Thinking Forward

The year was 1985. *Dynasty* was all the rage on television, and ridiculously big shoulder pads took over women's fashion. Rubik's Cubes puzzled us while Smurfs toys outsold Star Wars and Mickey Mouse. Video arcades were the "in" place to hang out, but Nintendo was gaining popularity by the day. We asked ourselves, *"Where's the beef?"* while listening to Wham's *"Wake Me Up Before You Go-Go."* Ronald Reagan was president, and *The Breakfast Club* and *Back to the Future* stormed the box office. And, certainly not least, the traits of writing were born.

In fact, the 1980s were a boom time for writing instruction. Thanks to the groundbreaking work of Donald Graves, Donald Murray, Frank Smith, Lucy Calkins, and other teacher-researchers, we came to understand that writing is a recursive process of thinking, writing, reading, thinking, revising, reading, thinking, editing, reading, thinking, and publishing.

The traits were a breakthrough for writing assessment and were eagerly embraced by teachers right from their inception. But, based on what I observed from my own teaching, I began to consider the potential of traits not only to assess drafts but also to address revision—a huge hurdle in the writing process. It turns out that the road to revision is paved with the traits. (More on this in later chapters.)

Using the traits as a framework to discuss strengths and weaknesses in writing made it possible for my students to begin making wise choices about

> It turns out that the road to revision is paved with the traits.

what to do next with their writing—choices that were previously unknown to them. It became obvious that writing well required more than just getting something down on paper. They had to revise. Revision, Donald Murray taught us, "is not the end of the writing process, but the beginning. First emptiness, then terror, at last one word, then a few words, a paragraph, a page, finally a draft that can be revised" (2013, 1).

Roald Dahl, famed children's author, echoes this thinking in his widely quoted observation, "Good writing is essentially revision. I am positive of this." Although every writer takes a somewhat different path to develop a piece during revision, we use the same thinking process no matter the purpose for writing: narrative, informational, or opinion/argument.

Sometimes the best way to represent big ideas is through a visual image. As we think about how to use the traits to teach revision, it's important to remember the end game: smart thinking. Bryan Mathers got it right in his "visual thinkery" image, shown in Figure 1.1, which represents the difference between assessment for learning's sake and assessment for grading. If the purpose of writing were simply to receive a grade, then revision wouldn't matter so much. We could teach students the "rules" of language in our writing classes and leave it at that; they could follow any old recipe and churn out decent yet forgettable soup. But we know that the greater purpose of school is to prepare young minds for an unknown world—to teach them how to recognize a problem and find a solution. We want them to be able to taste the soup as they're cooking it, adding a dash of paprika or a pinch of cinnamon as needed to make it unique and memorable.

Figure 1.1 *The difference between formative and summative assessment.* © *Bryan Mathers. Reprinted with permission. http://bryanmmathers.com.*

Revision is about solving problems in writing. It's about applying both craft knowledge and skill in creative and purposeful ways to make writing work. It's thinking and rethinking, as many times as necessary. Again, Donald Murray revealed a critical insight: "As we read during revision, we deal with a complex blend of overlapping concerns. It is helpful, especially in the beginning, to develop your own checklist of the elements that contribute to voice" (2013, 187-188).

What are those "overlapping concerns," and where is that checklist? This was the rallying cry of writing teachers during the mid-1980s. To answer these questions, educators rolled up their sleeves and got to work. The truth was, we had no effective tools to read the writing; the result of that call to action was the "traits of writing" model. As we move through this book together, you'll learn much more about how the traits help demystify revision, the powerhouse phase of the writing process.

The Traits of Writing Model

The traits of writing model, as we know it today, has roots in the Beaverton School District in Beaverton, Oregon. As a teacher, I joined (or, more accurately, was drafted into) the district assessment committee and helped to develop, try out, and revise the traits model to assess student writing. In the years that followed, I created materials to support other teachers as they helped students learn how to write. During the process of establishing the essential link between assessment and instruction, the road to revision began to materialize. I followed the lead of the traits and found an on-ramp to one of the trickiest parts of teaching writing: revision. I realized it all starts with understanding how to read student writing, apply common terminology and criteria, and articulate what is strong and what needs more work in each student's piece.

What follows are the meat and potatoes of the traits. By carefully defining the traits and their recently refined key qualities, we create a shared language to talk about writing. This language, and how we use it in the classroom to teach and learn, is the core of the work. Consider how knowing what is going on in a piece of writing—really "reading the writing"—affects instruction. For example, if Kanisha is excited about her idea when she talks about it, but it's coming across as pretty "blah" when written, we know she needs to work on voice and word choice. Or, if Michael stumbles or falters when he reads his piece aloud, we know to focus on sentence fluency. To be helpful, to make our conversations with students as useful as possible, we need a specific, common language that clarifies what and how students are doing in their writing—a language that follows them as student writers from year to year. This is how we help them take the next logical steps to revise their writing regardless of where they begin.

$\mathcal{P}$*ause and* $\mathcal{C}$*onsider* What are the natural outcomes of using shared terminology across grades and schools when teaching writing? What are some of the pitfalls if we don't?

What's a Key Quality?

As first conceived, each trait was defined as a core feature of writing. They were described on the scoring guide using bullets and short phrases at different levels of accomplishment in order to match student writing to different performance zones. After using scoring guides for more than twenty years and taking in feedback from users to continue tweaking them, I found that a major refinement to clarify definitions of the traits was in order. Enter the key qualities.

The definition of each trait now includes four key qualities, written in complete sentences. A trait, after all, is a big place in writing. If a teacher wants to focus on organization, for example, the question becomes *What part of organization do you want to tackle? The beginning, the sequence and transition words, the body, the ending?* Lessons and writing activities should focus on one of these areas at a time, not all four.

Using sentences instead of bulleted lists and phrases makes it much easier for users to find the specific language that matches student writing performance. And anything that makes this process easier is always welcome.

Revision of the scoring guides to include key qualities is a major development for the traits. You'll see just how important they are to assessment and instruction as the chapters unfold.

Definitions of the Traits and Their Key Qualities

What follows is a down-and-dirty guide to the seven traits as well as the key qualities within each trait. The first five traits—ideas, organization, voice, word choice, and sentence fluency—are critical during revision, whereas the final two—conventions and presentation—are most important during editing and creating the final draft. Consider this a starting point; if you want to dig deeper into the history and development of traits, there are plenty of free resources on my website (www.culhamwriting.com). You'll be able to practice using traits and key qualities for assessment, conferring, and planning instruction as you move through the rest of this book on your own or with colleagues. And you'll start to understand how traits and key qualities can have a strong impact on student revision—how students can internalize traits and develop as confident writers over time.

Please keep in mind, too, that in this book we're focusing on writing that is a paragraph or more in length. You can find scoring guides and key qualities "lite" for less-experienced writers on the primary scoring guides available for free download on my website. A fourth or fifth grader who is new to writing in English or struggling for other reasons might benefit from feedback on the G1-2 continuum, for instance. Or, a kindergartner who is a fluent writer—using sentences and demonstrating skill by expressing ideas in multiple sentences—might have grown out of the developmental continuum and into the one for writers who can create a cohesive paragraph. As we score writing samples together in Chapter 2, you'll see how matching the feedback for the writer to their current level of writing skill is beneficial. For now, let's get acquainted with the traits and their key qualities.

Ideas

The piece's content; its central message and details that support that message.

A. Finding a Topic

The writer offers a clear, central theme or a simple, original story line that is memorable.

B. Focusing the Topic

The writer narrows the theme or story line to create a piece that is clear, tight, and manageable.

C. Developing the Topic

The writer provides enough critical evidence to support the theme and shows insight into the topic, or he or she tells the story in a fresh way through an original, unpredictable plot.

D. Using Details

The writer offers credible, accurate details that create pictures in the reader's mind, from the beginning of the piece to the end. Those details provide the reader with evidence of the writer's knowledge about and/or experience with the topic.

Organization

The internal structure of the piece—the thread of logic, the pattern of meaning.

A. Creating the Lead

The writer grabs the reader's attention from the start and leads him or her into the piece naturally. The writer entices the reader, providing a tantalizing glimpse of what is to come.

B. Using Sequence Words and Transition Words

The writer includes a variety of carefully selected sequence words (such as *later*, *then*, and *meanwhile*) and transition words (such as *however*, *also*, and *clearly*), which are placed wisely to guide the reader through the piece by showing how ideas progress, relate, and/or diverge.

C. Structuring the Body

The writer creates a piece that is easy to follow by fitting details together logically. He or she slows down to spotlight important points or events and speeds up to move the reader along.

D. Ending with a Sense of Resolution

The writer sums up his or her thinking in a natural, thoughtful, and convincing way. He or she anticipates and answers any lingering questions the reader may have, providing a strong sense of closure.

Voice

The tone of the piece—the personal stamp of the writer, which is achieved through a strong understanding of purpose and audience.

A. Establishing a Tone

The writer cares about the topic, and it shows. The writing is expressive and compelling. The reader feels the writer's conviction, authority, and integrity.

B. Conveying the Purpose

The writer makes clear his or her reason for creating the piece. He or she offers a point of view that is appropriate for the mode (narrative, expository, or persuasive), which compels the reader to read on.

C. Creating a Connection to the Audience

The writer speaks in a way that makes the reader want to listen. The writer has considered what the reader needs to know and the best way to convey it by sharing his or her fascination, feelings, and opinions about the topic.

D. Taking Risks to Create Voice

The writer expresses ideas in new ways, which makes the piece interesting and original. The writing sounds like the writer because of his or her use of distinctive, just-right words and phrases.

Word Choice

The specific vocabulary the writer uses to convey meaning and enlighten the reader.

A. Applying Strong Verbs

The writer uses many "action words," giving the piece punch and pizzazz. He or she has stretched to find lively verbs that add energy to the piece.

B. Selecting Striking Words and Phrases

The writer uses many finely honed words and phrases. His or her creative and effective use of literary techniques, such as alliteration, simile, and metaphor, makes the piece a pleasure to read.

C. Using Words That Are Specific and Accurate

The writer uses words with precision. He or she selects words the reader needs to fully understand the message. The writer chooses nouns, adjectives, adverbs, and so forth that create clarity and bring the topic to life.

D. Utilizing Language Effectively

The writer uses words to capture the reader's imagination and enhance the piece's meaning. There is a deliberate attempt to choose the best word over the first word that comes to mind.

Sentence Fluency

The way words and phrases flow through the piece. This is the auditory trait and is therefore "read" with the ear as much as the eye.

A. Capturing Smooth and Rhythmic Flow

The writer thinks about how the sentences sound. He or she uses phrasing that is almost musical. If the piece were read aloud, it would be easy on the ear.

B. Crafting Well-Built Sentences

The writer carefully and creatively constructs sentences for maximum impact. Transition words such as *but*, *and*, and *so* are used successfully to join sentences and sentence parts.

C. Varying Sentence Patterns

The writer uses various types of sentences (simple, compound, and/or complex) to enhance the central theme or story line. The piece includes long, complex sentences and short, simple ones.

D. Breaking the "Rules" to Create Fluency

The writer diverges from standard English to create interest and impact. For example, he or she may use a sentence fragment—such as "All alone in the forest"—or a single word—such as "Bam!"—to accent a particular moment or action. The writer might begin with informal words such as *well*, *and*, or *but* to create a conversational tone, or he or she might break rules intentionally to make dialogue sound authentic.

Conventions

The mechanical correctness of the piece. Correct use of conventions (spelling, capitalization, punctuation, paragraphing, and grammar and usage) guides the reader through text easily.

A. Checking Spelling

The writer spells sight words, high-frequency words, and less-familiar words correctly. When he or she spells less-familiar words incorrectly, those words are phonetically correct. Overall, the piece reveals control in spelling.

B. Punctuating and Paragraphing Effectively

The writer handles basic punctuation skillfully. He or she understands how to use periods, commas, question marks, and exclamation marks to enhance clarity and meaning. Paragraphs are indented in the right places. The piece is ready for a general audience.

C. Capitalizing Correctly

The writer uses capital letters consistently and accurately. A deep understanding of how to capitalize dialogue, abbreviations, proper names, and titles is evident.

D. Applying Grammar and Usage

The writer forms grammatically correct phrases and sentences. He or she shows care in applying the rules of standard English. The writer may break from those rules for stylistic reasons but otherwise abides by them.

Presentation

The physical appearance of the piece. A visually appealing text provides a welcome mat, inviting the reader in to enjoy the writing.

A. Applying Handwriting Skills

The writer uses handwriting that is clear and legible. Whether he or she prints or uses cursive, letters are uniform and slant evenly throughout the piece. Spacing between words is consistent.

B. Using Word Processing

The writer uses a font style and size that are easy to read and a good match for the piece's purpose. If he or she uses color, it enhances the piece's readability.

C. Utilizing White Space

The writer frames the text with appropriately sized margins. There are no cross-outs, smudges, or tears on the paper.

D. Incorporating Text Features

The writer effectively places text features such as headings, page numbers, titles, and bullets on the page and aligns them clearly with the text they support.

This may seem like a lot of information, but think about what it means to us as writing teachers: terminology and definitions that not only help us accurately and reliably assess student writing to reveal strengths and areas to further develop but also serve as a road map for designing specific lessons and activities to teach students in each essential area of writing. We can now marry formative assessment to instruction in distinct ways via the traits, which are broad characteristics of writing, and the key qualities, which are more specific and identifiable in student work. We can avoid gray areas or lapses in what is taught systematically each and every year; we now have a 100 percent match between what is assessed and what should be taught. And, most important, we have a shared language for talking about writing in every classroom.

So, What's Next?

You now have, in your hands, twenty-eight key qualities of seven traits. Every student, no matter his or her grade level or ability, needs work on every key quality every year. After all, teaching writing well requires a cumulative approach over time. Knowing the traits and their key qualities means you can differentiate instruction and expectations based on students' needs regardless of their skills when your work together begins. The traits and their key qualities are the road map for teachers and students as you both learn more about writing at a deeper level of complexity over time. (Chapter 5, "Rethinking Revision: The Real Work of Writing," provides more about how to plan a year's curriculum based on the key qualities.)

Before we can use the traits to improve student writing, however, we must learn how to find them in the writing. The next chapter will model and teach you how to use these trait definitions for formative assessment using the Grades 3 and Up Scoring Guide, which can be found in its entirety in Appendix B and online at sten.pub/tww. The scoring guide provides differentiated levels of performance, trait by trait, so you can pinpoint the degree to which student writing is successful at any point in its development. There are specific strategies and procedures for applying the scoring guide that make it a straightforward and relatively simple tool to use. I invite you to walk the walk with me.

2

Formative Assessment: The Heart of the Matter

When I think about how much we've learned, as a profession, about the value of formative assessment, I smile. After all, it's hard to argue with the idea that you need to know what students already understand before you can plan meaningful instruction on what they don't. That is the simple yet compelling lure of the traits of writing. They show us, clearly and consistently, where students are learning, where they are stalled, and where they are clueless—exactly what is needed to help them. Every great what deserves a great how. What an incredible tool the traits have turned out to be.

Thirty years ago, when traits were first brought to light, I had only a scoring guide in my hands to assess and teach. That's it. No connection to mentor texts, no big books of lesson ideas, no spiraling key qualities, no Writing Wallets (we'll learn more about these in Chapter 5), no additional tools and resources at all to help me support young writers. Just the traits. And yet, with that scoring guide I found I had what I needed to move forward with my students. I had language and criteria that made sense to them and to me. As I assessed student writing during the writing process, it became clear to me, for the first time, where to help students take the next steps in their work. It was exhilarating—not a word one typically associates with teaching writing.

The work grew from there. There is a great deal in this book about ways to use the traits to create a textured, layered, and constructive writing classroom. All of the ideas in this book have developed and gelled over time. This chapter, however, is devoted to learning to use the traits as an assessment tool with fidelity, reliability, and clarity. To read student writing is to understand student writing; we simply need the right lens to peer through.

> To read student writing is to understand student writing.

What follows are examples of student papers that are assessed for one trait each and one paper that is assessed for all the traits. They were selected randomly from hundreds of papers to represent typical writing at their respective grade levels. They are neither the best nor the worst of what students write, but they do showcase different issues that surface at varying ages and stages of writing development. I'll walk you through the writing and the scoring guides so you can follow along with my assessment, trait by trait.

In Appendix A and on the online companion site (sten.pub/tww), you'll find eight more writing samples from grades two through six that have been assessed for all the traits and commented upon as well. They exemplify a wide range of skill—from just beginning to showing control—in each of the traits and are examples of students writing multiple sentences (at least a paragraph) on a topic. The practice papers in this chapter and the appendix will give you and your colleagues hands-on experience to gain skill and confidence in trait-based assessment. Consider using these writing samples with your students, too, as you teach each trait and its key qualities; we'll dive deeper into modeling in a writing lesson in Chapter 6.

The writing samples and notes included here walk you through trait-based assessment. Feel free to score the sample papers first and then follow along with my process. Then take some time to practice using the sample papers in the appendix. Together, we will achieve new understandings of formative assessment and what good writing looks like. Sometimes we'll agree, and sometimes we may not (although I have found over the years that after reading and assessing a handful of papers together, we're likely to agree on the scores within one point more than 90 percent of the time). We can resolve any differences by turning to the scoring guide and its clarifying language as the arbitrator and having meaningful discussions with colleagues about our perceptions of quality. As we consider our responses to texts, we learn—from the scoring guide and from each other. Learning how to assess is powerful stuff, and practice is the most important way to gain confidence and skill to do it well. Get ready to roll up your sleeves and get your hands dirty as we

> Learning how to assess is powerful stuff, and practice is the most important way to gain confidence and skill to do it well.

- *decide* which trait or traits you will assess;

- *read* the writing;

- *use* the scoring guide and ask ourselves, *Has the writing met the criteria? Has it almost hit the mark? Is it just beginning?;*

- *select* language and scores from the scoring guide that match the writing;

- *discuss* the results;

- *listen* to other's reactions and rationales; and

- *come to agreement* based on the language of the scoring guide.

Be Aware of Bias

Certain issues may jeopardize your ability to fairly assess student writing. Avoid these at all costs. Honesty and reliability should be your assessment goals. Before we get started, keep an eye out for the following issues that may arise during writing assessment.

- *Worrying too much about grade level.* Yes, grade level matters. I think of it this way: the scoring guide is half of what you need to assess accurately, and the other half is a set of benchmark papers that shows the range of how students write at different developmental stages or grade levels. In other words, what does a score of 6 in ideas look like in third grade compared with sixth grade? The criteria remain the same, but our expectations about what students should be able to do regarding complexity and clarity increase over time. Avoid using phrases such as "not very good for a fourth grader," for example. Students exist at varied levels of writing skill at every age. The typical reason they are together in a class is their age, not their skill level. Grade-level comparisons are often unhelpful.

- *The student's prior performance.* You may know a student well and therefore recognize that a particular performance is either above or below what is typical, so you score it too high or too low based on effort. Instead, anchor your scoring in the criteria of the scoring guide. You can comment on your prior observations to the writer when appropriate. Read the writing and use the scoring guide to reflect on the student's piece at this point in its development.

- *The student's ability.* The only reason to use formative assessment is to provide accurate feedback to the writer for the purpose of improving his or her work. If a student is a vulnerable writer for any reason, documented or not, be careful not to over-score the writing because you don't want to discourage the writer. Conversely, don't under-score the work of a talented writer because you feel the writer could have done more. Using the scoring guide, which is neutral on these issues, explain to students where the writing succeeded and where it could still grow, setting reasonable goals.

- *The student's effort.* It's heartbreaking to watch a student pore over his writing and put his heart into it only to find, when it comes time to assess the writing, that it just didn't turn out very well. You may be tempted to score a piece like this higher just because of the extraordinary effort. Use the scoring guide and be honest in your assessment, but make sure the student knows you noticed his effort and how it will pay off over time (because it will!).

- *Writing that doesn't follow the prompt.* For the purpose of assessing, do not factor in how closely the student followed a prompt (if there was one). Assess the writing, whatever it turns out to be. You can direct the student back to the task at hand and refocus to create the paper that you assigned during the writing process, or you can encourage the writer to keep working on this piece during open writing time when choice of topic matters. In other words, do not assess whether the student followed the directions as part of assessing with the traits. The piece may have a great idea but a different one than you expected. Deal with that issue separately.

- *Bias of any type.* Race, gender, personal issues with the student, age, work habit, style of writing, and on and on: these are all things that will creep into our thinking about a student and his or her writing. We don't want to admit it, but it's true. You must do everything possible to assess the writing, not the student. Use the scoring guide as the mediator to resolve any issues raised by your background knowledge of the student.

Getting Ready and Getting Started

Learning to read the writing for the traits requires two new skills: using a clearly articulated scoring guide and sorting out one trait from the other as you assess.

Above all, don't use an abbreviated scoring guide or one that is not clearly written. In the latest iteration of the traits scoring guides, you'll find that the descriptors are written in sentences. This change from bullets and phrases on previous versions is quite deliberate and designed to take the guesswork out of assessment. The traits scoring guides also include four key qualities for each trait that make it possible to focus on the details of the writing like never before. In other words, be sure you're using a scoring guide from this book or from my website, not from a separate website or resource.

When it comes to assessing one trait at a time, rest assured that as the definition and key qualities of each trait become more familiar to you, you'll know immediately which issue in the writing aligns to which trait. At first, however, it may be a little murky. You may notice a problem but won't know which trait to tag for it. The opposite might occur as well—something great will show up and you won't know where to give credit. Practice will take care of these issues. Practice, practice, practice.

Familiarize Yourself with the Traits

It helps to work with a partner or in a small group as you first start assessing with the traits scoring guides. What follows is a step-by-step model that has been successful in countless schools:

1. Download the four papers assessed in this chapter and a scoring guide for each. These resources can be found online at sten.pub/tww so you'll have a paper copy to mark up.

2. Gather your supplies: note paper, pencil, and a highlighter.

3. Together with colleagues, review how the scoring guide works:

   • You'll find a page for each trait.

   • A continuum arrow along the left side indicates that the writing in that trait falls somewhere between just beginning and strong.

   • Three performance zones are included: high, middle, and low. Each performance zone has two scores:

     » Low or just beginning: 1–2

     » Middle or on the way: 3–4

     » High or strong: 5–6

   • In each of the performance zones, the trait's key qualities are listed and described to match what the writing may demonstrate at that level. This is the good stuff—the heart and soul of the assessment.

Take time to explore the scoring guide with a partner or a small group of colleagues. It can feel overwhelming to be handed seven pages of criteria that are unfamiliar. Point out how the key qualities appear on the page three times, for each of the different levels. The descriptions of each key quality are carefully written to help teachers dig into the writing and match descriptors to what students have done. Notice, however, that no scoring guide can cover every single thing students do in writing, so it's important to internalize the intent of the guide at each level in order for the best assessment to take place.

Pause and Consider

Assessing the Writing

Reading papers and assessing them for all the traits is time consuming. But take heart! After you familiarize yourself with the process and become comfortable with the scoring guide, the amount of time it takes to read a paper and assess it is greatly reduced. And don't forget, on most occasions you are not reading and responding to all the traits at once—often you will focus on one trait at a time, which is even faster yet. Regardless, the time you spend understanding the criteria and applying them to student writing pays off when you learn what students are doing well and what needs to come next in your teaching and their learning.

1. Read the paper from beginning to end. Don't stop, don't skim, don't hurry.

2. Select a trait on which to focus and pull out the scoring guide for that trait.

3. Ask yourself: *Which of the three zones of performance do I feel is applicable for this trait in this piece?* Trust your instincts. Is the writing stronger than weak or weaker than strong? Or, start in the middle zone and work your way up or down according to what you find in the writing.

4. Read the first key quality descriptor for the trait and ask yourself: *Does this match what I'm seeing in this paper?* If the answer is yes, use your highlighter to mark the words and phrases that describe the student's writing on the scoring guide. If the answer is no or sort of, then go up a level or down a level to the same key quality and see if the description there is a better match. You'll know which direction, trust me.

5. As you read the higher or lower version of the key quality, use the highlighter to mark any words and phrases that match. Don't fret if the student's work isn't all in one level or another. Honestly? It will rarely be all one score without elements of another coloring the result. This is student writing, after all, and it doesn't come in nice, neat little packages.

6. Repeat the process with the other three key qualities. Use the highlighter to mark the language on the scoring guide that matches what you find in the writing.

7. Sit back and look at the highlighted sections of the scoring guide for one trait. They may cluster in a performance zone, or they may be scattered: this is the score. If your highlights are mostly in the middle with a few in the high level, the score is in the 4–5 range, depending on the number

of marks in each section. If your highlights are mostly in the low section with a few marks in the middle, the score is in the 2–3 range. Make sense? Record your score for the trait using a recordkeeping tool (see my website, www.culhamwriting.com) and move on.

8. Repeat this process with each trait. You can stop and discuss your scores with your partner or team after each individual trait or when all the traits are scored. Having highlighted the qualities from the scoring guide to match the writing will make your discussions informed and lively. Don't be surprised if you find yourself enjoying this part of the process—it's affirming and enlightening.

Pause and Consider

From years of experience, I know how hard it is to separate the writing from the child and knowledge of the child's past performances. As you share ideas about using a scoring guide as a way to provide feedback to students and focus on revision and editing decisions ahead, remind yourself that you are not assessing the child—you are assessing the writing at this moment in its development with an eye toward what to nudge the student to try next. How do you make sure your assessment is accurate and reliable? React to these situations: The writing in one or more traits might be a 1 at this time; however, it doesn't feel good to assign a score of 1. Or, the writing is a 6 in one or more traits but you feel you should hold back and assign a 5 because it's written by a capable writer. (Keep this in mind during your discussion: we assess the writing, not the writer.)

A Few Caveats About Scoring

- If a paper is highly flawed in conventions, I typically read it once and score the conventions first. Then I do a thoughtful second read, this time pretending the conventions are clean and well edited so I can concentrate on the message. I find that once I sweep conventions off the table, I just might have a really strong paper to read and enjoy.

Writing is complicated. It's thinking aloud on paper, and we come to it with our own baggage as readers and writers.

- You don't always have to score a paper for every trait. On the first three papers, we're practicing in just one area so you can focus on it and teach students as they revise their writing. On the fourth paper, we're assessing all the traits as if the paper is finished and you want a final score for the whole piece.

- After you've read and practiced on a full class set of writing samples, you'll be able to read and score a paper for all the traits in just three to five minutes. Really. This does not include time to make comments, however. More about that later.

- It's always helpful to work with another teacher or professional, especially at first. You can read a paper and score it, then compare your assessment with that of your partner. The discussion that ensues should help you reach agreement on a score within one point; even more important, your partner can help you figure out a nudge that will help the writer take the next step to improve the piece.

Let's Practice Together

Here we go. Let's score real student writing examples together so you can get comfortable with the process. I'm going to begin with three third-grade writing samples and assess each for one trait. This may be the bulk of how you use formative assessment—one trait at a time, always looking for what the student is doing well and where to find the instructive nudges. Then I'll share a fifth-grade writing sample and assess it for all the traits. Remember that Appendix A includes plenty more writing samples from students at different grade levels and performance zones, as well as in different modes. (The next chapter goes into more detail on modes, or purposes for writing, including narrative, informative, and opinion.) Finally, because I know we need to provide grades on writing from time to time, I'll show you how to convert the scoring guide information into percentages using a nifty conversion chart you won't want to live without (see Appendix B for your own copy).

Getting comfortable with the process

Please keep in mind, as you walk through these student writing samples with me, that it's perfectly reasonable to be one point higher or lower on the scoring guide than I am or some of your colleagues are. If you, for example, assess a trait at a 3 and I assign a 2, we can consider that agreement. After all, we're sending a similar message to the writer: "You've got some good stuff in here worth working on." But if you assign a 2 and I assess the trait at a 6, that is a confusing message. You are saying, "It's a good start, with many places to grow and improve." I am saying, "Good for you! You met the criteria." That mixed signal can really undermine a writer's sense of what he or she has accomplished. Scores more than a point apart must be reconciled before giving feedback to the writer.

Use the scoring guide as the arbitrator. Imagine yourself having to defend your scores to an unhappy parent or guardian. Could you point to places in the text and match them to the descriptors on the scoring guide to show why you assigned the score you did? You should always be able to state clearly why a piece of writing was assessed the way it was. And, you should always be willing to take a second look if your assessment turns out to be off by a point or more. No one (myself included) gets it right every single time. Writing is complicated. It's thinking aloud on paper, and we come to it with our own baggage as readers and writers. Don't be afraid to reread and rescore as you get more and more comfortable with this formative assessment. It's the sign of a good teacher that you have an open mind and, with the right evidence, would be willing to look at the work again and again.

Assessing for One Trait

As everyday practice, you'll be assessing for one trait and using the information you gather to plan and differentiate instruction. This can also be an excellent way to track growth as you document progress during the school year—something students, parents, administrators, and you (of course!) will want at your fingertips. You can use the results as you confer with kids individually or in small groups. So, zooming in on one aspect of the writing will likely be your most useful and routine formative assessment tool. It's quick, it's specific, and it leads to clear feedback and information for the writer about what to do next. Try assessing for the ideas trait on the writing samples that follow.

Grade 3: Ideas Trait

As you assess the pieces of writing in this section with me, focus only on the ideas trait and each of its key qualities. Do your best to put other issues, such as spelling, on the back burner. There will be time to address editing later, once this piece is fully revised and you want to assess it for all the traits. We'll use the ideas trait scoring guide (a full-page version is available in Appendix B and online) as we assess the three student pieces in this section.

LUSSIMIA

The first planet ever to be in the universe was a planet called Lussimia. Lussimia was like earth it had wars, bulling, and hating, but it wasn't like the underworld because it had Love, friendships, and peace. The people who lived on Lussimia were like humans they had all the same forms as people who live on earth. The planets of Earth and Lussimia were the exacly the same coalers too. But like earth they both had bad people. There was a person living on Lussimia his name was Black Eye but people also called him the walking Zombie. He was very vichous to his family, to kids, to anyone he meet. He bealived that every planet should be ruled by him and that every planet should be in his power.

Grade 3, Writing Sample 1: "Lussimia"

This writer has a terrific idea and no lack of imagination! This feels like the beginning of a much longer piece where the action will play out. As it is, the writer has a good command of some of the key qualities for the ideas trait, but not for others, which ultimately will make it easier for us to advise him or her about what to do next. Take a look at how I scored the piece, as shown in Figure 2.1. This writing reflects a mix of strengths and weaknesses in this trait. The writer has a strong overall idea but hasn't zeroed in on the direction the writing will take as it develops. Still, this portion of the writing includes strong details. It would receive a score of 4 in the ideas trait because what is written is solid—the idea just needs to be fleshed out and expanded. It's a great start.

Key Quality Scores

Finding a Topic: 5

Focusing the Topic: 4

Developing the Topic: 3

Using Details: 5

Overall ideas score: 4

TEACH WRITING WELL

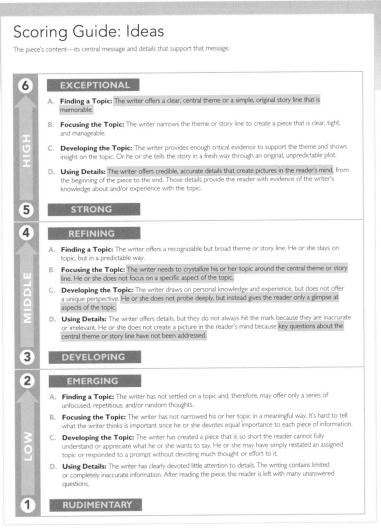

Scoring Guide: Ideas

The piece's content—its central message and details that support that message.

6 | EXCEPTIONAL

(HIGH)

A. **Finding a Topic:** The writer offers a clear, central theme or a simple, original story line that is memorable.

B. **Focusing the Topic:** The writer narrows the theme or story line to create a piece that is clear, tight, and manageable.

C. **Developing the Topic:** The writer provides enough critical evidence to support the theme and shows insight on the topic. Or he or she tells the story in a fresh way through an original, unpredictable plot.

D. **Using Details:** The writer offers credible, accurate details that create pictures in the reader's mind, from the beginning of the piece to the end. Those details provide the reader with evidence of the writer's knowledge about and/or experience with the topic.

5 | STRONG

4 | REFINING

(MIDDLE)

A. **Finding a Topic:** The writer offers a recognizable but broad theme or story line. He or she stays on topic, but in a predictable way.

B. **Focusing the Topic:** The writer needs to crystallize his or her topic around the central theme or story line. He or she does not focus on a specific aspect of the topic.

C. **Developing the Topic:** The writer draws on personal knowledge and experience, but does not offer a unique perspective. He or she does not probe deeply, but instead gives the reader only a glimpse at aspects of the topic.

D. **Using Details:** The writer offers details, but they do not always hit the mark because they are inaccurate or irrelevant. He or she does not create a picture in the reader's mind because key questions about the central theme or story line have not been addressed.

3 | DEVELOPING

2 | EMERGING

(LOW)

A. **Finding a Topic:** The writer has not settled on a topic and, therefore, may offer only a series of unfocused, repetitious, and/or random thoughts.

B. **Focusing the Topic:** The writer has not narrowed his or her topic in a meaningful way. It's hard to tell what the writer thinks is important since he or she devotes equal importance to each piece of information.

C. **Developing the Topic:** The writer has created a piece that is so short the reader cannot fully understand or appreciate what he or she wants to say. He or she may have simply restated an assigned topic or responded to a prompt without devoting much thought or effort to it.

D. **Using Details:** The writer has clearly devoted little attention to details. The writing contains limited or completely inaccurate information. After reading the piece, the reader is left with many unanswered questions.

1 | RUDIMENTARY

Figure 2.1 *Ideas scored page for "Lussimia"*

Here's a possible comment to the writer:

Lussimia sounds like a dark and scary place, and you've done a good job using details that make it clear for the reader what a positive place it once was. It's interesting how you contrasted it with the underworld and what we've been talking about in Greek mythology. Let's create a story map about where this story is going next. You've introduced a character, Black Eye (and made a great comparison to a walking zombie), but as the reader, I have some questions that maybe you can answer as the piece develops in the next draft.

Now, contrast the amount of control shown in the ideas trait in "Lussimia" with this next third-grade piece. Please note, we don't ever assess one student against another. But, for the purposes of learning how to assess using the scoring guide, it can be helpful to use these anonymous samples to see the performance range at a particular grade level.

I licke sumer but not as Much as spring. there are baby annimales in the spring. They live on farms If I had a pet it wold be a HORNY tode. jesse wuld come to my room & screem. My favorit movee is lego movee but isnt not scary

Grade 3, Writing Sample 2: "Summer"

Yikes! This writer doesn't know what he or she wants to write about. There's potential here—but as is, it reads like a list of possible topics. Take a look at what is highlighted at the low level of the ideas scoring guide (see Figure 2.2)—it fits. The most helpful advice to this student would be to pick one of these potential topics and say more about it and only it. This draft could go from an ideas score of 1 to 3 very quickly, depending on the amount of detail and elaboration included.

Key Quality Scores

Finding a Topic: 1

Focusing the Topic: 1

Developing the Topic: 1

Using Details: 1

Overall ideas score: 1

TEACH WRITING WELL

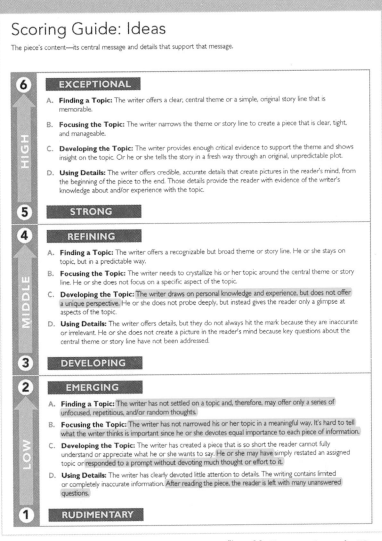

Scoring Guide: Ideas

The piece's content—its central message and details that support that message.

6 — EXCEPTIONAL

HIGH

A. **Finding a Topic:** The writer offers a clear, central theme or a simple, original story line that is memorable.

B. **Focusing the Topic:** The writer narrows the theme or story line to create a piece that is clear, tight, and manageable.

C. **Developing the Topic:** The writer provides enough critical evidence to support the theme and shows insight on the topic. Or he or she tells the story in a fresh way through an original, unpredictable plot.

D. **Using Details:** The writer offers credible, accurate details that create pictures in the reader's mind, from the beginning of the piece to the end. Those details provide the reader with evidence of the writer's knowledge about and/or experience with the topic.

5 — STRONG

4 — REFINING

MIDDLE

A. **Finding a Topic:** The writer offers a recognizable but broad theme or story line. He or she stays on topic, but in a predictable way.

B. **Focusing the Topic:** The writer needs to crystallize his or her topic around the central theme or story line. He or she does not focus on a specific aspect of the topic.

C. **Developing the Topic:** The writer draws on personal knowledge and experience, but does not offer a unique perspective. He or she does not probe deeply, but instead gives the reader only a glimpse at aspects of the topic.

D. **Using Details:** The writer offers details, but they do not always hit the mark because they are inaccurate or irrelevant. He or she does not create a picture in the reader's mind because key questions about the central theme or story line have not been addressed.

3 — DEVELOPING

2 — EMERGING

LOW

A. **Finding a Topic:** The writer has not settled on a topic and, therefore, may offer only a series of unfocused, repetitious, and/or random thoughts.

B. **Focusing the Topic:** The writer has not narrowed his or her topic in a meaningful way. It's hard to tell what the writer thinks is important since he or she devotes equal importance to each piece of information.

C. **Developing the Topic:** The writer has created a piece that is so short the reader cannot fully understand or appreciate what he or she wants to say. He or she may have simply restated an assigned topic or responded to a prompt without devoting much thought or effort to it.

D. **Using Details:** The writer has clearly devoted little attention to details. The writing contains limited or completely inaccurate information. After reading the piece, the reader is left with many unanswered questions.

1 — RUDIMENTARY

Figure 2.2 *Ideas scored page for "Summer"*

You might gently ask this writer to focus on one detail to develop, like this:

You've provided a lot to think about as you develop your draft and move forward so this piece's idea crystalizes. Is there a favorite detail or a sentence in here you like best? I see so many possibilities! Tell me more about the one you want to commit to and write more about. Then we can make a list of what could be included, where you'd find that information, and what you think is important for the reader to know about your topic and its focus.

I am writing about my favorite kind of dessert. I like a lot of desserts but my favorite kind is sweat potato pie. I like this kind of dessert because when you tack your first bite it feels as if you've falan in to heaven. The midal is as soft as 10,000 marshmelos made of clouds and loshen and the crust is as chewy as 60 rasens. The best part of sweat potato pie is that it's filled with love in every bite because my mom makes it.

I think that how ever doesn't like sweat potato pie is a tiny bit werd. If I can't have sweat potato pie I wount have any, do you hear me, any kind of dessert. I love my sweat potato pie and no one can tack it away from me!!!!!

Grade 3, Writing Sample 3: "Sweet Potato Pie"

Key Quality Scores

Finding a Topic: 6

Focusing the Topic: 6

Developing the Topic: 6

Using Details: 6

Overall ideas score: 6

Now take a look at one more third-grade piece of writing for the ideas trait. Keep your ideas trait scoring guide in hand, so you can validate your assessment using the specific details of each key quality. (You might choose to note the voice and word choice traits on this piece, too. Traits work together and highly influence one another—for good and for not-so-good—in actual writing.)

This one should be easy. It's a 6, pure and simple (see Figure 2.3). Is it perfect? No. But I'd challenge you to keep this in mind: if all third graders wrote this clearly about their ideas and were able to communicate as effectively, we would be much happier with our writing instruction and how students were progressing.

When you look at this piece and read it like a writer, you see strength in several traits: ideas, voice, and word choice. It has a complete (and yummy!) idea, based on the writer's own experience, and it's expressed with the right amount of elaboration. We want to make sure this writer knows what he or she has done well and then begin to work on other traits and their key qualities that may not show as much strength. This is how I might respond to this writer:

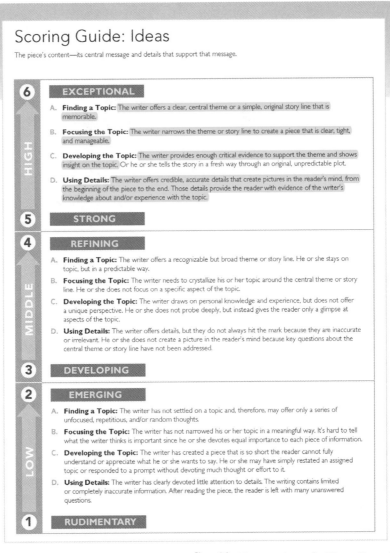

Scoring Guide: Ideas

The piece's content—its central message and details that support that message.

6 EXCEPTIONAL

HIGH

A. **Finding a Topic:** The writer offers a clear, central theme or a simple, original story line that is memorable.

B. **Focusing the Topic:** The writer narrows the theme or story line to create a piece that is clear, tight, and manageable.

C. **Developing the Topic:** The writer provides enough critical evidence to support the theme and shows insight on the topic. Or he or she tells the story in a fresh way through an original, unpredictable plot.

D. **Using Details:** The writer offers credible, accurate details that create pictures in the reader's mind, from the beginning of the piece to the end. Those details provide the reader with evidence of the writer's knowledge about and/or experience with the topic.

5 STRONG

4 REFINING

MIDDLE

A. **Finding a Topic:** The writer offers a recognizable but broad theme or story line. He or she stays on topic, but in a predictable way.

B. **Focusing the Topic:** The writer needs to crystallize his or her topic around the central theme or story line. He or she does not focus on a specific aspect of the topic.

C. **Developing the Topic:** The writer draws on personal knowledge and experience, but does not offer a unique perspective. He or she does not probe deeply, but instead gives the reader only a glimpse at aspects of the topic.

D. **Using Details:** The writer offers details, but they do not always hit the mark because they are inaccurate or irrelevant. He or she does not create a picture in the reader's mind because key questions about the central theme or story line have not been addressed.

3 DEVELOPING

2 EMERGING

LOW

A. **Finding a Topic:** The writer has not settled on a topic and, therefore, may offer only a series of unfocused, repetitious, and/or random thoughts.

B. **Focusing the Topic:** The writer has not narrowed his or her topic in a meaningful way. It's hard to tell what the writer thinks is important since he or she devotes equal importance to each piece of information.

C. **Developing the Topic:** The writer has created a piece that is so short the reader cannot fully understand or appreciate what he or she wants to say. He or she may have simply restated an assigned topic or responded to a prompt without devoting much thought or effort to it.

D. **Using Details:** The writer has clearly devoted little attention to details. The writing contains limited or completely inaccurate information. After reading the piece, the reader is left with many unanswered questions.

1 RUDIMENTARY

Figure 2.3 *Ideas scored page for "Sweet Potato Pie"*

I'm positively drooling over this piece. You picked a focused idea, explained it so readers can picture it, and used the "just right" amount of details that really work to develop your main idea. Nice work! Because you were so imaginative with your word choice, your voice rings true from beginning to end. You even directly reached out to the reader—very powerful. Now that you have started such a strong piece, let's take a look at how it actually begins. I bet you can think of a book you love that has a lead that really got your attention. Try using that same technique, and let's see how it goes. But wait! First I have to go find some sweet potato pie to gobble up right now!

Assessing for All the Traits

The best time to assess for all traits at once is at the end of a big unit paper or project. And even then, I'd go through the whole process only if you need those scores for some administrative reason: report cards, for instance. Once the paper is finished—really finished—read it, assess it, make a comment about what improved during the drafting, revising, and editing process, and leave a seed of thought about what the student might work on next. Done. Don't edit every line, write marginal comments about what to change, and generally obsess over all that could be said about the writing. Why? The student is not going to use that information to revise their work. Remember: the paper is finished, and you (and they) are moving forward to work on something new.

> Save your energy, time, expertise, and goodwill for during the writing process.

Assessing for all the traits will take more time. However, it yields a world of information about the interconnectedness of the traits—for instance, when a student works on word choice, the voice may also improve. When he or she focuses on structuring the body, the idea might get stronger. After you teach different parts of speech (in context), the student's sentences begin to flow. It's useful to note how the student's writing skills improve in a holistic way—but not as helpful as trait-by-trait, one-at-a-time feedback to the writer who can easily become overwhelmed by too much information and not know what to do next.

Save your energy, time, expertise, and goodwill for during the writing process. This is when you can share ideas with students about what to try next—while there is still time for them to do something about it. In revision, students learn to think and talk like writers; that doesn't necessarily happen if they receive a grade and a whole bunch of comments on a finished piece of writing returned by a grumpy, exhausted teacher who spent way more time marking papers than is useful. Save yourself. Save writing teachers everywhere.

With that said, it's still important to know how to assess a single piece of writing for all the traits. What follows is a piece of writing by a fifth-grade student that we'll use to practice. It is a finished piece that has gone all the way through the writing process—planning, drafting, receiving feedback, revising (more than once), editing, rewriting, and finishing/publishing. I'll walk you through each trait and show highlighted thumbnail scoring guides, and then you can practice with the student writing samples in Appendix A to hone your trait-based assessment skills. Full-size versions of the traits scoring guides can be found in Appendix B, and they're also downloadable from sten.pub/tww.

Grade 5, Writing Sample 3: "Hula Hooping"

5-F
4/12/1.

Hula Hooping
The sun glissens on the shiny tape.
The hoop moves faster than the speed
of light, swirling around my body. Up and
down. Up and down. I absolutly love
to hula hoop, and no one ever thinks
of it as a "sport,... but it is! The whole
thing is a sport, tricks and all!
    The best thing about hula hooping
is showing off. I think of it as
a kind way of bragging. My favorite
way to show off is the illusion tricks.
In one of the tricks, the hoop
looks like it's levitating! Another trick
is the eagle. It is a Native hoop
dance move, and it always impresses!
You use some hoops to make wings,
and then twirl around, faster and faster!
You can also lift the hoops up as you twirl!

    When my friends at my hooping
class are ready to share what's up,
we have little "hoop meetings." We arrange
our hoops in a circle, and talk about upcoming or recent events. We sometimes do little, fun games to warm up,
and we talk so much, it takes a half
hour!
    I get excited when it's hooping
class time, because I get to see all
my friends. I love to talk and talk
with them. It's really awesome to
hang out with friends every week!
In my opinion, hula hooping brings
us together. It makes us have fun
and feels comfortable!
    When I see a hula hoop, I can
pick it up and wow a crowd... well,
most of the time. It's instant heaven
to me! The thing is, I can never think
of a world without hula hooping!

Scoring Guide: Ideas

The piece's content—its central message and details that support that message.

6 | EXCEPTIONAL

HIGH

A. **Finding a Topic:** The writer offers a clear, central theme or a simple, original story line that is memorable.

B. **Focusing the Topic:** The writer narrows the theme or story line to create a piece that is clear, tight, and manageable.

C. **Developing the Topic:** The writer provides enough critical evidence to support the theme and shows insight on the topic. Or he or she tells the story in a fresh way through an original, unpredictable plot.

D. **Using Details:** The writer offers credible, accurate details that create pictures in the reader's mind, from the beginning of the piece to the end. Those details provide the reader with evidence of the writer's knowledge about and/or experience with the topic.

5 | STRONG

4 | REFINING

MIDDLE

A. **Finding a Topic:** The writer offers a recognizable but broad theme or story line. He or she stays on topic, but in a predictable way.

B. **Focusing the Topic:** The writer needs to crystallize his or her topic around the central theme or story line. He or she does not focus on a specific aspect of the topic.

C. **Developing the Topic:** The writer draws on personal knowledge and experience, but does not offer a unique perspective. He or she does not probe deeply, but instead gives the reader only a glimpse at aspects of the topic.

D. **Using Details:** The writer offers details, but they do not always hit the mark because they are inaccurate or irrelevant. He or she does not create a picture in the reader's mind because key questions about the central theme or story line have not been addressed.

3 | DEVELOPING

2 | EMERGING

LOW

A. **Finding a Topic:** The writer has not settled on a topic and, therefore, may offer only a series of unfocused, repetitive, and/or random thoughts.

B. **Focusing the Topic:** The writer has not narrowed his or her topic in a meaningful way. It's hard to tell what the writer thinks is important since he or she devotes equal importance to each piece of information.

C. **Developing the Topic:** The writer has created a piece that is so short the reader cannot fully understand or appreciate what he or she wants to say. Or he or she may have simply restated an assigned topic or responded to a prompt without devoting much thought or effort to it.

D. **Using Details:** The writer has clearly devoted little attention to details. The writing contains limited or completely inaccurate information. After reading the piece, the reader is left with many unanswered questions.

1 | RUDIMENTARY

Figure 2.4   *Ideas scored page for "Hula Hooping"*

Ideas trait summary

Take a look at Figure 2.4 to see how I highlighted the ideas scoring guide for "Hula Hooping." There is no doubt that this writer loves hula hooping! In the body of the text, she provides specific information that helps me visualize. More examples, more details, and more information about her original assertion would be helpful. When I read this piece, I find myself smiling at her passion for an activity that I had never really considered a sport. Interesting. I would like to hear more about her rationale for this statement. I'd also like to see her push the use of everyday words toward those that are more specific and accurate in the next draft.

We understand this writer's love of hula hooping and why she thinks it's a great activity, but I'm confused about the intent of the piece. She begins by building a case that hula hooping should be considered a sport but digresses into fun and lively discourse about her experiences hula hooping; she doesn't stay on track with the sport assertion. This student, a skilled writer, should make a decision about the focus of the piece and stick with it in the next draft (if there is one). Discussion about this paper's ideas score should be about whether it is a 4 or a 5—it's an uneven performance but pretty good overall.

Organization trait summary

This may be one of the best introductions I've seen from a student writer. I hope the writer got the idea for this fabulous lead by reading a mentor text that showed how to tantalize in such a visual way. Regardless, this writer is spot-on for the first key quality. Take a look at the organization scoring guide (Figure 2.5) to see how I scored the remaining key qualities for organization.

Overall the piece is very strong in organization. I think once the ideas issue is resolved, the organization will tighten up to show the logical thread of meaning more clearly. The fourth paragraph is the weakest, which leaves me wondering if the writer had been told to write five paragraphs. By the way, I'm no fan of telling students how long the writing should be, or in what format, before the piece is written. I've found that young writers will shoehorn in an extra paragraph just to satisfy the structure requirements rather than letting the idea drive the logical organization.

When I read this piece, I have the urge to speed up the pacing. The ending will likely get stronger when the purpose comes into focus. It's hard to wrap up something that's wandered off course. However, this writer shows control of the basic organizational issues that matter most.

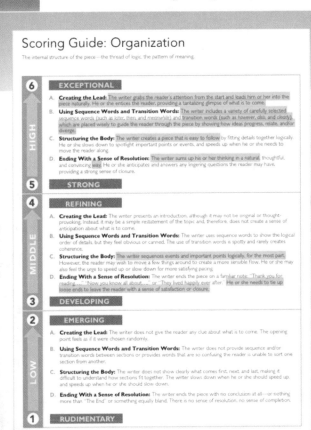

Scoring Guide: Organization

The internal structure of the piece — the thread of logic, the pattern of meaning.

6 EXCEPTIONAL

A. **Creating the Lead:** The writer grabs the reader's attention from the start and leads him or her into the piece naturally. He or she entices the reader, providing a tantalizing glimpse of what is to come.

B. **Using Sequence Words and Transition Words:** The writer includes a variety of carefully selected sequence words (such as later, then, and meanwhile) and transition words (such as however, also, and clearly), which are placed wisely to guide the reader through the piece by showing how ideas progress, relate, and/or diverge.

C. **Structuring the Body:** The writer creates a piece that is easy to follow by fitting details together logically. He or she slows down to spotlight important points or events, and speeds up when he or she needs to move the reader along.

D. **Ending With a Sense of Resolution:** The writer sums up his or her thinking in a natural, thoughtful, and convincing way. He or she anticipates and answers any lingering questions the reader may have, providing a strong sense of closure.

5 STRONG

4 REFINING

A. **Creating the Lead:** The writer presents an introduction, although it may not be original or thought-provoking. Instead, it may be a simple restatement of the topic and, therefore, does not create a sense of anticipation about what is to come.

B. **Using Sequence Words and Transition Words:** The writer uses sequence words to show the logical order of details, but they may feel obvious or canned. The use of transition words is spotty and rarely creates coherence.

C. **Structuring the Body:** The writer sequences events and important points logically, for the most part. However, the reader may wish to move a few things around to create a more sensible flow. He or she may also feel the urge to speed up or slow down for more satisfying pacing.

D. **Ending With a Sense of Resolution:** The writer ends the piece on a familiar note: "Thank you for reading...." "Now you know all about..." or "They lived happily ever after." He or she needs to tie up loose ends to leave the reader with a sense of satisfaction or closure.

3 DEVELOPING

2 EMERGING

A. **Creating the Lead:** The writer does not give the reader any clue about what is to come. The opening point feels as if it were chosen randomly.

B. **Using Sequence Words and Transition Words:** The writer does not provide sequence and/or transition words between sections or provides words that are so confusing the reader is unable to sort one section from another.

C. **Structuring the Body:** The writer does not show clearly what comes first, next, and last, making it difficult to understand how sections fit together. The writer slows down when he or she should speed up, and speeds up when he or she should slow down.

D. **Ending With a Sense of Resolution:** The writer ends the piece with no conclusion at all—or nothing more than "The End" or something equally bland. There is no sense of resolution, no sense of completion.

1 RUDIMENTARY

HIGH / MIDDLE / LOW

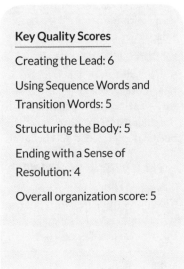

Key Quality Scores

Creating the Lead: 6

Using Sequence Words and Transition Words: 5

Structuring the Body: 5

Ending with a Sense of Resolution: 4

Overall organization score: 5

Figure 2.5 *Organization scored page for "Hula Hooping"*

Key Quality Scores

Establishing a Tone: 6

Conveying the Purpose: 5

Creating a Connection to the Audience: 6

Taking Risks to Create Voice: 6

Overall voice score: 6

Scoring Guide: Voice

The tone and tenor of the piece—the personal stamp of the writer, which is achieved through a strong understanding of purpose and audience.

6 EXCEPTIONAL

A. **Establishing a Tone:** The writer cares about the topic, and it shows. The writing is expressive and compelling. The reader feels the writer's conviction, authority, and integrity.

B. **Conveying the Purpose:** The writer makes clear his or her reason for creating the piece. He or she offers a point of view that is appropriate for the mode (narrative, expository, or persuasive), which compels the reader to read on.

C. **Creating a Connection to the Audience:** The writer speaks in a way that makes the reader want to listen. He or she has considered what the reader needs to know and the best way to convey it by sharing his or her fascination, feelings, and opinions about the topic.

D. **Taking Risks to Create Voice:** The writer expresses ideas in new ways, which makes the piece interesting and original. The writing sounds like the writer because of his or her use of distinctive, just-right words and phrases.

5 STRONG

4 REFINING

A. **Establishing a Tone:** The writer has established a tone that can be described as "pleasing" or "sincere," but not "passionate" or "compelling." He or she attempts to create a tone that hits the mark, but the overall result feels generic.

B. **Conveying the Purpose:** The writer has chosen a voice for the piece that is not completely clear. There are only a few moments when the reader understands where the writer is coming from and why he or she wrote the piece.

C. **Creating a Connection to the Audience:** The writer keeps the reader at a distance. The connection between reader and writer is tenuous because the writer reveals little about what is important or meaningful about the topic.

D. **Taking Risks to Create Voice:** The writer creates a few moments that catch the reader's attention, but only a few. The piece sounds like anyone could have written it. It lacks the energy, commitment, and conviction that would distinguish it from other pieces on the same topic.

3 DEVELOPING

2 EMERGING

A. **Establishing a Tone:** The writer has produced a lifeless piece—one that is monotonous, mechanical, repetitious, and/or off-putting to the reader.

B. **Conveying the Purpose:** The writer chose the topic for mysterious reasons. The piece may be filled with random thoughts, technical jargon, or inappropriate vocabulary, making it impossible to discern how the writer feels about the topic.

C. **Creating a Connection to the Audience:** The writer provides no evidence that he or she has considered what the reader might need to know to connect with the topic. Or there is an obvious mismatch between the piece's tone and the intended audience.

D. **Taking Risks to Create Voice:** The writer creates no highs and lows. The piece is flat and lifeless, causing the reader to wonder why he or she wrote it in the first place. The writer's voice does not pop out, even for a moment.

1 RUDIMENTARY

Figure 2.6 *Voice scored page for "Hula Hooping"*

Voice trait summary

This writer has voice down! Her enthusiasm is infectious, and her knowledge of hula hooping is evident. The voice scoring guide shown in Figure 2.6 recognizes this writer's strong command of the voice trait.

Reading this piece makes me want to meet the writer. I want to hear her talk more about her passion for hula hooping. Her writing is expressive and real—two voice-related issues that are essential for drawing in the reader. The only nudge might be to make the purpose for the piece clearer. However, there's personal experience and believability here—we love both in a piece of writing.

Word Choice trait summary

The word choice trait is priceless during the revision process. Writers can always find a more precise word, a crisper way to express an idea. And, the specificity with language we crave as readers will come only through revision. Although this writer shows good control of word choice, you can see areas where she could use more imaginative language; I've marked that on the word choice scoring guide in Figure 2.7.

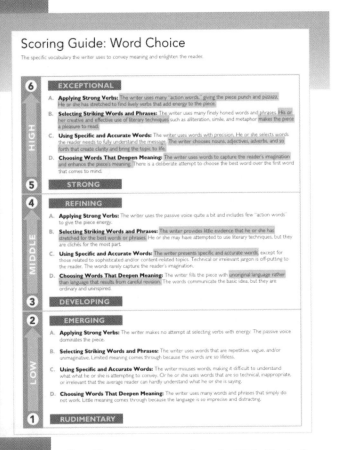

Scoring Guide: Word Choice

The specific vocabulary the writer uses to convey meaning and enlighten the reader.

6 EXCEPTIONAL

HIGH

A. **Applying Strong Verbs:** The writer uses many "action words," giving the piece punch and pizzazz. He or she has stretched to find lively verbs that add energy to the piece.

B. **Selecting Striking Words and Phrases:** The writer uses many finely honed words and phrases. His or her creative and effective use of literary techniques such as alliteration, simile, and metaphor makes the piece a pleasure to read.

C. **Using Specific and Accurate Words:** The writer uses words with precision. He or she selects words the reader needs to fully understand the message. The writer chooses nouns, adjectives, adverbs, and so forth that create clarity and bring the topic to life.

D. **Choosing Words That Deepen Meaning:** The writer uses words to capture the reader's imagination and enhance the piece's meaning. There is a deliberate attempt to choose the best word over the first word that comes to mind.

5 STRONG

4 REFINING

MIDDLE

A. **Applying Strong Verbs:** The writer uses the passive voice quite a bit and includes few "action words" to give the piece energy.

B. **Selecting Striking Words and Phrases:** The writer provides little evidence that he or she has stretched for the best words or phrases. He or she may have attempted to use literary techniques, but they are clichés for the most part.

C. **Using Specific and Accurate Words:** The writer presents specific and accurate words, except for those related to sophisticated and/or content-related topics. Technical or irrelevant jargon is off-putting to the reader. The words rarely capture the reader's imagination.

D. **Choosing Words That Deepen Meaning:** The writer fills the piece with unoriginal language rather than language that results from careful revision. The words communicate the basic idea, but they are ordinary and uninspired.

3 DEVELOPING

2 EMERGING

LOW

A. **Applying Strong Verbs:** The writer makes no attempt at selecting verbs with energy. The passive voice dominates the piece.

B. **Selecting Striking Words and Phrases:** The writer uses words that are repetitive, vague, and/or unimaginative. Limited meaning comes through because the words are so lifeless.

C. **Using Specific and Accurate Words:** The writer misuses words, making it difficult to understand what what he or she is attempting to convey. Or he or she uses words that are so technical, inappropriate, or irrelevant that the average reader can hardly understand what he or she is saying.

D. **Choosing Words That Deepen Meaning:** The writer uses many words and phrases that simply do not work. Little meaning comes through because the language is so imprecise and distracting.

1 RUDIMENTARY

Key Quality Scores

Applying Strong Verbs: 5

Selecting Striking Words and Phrases: 4

Using Accurate and Specific Words: 5

Choosing Words That Deepen Meaning: 4

Overall word choice score: 4 ↑

Figure 2.7 *Word Choice scored page for "Hula Hooping"*

Sometimes, a most-accurate score straddles two performance zones. In this case, there are some strengths in word choice right along with examples of mundane language. I sometimes use the arrow-up symbol (↑). It's not a 6, because the words still need refining in places, but it's not a 3 either, because of the piece's strengths in word choice. Some teachers prefer to give split scores (4/5) in cases like these, whereas others use half points (4.5) or pluses and minuses (4+/4-). I like the arrow; it says, *"Just a little more work and you'll be in a whole new zone with word choice. Exciting—good for you!"*

Sometimes, a most-accurate score straddles two performance zones.

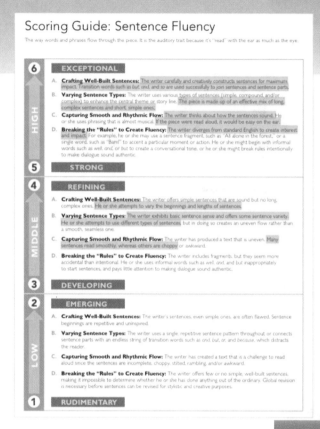

Figure 2.8 *Sentence Fluency scored page for "Hula Hooping"*

Sentence Fluency trait summary

Some parts of this piece show mastery over sentence fluency, and other parts are rather ordinary. Generally, the first half of the piece is stronger than the second, but the strengths are executed well and outweigh any places that lapse. Figure 2.8 shows my highlighted marks on the sentence fluency scoring guide.

You can help the writer reach the next level in sentence fluency by pointing out what is strong and suggesting where the sentences could be revised to show more variety and read more smoothly. Use a highlighter on the text to visually pinpoint areas where some basic sentence combining might work. For example, these two sentences—*"In my opinion, hula hooping brings us together. It makes us have fun and feels comfortable."*—could be joined together: *"In my opinion, hula hooping brings us together because we have fun and feel comfortable playing our favorite sport."*

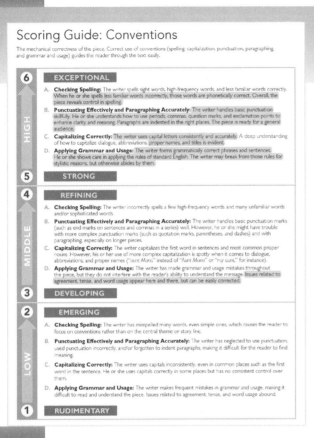

Scoring Guide: Conventions

The mechanical correctness of the piece. Correct use of conventions (spelling, capitalization, punctuation, paragraphing, and grammar and usage) guides the reader through the text easily.

6 EXCEPTIONAL

A. **Checking Spelling:** The writer spells sight words, high-frequency words, and less familiar words correctly. When he or she spells less familiar words incorrectly, those words are phonetically correct. Overall, the piece reveals control in spelling.

B. **Punctuating Effectively and Paragraphing Accurately:** The writer handles basic punctuation skillfully. He or she understands how to use periods, commas, question marks, and exclamation points to enhance clarity and meaning. Paragraphs are indented in the right places. The piece is ready for a general audience.

C. **Capitalizing Correctly:** The writer uses capital letters consistently and accurately. A deep understanding of how to capitalize dialogue, abbreviations, proper names, and titles is evident.

D. **Applying Grammar and Usage:** The writer forms grammatically correct phrases and sentences. He or she shows care in applying the rules of standard English. The writer may break from those rules for stylistic reasons, but otherwise abides by them.

5 STRONG

4 REFINING

A. **Checking Spelling:** The writer incorrectly spells a few high-frequency words and many unfamiliar words and/or sophisticated words.

B. **Punctuating Effectively and Paragraphing Accurately:** The writer handles basic punctuation marks (such as end marks on sentences and commas in a series) well. However, he or she might have trouble with more complex punctuation marks (such as quotation marks, parentheses, and dashes) and with paragraphing, especially on longer pieces.

C. **Capitalizing Correctly:** The writer capitalizes the first word in sentences and most common proper nouns. However, his or her use of more complex capitalization is spotty when it comes to dialogue, abbreviations, and proper names ("aunt Marie" instead of "Aunt Marie" or "my aunt," for instance).

D. **Applying Grammar and Usage:** The writer has made grammar and usage mistakes throughout the piece, but they do not interfere with the reader's ability to understand the message. Issues related to agreement, tense, and word usage appear here and there, but can be easily corrected.

3 DEVELOPING

2 EMERGING

A. **Checking Spelling:** The writer has misspelled many words, even simple ones, which causes the reader to focus on conventions rather than on the central theme or story line.

B. **Punctuating Effectively and Paragraphing Accurately:** The writer has neglected to use punctuation, used punctuation incorrectly, and/or forgotten to indent paragraphs, making it difficult for the reader to find meaning.

C. **Capitalizing Correctly:** The writer uses capitals inconsistently, even in common places such as the first word in the sentence. He or she uses capitals correctly in some places but has no consistent control over them.

D. **Applying Grammar and Usage:** The writer makes frequent mistakes in grammar and usage, making it difficult to read and understand the piece. Issues related to agreement, tense, and word usage abound.

1 RUDIMENTARY

Figure 2.9 *Conventions scored page for "Hula Hooping"*

Key Quality Scores

Checking Spelling: 5

Punctuating Effectively and Paragraphing Accurately: 6

Capitalizing Correctly: 5

Applying Grammar and Usage: 6

Overall Conventions score: 5 ↑

Conventions trait summary

Because this is a finished piece, the writer has already edited for conventions, so this is a good time to see if she needs more help with anything in this area. It's difficult to assess conventions as one unit; you would be wise to think about each of the four key qualities separately. Don't lump everything together, or you might miss the fact that the punctuation shows a range of skill. Figure 2.9 shows how I'd score this paper for conventions.

You probably noticed that there are a few spelling errors, but nothing all that serious. There are some small issues in capitalization, but the grammar is strong. This is an example of why holistic scores are not as useful as analytical ones: when one score for conventions is assigned, you don't see the strengths and weaknesses in as much definition to know where to help the student. You may want to provide the student with feedback on each convention separately, over time, and zero in on what is expected at your grade-level standards. With regard to conventions overall, this piece is almost ready to share; it would need only a small amount of editing to publish it.

Scoring Guide: Presentation

The physical appearance of the piece. A visually appealing text provides a welcome mat. It invites the reader in.

6 EXCEPTIONAL

HIGH

A. **Applying Handwriting Skills:** The writer uses handwriting that is clear and legible. Whether he or she prints or uses cursive, letters are uniform and slant evenly throughout the piece. Spacing between words is consistent.

B. **Using Word Processing Effectively:** The writer uses a font style and size that are easy to read and are a good match for the piece's purpose. If he or she uses color, it enhances the piece's readability.

C. **Making Good Use of White Space:** The writer frames the text with appropriately sized margins. Artful spacing between letters, words, and lines makes reading a breeze. There are no cross-outs, smudges, or tears on the paper.

D. **Refining Text Features:** The writer effectively places text features such as headings, page numbers, titles, and bullets on the page and aligns them clearly with the text they support.

5 STRONG

4 REFINING

MIDDLE

A. **Applying Handwriting Skills:** The writer has readable handwriting, but his or her inconsistent letter slanting, spacing, and formation distract from the central theme or story line.

B. **Using Word Processing Effectively:** The writer uses an easy-to-read font but formats it in a way that makes the piece cluttered and distracting. His or her choice of font style and/or size may not match the piece's purpose. He or she may use color with varying degrees of success.

C. **Making Good Use of White Space:** The writer creates margins but they are inconsistent or ineffective as a frame for the piece. Spacing between letters, words, and lines makes reading difficult at times. An occasional cross-out or smudge blemishes the piece.

D. **Refining Text Features:** The writer includes complex text features such as charts, graphs, maps, and tables, but not clearly or consistently. However, he or she does a good job with less complex features such as the size and placement of the title, bullets, sidebars, subheadings, illustrations, and page numbers.

3 DEVELOPING

2 EMERGING

LOW

A. **Applying Handwriting Skills:** The writer forms letters and uses space in a way that makes the piece virtually illegible. The handwriting is a visual barrier.

B. **Using Word Processing Effectively:** The writer creates a dizzying display of different font styles and sizes, making the piece virtually unreadable. The misuse of color also detracts.

C. **Making Good Use of White Space:** The writer formats margins inconsistently and uses white space ineffectively, making the piece hard to read. Space between letters, words, and lines is nonexistent, or there is so much space it's distracting.

D. **Refining Text Features:** The writer does not include features or includes features that are confusing or indecipherable rather than useful to the reader. The paper is seriously marred with cross-outs, smudges, and/or tears.

1 RUDIMENTARY

Figure 2.10 *Presentation scored page for "Hula Hooping"*

Presentation trait summary

Let's approach this feature of the writing in a slightly different way—by thinking only about which key qualities from the scoring guide apply to the writing (see Figure 2.10). Presentation is, after all, more of a visual and fine motor skill than a cognitive writing skill. It matters to readers, without a doubt, but depending on the purpose and the medium of the writing (handwritten or word processed), you will need to reflect only on the parts of the scoring guide that apply. In addition, presentation matters most on a final, finished copy—something we don't have in our hands every day.

That said, in this piece we notice right away that the handwriting is easy to read. The letters and words stand out clearly, even to my old eyes. The use of margins and white space works fine; it's hard to keep words from spilling into the right margin, but this writer minimizes that issue. I'm not bothered by the fact that the last three lines are crammed into the bottom space. The title is set off nicely, though other text features such as page numbers, integration of art, or the use of bullets and subheads are not attempted. Overall, the piece is quite readable. I'd assign it an overall presentation score of 5.

"Hula Hooping" Wrap-Up

Review the scores for all the traits together. Does this spread of scores convey the message you'd like this writer to receive? The ideas and word choice require the most work; the other traits just need tweaking.

Ideas	Organization	Voice	Word Choice	Sentence Fluency	Conventions	Presentation
4	5	6	4	5	5	5

For instructional purposes, select a trait that has been demonstrated relatively well and one that needs additional work to comment upon. Go back to the scoring guide, look for what you highlighted in the key qualities for each trait, note the language, and frame your feedback using those details.

When you respond to the writer about this piece, you might say something like this:

> *I never thought that much about hula hooping until I read your paper. It really made me think about how fun and social it can be. I could tell this was your paper just because of the expressions you used and the energy you put into it—there's great voice here. Way to go! Now, let's take a look at your ideas and the purpose for your writing. I'm not sure if you are writing an opinion piece or an informational piece. Let's talk about the two different ways your idea could develop and how to revise to make your purpose for writing more clear as you begin your next piece.*

If you and I were sitting face-to-face, talking about this paper as colleagues, I would look you in the eye and make sure you understood that this numeric information is provided for formative assessment purposes only. Again: the numbers provided in the scoring guides are only there to help guide your instruction and document this student's writing growth. (I know you have to give a grade every now and then, though, so I'll show you how to convert rubric scores into grades next.) Use the scoring guides to help you look inside the writing and ferret out strengths and areas the student can work on throughout the writing process.

> The numbers provided in the scoring guides are only there to help guide your instruction and document this student's writing growth.

One paper does not provide enough feedback to students as they begin to revise for one, several, or all of the traits. You'll need to gain more experience. Every worthwhile skill takes practice, right? Formative assessment is complex but so informative—it is well worth the effort. Now would be an excellent time to try assessing a few more papers. Try assessing the writing samples in Appendix A. Use them, along with writing samples from your own classroom and school, to gain skill and confidence with traits-based assessment.

Discuss with colleagues: How will this type of formative assessment change how you read student writing? How can it help you differentiate instruction based on what evidence in the writing demonstrates that each student needs?

If You Have to Give a Grade

A grading conversion chart is necessary to convert rubric scores into percentages because, as you may have noticed, simply dividing the number of points earned by the number of possible points gives you a pure percentage that skews low for grading purposes. For example, on a 6-point scale, a student scoring a 3 should not get 50 percent (usually an F)—your gut instinct should tell you that is wrong. Shouldn't it be a midrange score—a C? Yet if you divide 3 by 6, you get .50. What's up with that?

The answer lies in a mathematical formula that will bring the score into the range we typically use in American grading scales. Perhaps you use this one: 90–100 = A; 80–89 = B; 70–79 = C; 60–69 = D; 59 and below = F. (If you use something similar, the same thinking applies.) Given the 90–100 = A example, walk through this with me as a writing teacher and not a math teacher:

How many ways are there to get an A? 11 (90, 91, 92, 93, 94, 95, 96, 97, 98, 99, 100)

How many ways are there to get a B? 10 (80, 81, 82, 83, 84, 85, 86, 87, 88, 89)

How many ways are there to get a C? 10 (70, 71, 72, 73, 74, 75, 76, 77, 78, 79)

How many ways are there to get a D? 10 (60, 61, 62, 63, 64, 65, 66, 67, 68, 69)

HOW MANY WAYS ARE THERE TO GET AN F? >59

The inequity is obvious. Using a traditional scale, we don't have an equal distribution from 1 to 100 for assigning grades. In essence, we use only the top forty points from 60 to 100. So, when working with a rubric scoring system, you must use a grading conversion chart where all the math has been done behind the scenes in order to make your grading accurate and fair.

Over the years, I've developed a chart that will give you a percentage score based on how many traits were scored, from 1 to 7. (You can see a thumbnail of this chart in Figure 2.11; a full-page version appears in Appendix B, and you can download it at sten.pub/tww.) You line up the total number of traits scored (x) with the number of points earned (y); the intersection of the x and y axes is the percentage.

The 6pt. Grading Chart

Grading Chart: Points to Percentages

Number of Traits Scored

Grade	Total Points	7	6	5	4	3	2	1
	1							60.00%
	2						60.00%	68.00%
	3					60.00%	64.00%	76.00%
	4				60.00%	62.67%	68.00%	84.00%
	5			60.00%	62.00%	65.33%	72.00%	92.00%
Grade	6		60.00%	61.60%	64.00%	68.00%	76.00%	100.00%
	7	60.00%	61.33%	63.20%	66.00%	70.67%	80.00%	
	8	61.14%	62.67%	64.80%	68.00%	73.33%	84.00%	
	9	62.29%	64.00%	66.40%	70.00%	76.00%	88.00%	
F	10	63.43%	65.33%	68.00%	72.00%	78.67%	92.00%	
	11	64.57%	66.67%	69.60%	74.00%	81.33%	96.00%	
	12	65.71%	68.00%	71.20%	76.00%	84.00%	100.00%	
	13	66.86%	69.33%	72.80%	78.00%	86.67%		
	14	68.00%	70.67%	74.40%	80.00%	89.33%		
	15	69.14%	72.00%	76.00%	82.00%	92.00%		
	16	70.29%	73.33%	77.60%	84.00%	94.67%		
D	17	71.43%	74.67%	79.20%	86.00%	97.33%		
	18	72.57%	76.00%	80.80%	88.00%	100.00%		
	19	73.71%	77.33%	82.40%	90.00%			
	20	74.86%	78.67%	84.00%	92.00%			
	21	76.00%	80.00%	85.60%	94.00%			
	22	77.14%	81.33%	87.20%	96.00%			
	23	78.29%	82.67%	88.80%	98.00%			
C	24	79.43%	84.00%	90.40%	100.00%			
	25	80.57%	85.33%	92.00%				
	26	81.71%	86.67%	93.60%				
	27	82.86%	88.00%	95.20%				
	28	84.00%	89.33%	96.80%				
	29	85.14%	90.67%	98.40%				
	30	86.29%	92.00%	100.00%				
B	31	87.43%	93.33%					
	32	88.57%	94.67%					
	33	89.71%	96.00%					
	34	90.86%	97.33%					
	35	92.00%	98.67%					
	36	93.14%	100.00%					
	37	94.29%						
A	38	95.43%						
	39	96.57%						
	40	97.71%						
	41	98.86%						
A+	42	100.00%						

Figure 2.11 *Grade conversion chart*

For example, if you assessed all seven traits, locate 7 horizontally across the top of the grading chart, "Number of Traits Scored." Next, add up the number of points the writer earned. In the case of Hula Hooping, the total score is 34. Follow the "Total Points" vertically on the left until you get to 34. Intersect the number of traits scored (x axis) with the number of points earned (y axis), and you'll find that this piece earns a 90.86 percent.

Say you want to score only one trait—for example, word choice. In Hula Hooping, the word choice score is 4. By moving across the x axis to one trait and then locating 4 points on the y axis, you'll arrive at a score of 84 percent. Voilá! (You're welcome.)

I challenged you at the beginning of this chapter to think about a disgruntled parent confronting you about your assessment of their child's writing. If you have based your assessment on the traits of writing criteria, you will have no problem showing where examples from the writing match the scoring guide.

Now you can convert that assessment into a grade that makes sense. I would not want to be in your shoes if you tried to explain to a parent that a child who earned 3 out of 6 points was failing. Let's not go there. Use the grading chart.

Wrap-Up: Assessment Is the Heart of the Matter

I can't stress strongly enough how important it is to read the writing—really read it. Taking the time to understand what the writer is trying to do will make it much easier to determine how to help him or her when it is time to revise. Your practice can continue with the papers in the appendix and then with papers from your own students. Think of it like getting ready for a *Saturday Night Live* broadcast that lasts ninety minutes but takes a frenzied week to prepare: you and fellow writers create the script; you rehearse and smooth things out; you do a final dress rehearsal in front of an audience; and then you perform. *"Live! It's Saturday Night!"* It's filmed and broadcast across the world—flaws and all—and then the whole process begins again. Your assessment of student writing, actual student writing from your own class, is the performance. Your students will take what you have to say seriously, so we want to get it right. Practice, practice, practice.

3

Modes of Writing:
Their Challenges and Why They Matter

Rhetorical modes of writing are a big part of today's writing instruction conversation; modes, in short, describe the purposes for writing. As we continue to learn about and refine the best ways to teach writing, there is a renewed and driving interest in what we write and for whom (modes), not just in how (traits). Part of this attention is a direct result of the standards movement that has swept our country from north to south, east to west. The writing standards clearly focus on making sure students develop proficiency in different modes of writing: narrative, expository, and persuasive. In many sets of standards, modes are more specifically identified: narrative, informative/explanatory, and opinion/argument.

Often the modes are referred to as purposes for writing; indeed, I have defined the term *mode* this way for more than twenty-five years. The two terms are more similar in meaning than not, but there is a subtle difference. Mode is a broader term that encompasses not only the purpose for the writing but also the audience. That's an important distinction because, as writing teachers, we need to instruct students to be mindful of both who they are writing to and why they are writing.

The National Council of Teachers of English frames it this way in their 2016 position statement:

> Writing with certain purposes in mind, the writer focuses attention on what the audience is thinking or believing; other times, the writer focuses more on the information she or he is organizing, or on her or his own emergent thoughts and feelings. Therefore, the thinking, procedures, and physical format in writing are shaped in accord with the author's purpose(s), the needs of the audience, and the conventions of the genre. (1)

Part of the work to be done as a writing teacher is to convince students they're not always writing for you, the teacher, but for a more authentic audience. How they craft the piece depends, in great measure, on who they believe will be reading it. So, for instance, if a student is writing an opinion piece about why dogs should be allowed in school, is he writing it for classmates or for the school board? Keeping in mind a clear picture of the audience will help any writer focus on purpose and help him or her move among the traits; decisions about organization, sentence fluency, ideas, voice, and so on—all will depend on a clear purpose and audience.

Writing standards have attempted to simplify modes, but I would argue that they've oversimplified them and, in doing so, stripped away some of the authenticity of student writing. We need to consider the different purposes for writing, no question, but also the audience. They go hand in hand, shaping the text in tandem.

Why Do We Care About Modes?

Remember: traits are *how* you write; modes are *what* you write. Two peas in a pod. In our attempt to prepare students for their writing lives in and outside of school, we sometimes miss a critical point: motivating students to write has a great deal to do with increasing their awareness of how much their writing matters in all its different shapes and forms, now and into the future. That means understanding the different purposes for which they write and how those purposes affect those who will read their work. Many students do what they are asked to do, but do not have a chance to explore what fascinates, intrigues, or engages them and then frame it in a way that is meaningful for a specific purpose and audience. They see writing as a school subject—a hard one!—that is done to please the teacher or the system, not themselves.

If we want students to care more about writing, we should, as teachers, explore what students want to write about and what form it could take, hand in hand with relevant instruction for students to do it well. Renowned researcher and author George Hillocks Jr. says it this way: *"We know, from a very wide variety of studies in English and out of it, that students who are authentically engaged with the tasks of their learning are likely to learn much more than those who are not"* (2011, 189).

Approaching modes with this in mind is key. Talking with students—asking them what they want to write about and how to approach the writing through the lens of the modes—can foster the enthusiasm that writing well demands. We want students to learn to write for many different purposes and acquire the skills needed to do so. However, when what students write is always determined for them, we create an atmosphere where school is about the teacher; students are just along for the ride. We need our writing classrooms to be meaningful, purpose-driven places where teachers guide—not control—the writing students generate. Here is what this type of writing classroom looks like:

Remember: traits are how you write. Modes are what you write.

- Nine months are spent talking, listening, considering, modeling, and sharing, which sets the stage for writing in each of the modes over the course of the year.
- Students are challenged to choose topics of interest and write about them in different modes based on models.
- Teachers urge students to try new formats and genres, and to explore each mode in different ways over time.

And here's what it sounds like:

Teacher: Will you tell me what you are writing about?

Student: NASCAR. I'm a big fan of NASCAR, so I was thinking that could be my idea.

Teacher: That's great. I'm curious about how you got interested in NASCAR racing. Tell me!

Student: [Talks about personal connections.]

Teacher: So, as you are getting ready to write, will you be planning a story that has NASCAR racing or a NASCAR racer in it? Will you explain the sport and give readers information they may not know about NASCAR racing? Or will you be generating an opinion about why NASCAR is a better sport to follow than others?

Student: Uhh . . .

Teacher: May I share an observation? You wrote a narrative piece about a talking cell phone last time; now would you consider giving readers a meaty piece that focuses on history and facts about NASCAR racing? If you like that idea, let's think about what it could look like. A Wikipedia-style article on the history of NASCAR? Or a PowerPoint show in the NASCAR Hall of Fame that documents the changes in design, speed, and safety over time? Or do you have another approach you'd like to try? I want this to be something you get excited about so it will be exciting for me to read too!

Teaching modes well requires listening, valuing student input, and knowing the student's writing history so you can help broaden its scope. First and foremost, however, conversations like the preceding one validate to the writer that what he or she cares about makes all the difference in the writing classroom. It has the added benefit of creating much stronger writing that is a pleasure to read.

A Quick Look at Modes

The three modes generally used to describe the types of writing and their purposes are narrative, expository (informative/explanatory), and persuasive (opinion/argument). Descriptive writing has also been considered a mode at times in our educational history. However, much like Pluto's standing as a planet, it's been demoted to a "dwarf mode" because all writing should be descriptive, whether it's narrative, expository, or persuasive.

Narrative Writing

Purpose: to tell a story. The writer typically

- offers a clear, well-developed story line;
- includes characters that grow and change over time;
- conveys time and setting effectively;
- presents a conflict and resolution; and
- surprises, challenges, and/or entertains the reader.

Narrative writing provides a glimpse into the thinker's laboratory—the place where life is explored and considered, whether fiction or nonfiction. Through narrative, we relate our observations of life's complexity and how it feels when things are unfair or unjust in the real or imagined world. We explore friendship, loss, love, betrayal, and joy. We reveal our perspective on what it is like to be part of a family or culture that we know or imagine—and much more. Narrative writing seeks the truth—truth that is not always dependent on facts.

> Narrative writing reveals what is unique to the writer's life experience.

Narrative writing reveals what is unique to the writer's life experience and imagination; it's organized by time, and the voice is often personal and emotional.

Expository Writing

Purpose: to explain and provide information. The writer typically

- informs the reader about the topic;
- goes beyond the obvious to explain what is interesting or curious about the topic;
- focuses on making the topic clear for the reader;
- anticipates and answers the reader's questions; and
- includes details that add information, support key ideas, and help the reader make personal connections.

Expository writing, sometimes called informative or explanatory writing, gets a bad rap for being flat and dry. It is, indeed, driven by facts and information. But it should be thrilling to explore new ideas through facts and details—just as energizing as reading and writing a powerful narrative. There is no quicker way to turn off a reader than by boring them or trying to impress them with how much you know. Good expository writing should not read like a textbook or a typical encyclopedia article; it should read like literature. If you really know a lot about something, chances are your expertise started out as a simple interest that grew over time and circumstance to a full-fledged fascination. The energy behind that process of discovery should fill every page. Without it, no matter how much data and how many facts you've included, the writing will be lackluster and forgettable.

In expository writing, the idea is driven by the information behind it. It's organized according to the best way to lay out the information so the reader understands it (compare/contrast, deductive logic, point-by-point analysis, and so on). The voice in expository writing is credible, authentic, and trustworthy.

Persuasive Writing

Purpose: to construct an argument using reason and logic. The writer typically

- states a position (claim) clearly and sticks with it;
- offers good, sound reasoning;
- provides solid facts, opinions, and examples;
- reveals weaknesses in other positions; and
- uses voice to add credibility and show confidence.

Persuasive writing's purpose is to convince the reader by constructing an argument based on opinion, personal experience, anecdotes, data, evidence from texts, and examples. Persuasive writing uses evidence that supports the writer's opinion with facts and information; it can also play on the reader's emotions. Persuasive writing includes academic essays as well as marketing and propaganda.

Argument is a specific form of persuasive writing that draws upon the critical thinking essential to logic, which gets at argument's core. There is no room for personal appeal in argument writing; it is a purely academic form of discourse, which is why we study argument as a subset of persuasive writing. Argument writing is fine-tuned in the secondary grades. To prepare for academic writing, elementary students write fact-based opinions in order to persuade readers. The objective in opinion writing is to take a position and defend it with sound reasoning.

In persuasive writing, an idea is explored with a point of view (the author's or the reader's) in mind. Much like expository writing, it's built on facts and information, and it's organized similarly too. The voice must be believable and convincing. Persuasive writing is just good expository writing with an attitude.

Challenges in Modes—Trait by Trait

As you find ways to fuse the traits and modes to create a robust writing curriculum, areas of confusion can pop up and present challenges. Of course. You are helping students with big ideas for writing. It will take time for them to grasp how craft and purpose relate—in other words, how the traits are present in every mode of writing but may show themselves differently, depending on the purpose and audience. What follows is a discussion of the typical issues that arise and ideas for resolving them.

What Challenges Students in the Narrative Mode?

Ideas

They haven't learned to control the idea. For a long time, students tend to write simple stories without the insight or evidence of complex thinking that readers crave. Narrative writing seeks a bigger truth—something we can feel or believe rather than something we can measure. Therefore, narrative writing may well be the most challenging mode to master. It contains many different genres, from personal narrative to fantasy and memoir. And the basic elements of story line or plot in narrative genres—setting, time line, problem and resolution, characters and how they reveal themselves—are a lot to understand. *Suggestion: Look to mentor texts and point out examples that show mastery in each area of narrative writing that students can discuss and emulate.*

Organization

They run like thoroughbreds. Sometimes writers take off, never looking back, and write and write and write. They start out with one idea, but as it travels across paragraphs and pages, it morphs into something quite different by the end. Mostly this happens when there is a lack of clear organization; a loose focus is fine for notes or a very rough draft, but it doesn't work for a finished, polished piece of writing. Writers sometimes meander and wander around and through the story when instead they need to work toward staying on track, developing the piece thoughtfully and with direction. *Suggestion: This issue can be resolved by allowing time for planning and prewriting—thinking about and organizing ideas ahead of time—as much as possible.*

Voice

Young writers don't consider how important it is to relate to the reader. Many students write to please the teacher, to get a good grade, or simply to be finished. These writers have yet to discover the power of voice. They don't think about the reader, so the words and sentences they write can be technically correct but lack elements of interest. As they revise for voice, students need to keep in mind that readers not only want a story that is complete and well developed, they also want to be surprised, enthralled, teased, astonished, and blown away by a great story told with strong voice. For example, a student might write "It was scary" in a first draft. Imagine this instead in a final piece: "There it was again. That feeling that made the hairs of my neck prickle and my heart beat through my chest." That's voice. *Suggestion: Make sure students are writing about things that matter to them and that they are clear about who the audience is. Students will likely add humor, for instance, if they are writing for a classmate or friend.*

> Students need larger writing vocabularies, for sure, but they also need to apply the words they know with care.

Word Choice

They use the same words over and over. Knowing words and knowing how to use them effectively are two different things. Students need larger writing vocabularies, for sure, but they also need to apply the words they know with care. Many students write the first word they think of and call it done. For more dedicated writers, however, this word serves as a placeholder. On a second and third pass, the writer looks at the words in the sentence and chooses the best way, the most precise way, or the most interesting way to say that same thing. On significant pieces, make sure students go through their entire piece—from soup to nuts—to revise their words and experience the thrill of finding a better choice to replace something ordinary. *Suggestion: Read to them and with them—the surest way to learn new words.*

Sentence Fluency

They try dialogue. Yay! They try dialogue. Sigh. Constructing effective dialogue can frustrate even the most confident writer. Dialogue should move the story forward, not simply show two characters speaking. Fragments show up in narrative writing more often than other modes, too. You'll likely need to help students learn how to use them for stylistic effect. Young writers need to master sentence structure before they can use fragments to convey style or voice; otherwise, they'll simply confuse the reader. *Suggestion: Encourage students to examine mentor texts for the use of dialogue and come up with creative ways to show what is spoken aloud—speech bubbles, for instance.*

What Challenges Students in the Expository Mode?

Ideas

They get swamped because there's too much information available. As students sift through the world of possibilities, it's hard for them to choose what to include in their papers. Books, magazines, the Internet, movies, TV, interviews . . . the options are endless. Students often don't have the research skills needed to know what is useful and what isn't. They grab onto the first website that pops up and start using information from it even though it's only tangentially related to their topic. You'll need to remind students, "Just because it's on Wikipedia doesn't mean it's right for your paper." *Suggestion: Pick a topic and show students three examples of research you gather from the Internet: one with misinformation, one with general information, and one with specific and accurate information. Prioritize types of sites that generally include more trustworthy information—those ending in .edu and .gov instead of .com, for example.*

Organization

They settle for trite and predictable structures. Because organization is one of the hardest traits to master, students may glom onto a strategy and use it without much thought in different writing circumstances. If they are told "A paragraph has a topic sentence and three supporting details," they apply that structure every time, regardless of the content. Their writing becomes predictable and boring. It sounds forced and stilted. It doesn't work. The same is true for transitions, sequences, beginnings, and endings. Organization should position information to show the reader what matters, what's fascinating, what makes a difference. *Suggestion: Show students an organizational structure in a documentary movie, a blog, or a nonfiction book that demonstrates how the writer starts in one place and then circles back to that same place by the end. This thread of central meaning draws the reader in and then backs up to provide the background information needed to explore and explain the main idea.*

Voice

They think voice in expository writing should be boring and "academic." Often students have been served a heaping portion of textbooks and expository reading materials that lack energy, so it can be challenging for them (and for teachers!) to see the possibilities of voice in expository writing. Share lines like *"I believed then, as I do now, in the goodness of the published word: it seemed to contain an essential goodness, like the smell of leaf mold"* by E. B. White (Sweet 2016). Or *"The tentacles seize their prey. The surround their thrashing meal. They latch on with powerful sucker-studded clubs. Row after row of suckers. Suckers ringed with saw-like teeth that rip into skin and hold on tight"* (Fleming 2016). Conviction, authority, and credibility are the hallmarks of voice in expository writing. *Suggestion: There is no more powerful way to help students understand the role of voice in writing than through reading materials they relate to. Give students plenty of examples of interesting voice in expository texts.* Freedom in Congo Square *by Carole Boston Weatherford,* Penguin Day *by Nic Bishop, and* White Owl, Barn Owl *by Nicola Davies (or anything else by Nicola Davies!) are great books that show how writers create voice.*

> Conviction, authority, and credibility are the hallmarks of voice in expository writing.

Word Choice

They don't know the right words to use in content-specific writing. No matter the age of the writer, developing the right vocabulary for writing about content-specific information is a challenge. Every discipline has accurate and precise terminology that must be learned and applied correctly. In expository writing, the overuse of technical terms or jargon can get in the way of making meaning clear for a reader who is not familiar with the topic. Students struggle with unfamiliar words in texts as much because of the language as the concepts; when they do research for their own expository writing, it's easy for them to copy words and phrases they don't completely understand. *Suggestion: Encourage students to highlight words in their writing they are not sure about, look them up, and put them in their own terms.*

Fluency

They are busy thinking about other things. Many of the informative papers I've read from elementary students rely heavily on simple sentences. They may be focusing on how to integrate facts into running text, so the most effective sentence structures are not even on their radar. *Suggestion: Encourage students to read their work aloud, so they hear how choppy or sing-songy the sentences sound. Show them how to turn choppy sentences into longer, more interesting-sounding ones and how to include an interjection now and again to create interest. Remember, this trait relies on the ear as much as the eye.*

What Challenges Students in the Persuasive Mode?

Ideas

They haven't learned that all facts are not created equal. Opinion/argument relies on logic, so students need to determine which facts are most important to support their claim. When a writer discovers that two or more sources disagree on a key piece of information, he needs to do further research to determine which fact is the most accurate. Key questions they should be asking along the way are "Is this true?," How do I know?," and "Are there other places I can check to make sure my information is accurate?" Student writers also need to be sure they have acknowledged any strong ideas that reasonably dispute their claim, using facts and information.

Some heavy-duty thinking is required at the beginning, but the time spent up front can save a lot of frustration in the end.

Suggestion: Have students make a T-chart and list the facts and information they have included on one side and the sources of the facts on the other. It's not necessary to set a number, but you might give them a target of at least three or more facts and specific pieces of information to lend credibility to their idea.

Organization

They don't do enough planning, which leads to a disjointed paper. When a student says she will make the claim that Bigfoot is real, for instance, that should be just the start of her thinking about how to proceed with the topic. She'll need to focus on what she wants to write about Bigfoot, including history and location of sightings, physical appearance, fact versus fiction, and so on. She needs to plan where key information will go, how one idea will lead to the next, where to provide an opposing point of view, how to begin, and how to end. Without such planning, we receive papers from students that include a paragraph on this and a paragraph on that—but these paragraphs don't add up to a significant opinion or argument. Or the argument feels formulaic. Some heavy-duty thinking is required at the beginning, but the time spent up front can save a lot of frustration in the end. *Suggestion: Graphic organizers, as long as they are flexible and used sparingly with clear purpose, can be very helpful to students to plan their opinion writing.*

Voice

They think they have only one writing voice when, in fact, we all have many voices to draw upon. When we're passionate about an idea, we sound one way, but when we're confused or upset, we sound quite different. The voice and tone of opinion/argument writing are unlike those of its narrative counterpart—there is far less reliance on emotions such as happy, sad, thrilled, or scared. Instead, opinion/argument writing reveals the writer's commitment to the topic and compels the reader to read on. Ultimately, the purpose of opinion/argument is to convince the reader of the stance, and because purpose drives the voice in writing, the opinion/argument voice should be compelling, thoughtful, convincing, reliable, and credible. The writer needs to provide evidence from reliable sources along with well-reasoned conclusions and conviction. *Suggestion: Have students create a poster of different voice descriptors for opinion writing such as* knowledgeable, challenging, committed, enthusiastic, *and so on. Post the list so students can refer to it as they write and keep voice in mind for their opinion pieces. If time allows, make voice posters for the other two modes, narrative and expository, as well. Some attributes will be shared by all three modes, but many differences will exist among them too.*

Word Choice

They don't realize that they can be factual and still be creative. The writing we tend to find the most interesting takes some risks with word choice. Expressing an opinion or constructing an argument doesn't mean the writing must be boring and lifeless; in fact, it should be quite the opposite. The choice of sensory words and figurative language to inform readers about a persuasive topic can engage them on a deeper level. Interesting word choice will enhance voice as well. *Suggestion: Challenge students to look at the words they have used in a first draft and come up with stronger words that convey more authority and enhance their point in key places. Have them pick one or two places to zero in on for word choice revision. For example, why write "The invention of sticky notes was big" when you could write "The invention of sticky notes was accidental genius"?*

> The choice of sensory words and figurative language to inform readers about a persuasive topic can engage them on a deeper level.

Sentence Fluency

They bury key points that support the opinion or claim in long, complex sentences. There is logic to the length of sentences and their placement in this mode. Weaving information into the text, citing sources, providing examples, sharing anecdotes—all have to work together seamlessly. Students need to use their full arsenal of sentence types, lengths, and structures to make a claim about a topic, support the claim, and lead readers to the place where they seriously consider the claim. That requires long, short, simple, compound, complex, and compound/complex sentences, as well as sentences that do not all begin the same way. It's challenging, but ultimately sentences can underscore and punctuate an argument, which is extremely important in this mode. *Suggestion: Have students use questions in their writing—questions that the reader would logically have while reading the writer's opinion. Make sure they answer them. The inclusion of questions in the writing will change how the text sounds and keep the reader engaged.*

What Challenges Students in Conventions Across the Modes?

Students need skills in conventions every time they write and in every mode. Punctuating dialogue tends to plague students in the narrative mode, but dialogue could show up in the informative and opinion/argument modes too. Spelling vocabulary words can be challenging as well. Using capitalization effectively and for effect is something students should consider. And, of course, standard English grammar—unless it is in dialogue—should be applied. Citing sources correctly, following a specific style, is an issue of presentation for informative writing and opinion/argument modes. It's easy to get caught up in conventions on a first draft, which can stifle ideas, word choice, voice, and sentence fluency. Remind students that conventions help any piece of writing to be better understood. They should not worry too much about spelling, capitalization, and punctuation in a first draft, but this is a trait that definitely needs to be addressed in editing, after the idea is fully developed. *Suggestion: During editing, coach students to focus on one item at a time, such as capitalization or end punctuation, so they don't get overwhelmed. A checklist might help, and it's helpful to have peers read and comment too, because sometimes a fresh pair of eyes sees things we miss in our own writing.*

Mixing Modes

Although it's important for the writer to have a dominant mode in mind when he or she writes, weaving in other modes at carefully timed moments can bring the piece to life. This should be done in a way that makes the writing more clear and coherent—not stand out like an LED light on Rudolph's nose.

In fact, the best pieces of writing often mix modes. This is tricky for students to understand and then try on their own. We tend to want to put pieces in a neat-and-tidy writing box and label them narrative, informative, or opinion/argument. In fact, the models we show and discuss with students should have a dominant mode yet be strengthened by the use of other modes. You'll find this to be an interesting avenue to explore with students through mentor texts.

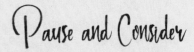

Keep the dominant mode in mind as you share picture books, chapter books, and everyday texts with your students and point out places where the author temporarily shifts to another mode to make the piece stronger.

Use the terms for modes consciously and consistently. Whether you and your schools choose the traditional terms (*narrative, expository, persuasive*) or the language of the Common Core State Standards (*narrative, informative/explanatory, opinion/argument*), choose one set of terms and stick with it.

Here's a passage from *90 Miles to Havana* by Enrique Flores-Galbis that illustrates this concept; I've labeled the different modes in brackets. It's a narrative that chronicles the true, heartbreaking story of a young boy and his brother who are exiled from Cuba, their homeland, to Miami, during operation Pedro Pan in 1961:

> My mother hasn't told me everything because she thinks I'm too young to understand and she doesn't want to scare me [Informative]. But I'm not too young to know that it's not her fault, and that she doesn't really want to send us away to a strange country all alone, and I'm not too young to feel terrible about it [Opinion]. (2010, 52)

I'm not suggesting we read every text and analyze it line by line for mode. I'm simply saying that the best-written texts often feature a blend of modes, and we should help students see how they work together to generate the strongest writing.

What About Genres?

The terms *mode* and *genre* are often confused in the writing teacher's lexicon. Think of the mode as the umbrella (the overall purpose of the writing) and the genre as the spokes (the specific categories within that mode).

The mode by itself is a target too broad for writers to hit with accuracy. *"Write an informative text"* is an overwhelming task and tends to produce writing that is superficial and unclear. *"Write a how-to text"* is a much clearer task because it's more specific—especially if good models have been shared and analyzed for content and form so students understand what writing looks like in that genre.

Genre refers to the type of writing associated with a specific form, content, and style. For example, literature has four main genres—poetry, drama, fiction, and nonfiction—all of which contain subcategories. Fiction includes familiar subgenres such as realistic fiction, historical fiction, fantasy, mystery, humor, science fiction, tall tales, and so on. Nonfiction includes biography, autobiography, diaries, memoirs, journals, essays, and more.

In my experience, *genre* is a word often associated with reading; *mode* is more often associated with writing. However, mode and genre work together as powerful allies in reading and writing. For example, it's possible—and even likely—for students to first read a memoir and then try writing a memoir (mode: narrative), read a brochure and write a brochure (mode: informative), or read a review and write a review (mode: opinion/argument).

Teacher-Friendly Scoring Guides

This chapter falls in the "Read the Writing" part of this book, so to that end, I've included scoring guides you can use to see how well students are satisfying the purpose of the mode. Figures 3.1, 3.2, and 3.3 show thumbnails of the scoring guides, but you'll find full-size, downloadable versions online at sten.pub/tww. (Student-friendly versions for different grade levels are in the next chapter and are also available online.)

If you wish, you can score papers on mode, right along with the trait(s), and your young writers can use the student versions to guide their revision and editing. This will provide a holistic score that answers the question "How close is this student to having satisfied the criteria for the mode?" The answer will reveal what the writer is doing well and what still needs work.

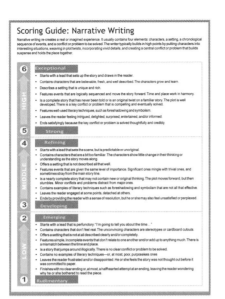

FIGURE 3.1 *Narrative Scoring Guide*

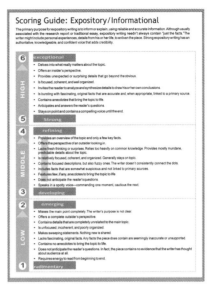

FIGURE 3.2 *Expository Scoring Guide*

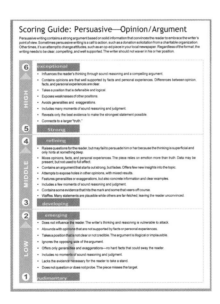

FIGURE 3.3 *Persuasive Scoring Guide*

Wrap-Up: Models of Modes

When students develop a clear understanding of what they are writing, it is easier for them to focus on how to write clearly and well. Once they know their writing purpose, they can dive into the traits of writing and the way each is applied to make the writing strong. A big part of this process involves showing students models, scoring guides, and examples of what "good" looks like in the traits and modes, and where these two writing instruction giants support each other. This, in turn, can motivate students to try something fresh, original, and satisfying. When we teach this way, students begin to make critical writing decisions, experiment with language and form, and learn that there is no limit to what they can do.

4

Tools and Talk
to Guide Revision

I learned a long time ago that the secret to home improvement is having the right tools. I need more than a hammer and a screwdriver to fix all the things that break in my house. So, every year, I march down to Home Depot and treat myself to a shiny new gizmo—a mallet, Allen wrenches, electronic measuring tape, pink duct tape, a level, a serious drill and drill bits—and now I have a toolbox that allows me to repair almost anything. I have to admit, however, that I usually watch a YouTube video or two before I try. I need an expert to show me how to use the tools to get the desired outcome. Otherwise, I'd have this great set of new tools but would still try to fix everything with the hammer and screwdriver because those are the ones I know how to use.

Likewise, consider this chapter your writing toolbox: a collection of resources to make the traits and modes user-friendly for student writers. Kids can do a lot with the right tools for writing. They just need us to show them how.

Isn't this what it's all about? We're working to help writers like Jermain go from here:

I was so happy. I felt good all over.

To here:

Inside me was a tingle. I started to feel a little taller. More like a giant. I made a fist, stretched my arm and stuck out my chest and said, "really me!"

How did Jermain make this leap? His teacher gave him the tools he needed to read, think about, and revise his own writing, and she showed him how to use them. Our ultimate goal for our students is that they read their own writing, determine what makes it work and what is holding it back, and develop their writing life. Once students begin thinking like writers, as Jermain has done, they carry this knowledge into every class and every situation for which they write—for the rest of their lives (no pressure on you, right?). Chapters 2 and 3 focused on helping you read student writing with new insights and perspectives. Now we turn our attention to helping students do the same thing.

Consider Donald Graves's wise words:

> We teach [children] how to read books but not how to read their own writing.... Unless we show children how to read their writing, their work will not improve. If we help children take knowledgeable responsibility in reading their own work, we not only help them to be effective lifelong writers, but we shift the responsibility for their writing to them, where it belongs. (1994, xvi)

We must teach them how to think and behave as writers, giving them the tools and language they need to succeed.

This is how insight about their writing develops and students improve. In order to nurture writers so they understand how to go from blah to brilliant, consider how the writing process looks and feels from the students' perspective. They must be actively involved in decision making right from the start. We must teach them how to think and behave as writers, giving them the tools and language they need to succeed. We must create classrooms where students learn how to read their own writing carefully and skillfully. Please step with me into the writer's world.

Tools Students Need to Read Their Writing

In a classroom where the writer has some autonomy and choice, students need many of the same resources I've shared previously in this text—but for their use, not just the teacher's. They need language; they need assessment tools; they need experience and practice learning to find the traits in mentor texts—both student and professional writing—so they can spot what is going on in their own work and make changes. It takes a skilled team of teacher, student, and peers to get the job done.

In their report *Informing Writing: The Benefits of Formative Assessment,* the Carnegie Corporation extols the value of using assessment to understand what students know about writing so we know how to build toward what comes next. The authors emphasize the importance of including students in the process:

When teachers monitor students' progress, writing improves. When students evaluate their own writing, writing improves. When students receive feedback about their writing, writing improves. When students are partners in writing assessment, giving and receiving peer feedback, students' writing improves. (Graham, Harris, and Hebert 2011, 27)

What's that old saying? *"Give a man a fish, and you feed him for a day. Teach a man to fish, and you feed him for a lifetime."* Or, as one third grader wrote in her paper, *"If you give a man a fish, he's happy. But if you teach him how to fish, he needs more room in the freezer."* Throughout this chapter you'll find some yummy fish to store in your writing-teacher freezer: writing process think abouts, student-friendly trait scoring guides, student-friendly mode scoring guides, and key quality think abouts.

You'll want to introduce some of these tools right away, and others you can hold back until you need them. I've included thumbnails of each of these tools in the sections of text that follow, but full-size reproducible versions can be found in Appendix B and online at sten.pub/tww. After all, we can't have too many resources and ideas to help student writers along their journey toward excellent writing.

> "If you give a man a fish, he's happy. But if you teach him how to fish, he needs more room in the freezer."

Begin with the Writing Process

The writing process think about (see Figure 4.1) can help students understand the ins and outs of the writing process. These are questions they can ask themselves during prewriting, drafting, revising, editing, and finishing/publishing. Perhaps you can post these questions for students to refer to as they write, or provide copies students can keep in their writing notebooks. Or, for younger students, you can abbreviate them to focus on what matters most. It's important to remind students from time to time that the stages of the writing process can loop and overlap and occur more than once; they don't necessarily have to happen step by step. For instance, prewriting is an early stage of the process when a writer plans and researches, but sometimes revision will send us back to reorganize or do more research, both of which are prewriting steps. (Look for a thorough exploration of all things revision in Chapter 5.)

For more reading about the writing process in its entirety, I recommend these original, powerful texts:

- Donald Graves: *A Fresh Look at Writing* (Heinemann 1994)
- Donald Murray: *A Writer Teaches Writing, Revised* (Wadsworth 2003)

And, to support your young writers, here are a few recent picture books that beautifully illustrate the writing process in action:

- *Rocket Writes a Story* by Tad Hills (author and illustrator)
- *Also an Octopus* by Maggie Tokuda-Hall (author) and Benji Davies (illustrator)
- *Written and Drawn by Henrietta* by Liniers (author and illustrator)
- *How This Book Was Made* by Mac Barnett (author) and Adam Rex (illustrator)
- *A Squiggly Story* by Andrew Larsen (author) and Mike Lowery (illustrator)

Figure 4.1 *Think About for Writing Process*

Focus on the Traits: Establish a Common Language

Once you get into the nitty-gritty of teaching with traits and asking students to think about traits as they write and revise, you'll want to share the language of the traits using the student-friendly scoring guides. These are quite similar to the scoring guides we worked with in Chapter 2, which you'll use to guide your assessment of student writing. However, they are simpler and avoid any jargon that might confuse students. Our young writers can use traits to guide their own reading and revision of their writing, too. It's all about establishing a common language for you and your students, and these student-friendly scoring guides do just that.

Introduce traits to students using the definitions and explanations that follow, and work together to create a poster for each trait that will hang in the classroom. You'll want each poster to show three specific elements: 1) the trait and a quick definition, 2) the key qualities, and 3) a visual metaphor for the trait. Keep it simple. The visual metaphor should be an image or icon that students feel represents the trait—a light bulb for ideas, a river for sentence fluency, and so on. (See Figure 4.2 for some great examples from an upper elementary classroom in Topeka, Kansas.) Encourage students to come up with something special and unexpected rather than the first thing that comes to mind. When they are finished, hang up the posters for reference all year. Truthfully, there are some awesome commercial trait posters out there, many I've had a hand in making myself, but none are as powerful as those that students create for themselves.

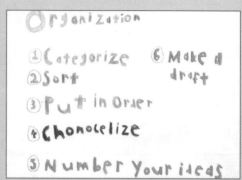

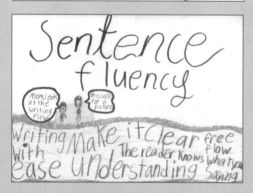

Figure 4.2 *Trait posters*

Figures 4.3 through 4.9 show thumbnails of the student-friendly trait scoring guides for the traits; full-page versions of these appear in Appendix B and at sten.pub/tww. (Thanks to the students of Debbie Stuart's classroom in Topeka, Kansas, for these examples.) You can find additional downloadable examples of student-friendly scoring guides at different levels, from those that have pictures and few words to far more detailed versions, on my website (www.culhamwriting.com). You can download and print any of them to use with students regardless of their age or skill level.

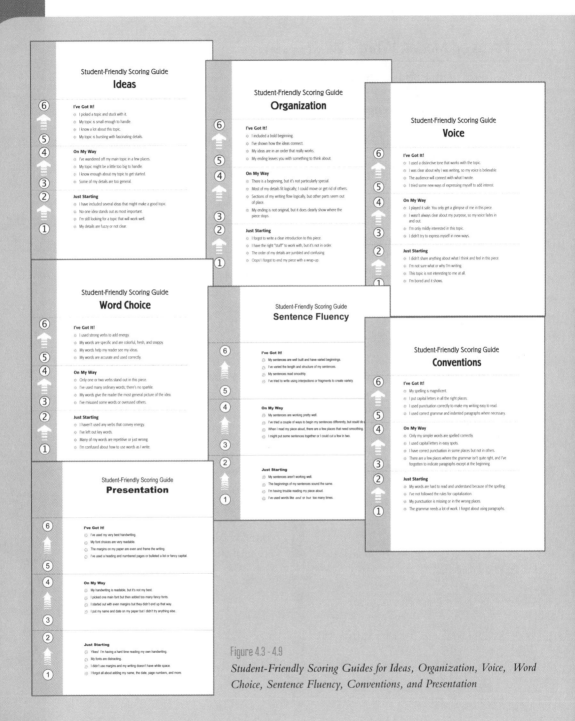

Student-Friendly Scoring Guide
Ideas

I've Got It!
- I picked a topic and stuck with it.
- My topic is small enough to handle.
- I know a lot about this topic.
- My topic is bursting with fascinating details.

On My Way
- I've wandered off my main topic in a few places.
- My topic might be a little too big to handle.
- I know enough about my topic to get started.
- Some of my details are too general.

Just Starting
- I have included several ideas that might make a good topic.
- No one idea stands out as most important.
- I'm still looking for a topic that will work well.
- My details are fuzzy or not clear.

Student-Friendly Scoring Guide
Organization

I've Got It!
- I included a bold beginning.
- I've shown how the ideas connect.
- My ideas are in an order that really works.
- My ending leaves you with something to think about.

On My Way
- There is a beginning, but it's not particularly special.
- Most of my details fit logically; I could move or get rid of others.
- Sections of my writing flow logically, but other parts seem out of place.
- My ending is not original, but it does clearly show where the piece stops.

Just Starting
- I forgot to write a clear introduction to this piece.
- I have the right "stuff" to work with, but it's not in order.
- The order of my details are jumbled and confusing.
- Oops! I forgot to end my piece with a wrap-up.

Student-Friendly Scoring Guide
Voice

I've Got It!
- I used a distinctive tone that works with the topic.
- I was clear about why I was writing, so my voice is believable.
- The audience will connect with what I wrote.
- I tried some new ways of expressing myself to add interest.

On My Way
- I played it safe. You only get a glimpse of me in this piece.
- I wasn't always clear about my purpose, so my voice fades in and out.
- I'm only mildly interested in this topic.
- I didn't try to express myself in new ways.

Just Starting
- I didn't share anything about what I think and feel in this piece.
- I'm not sure what or why I'm writing.
- This topic is not interesting to me at all.
- I'm bored and it shows.

Student-Friendly Scoring Guide
Word Choice

I've Got It!
- I used strong verbs to add energy.
- My words are specific and are colorful, fresh, and snappy.
- My words help my reader see my ideas.
- My words are accurate and used correctly.

On My Way
- Only one or two verbs stand out in this piece.
- I've used many ordinary words; there's no sparkle.
- My words give the reader the most general picture of the idea.
- I've misused some words or overused others.

Just Starting
- I haven't used any verbs that convey energy.
- I've left out key words.
- Many of my words are repetitive or just wrong.
- I'm confused about how to use words as I write.

Student-Friendly Scoring Guide
Sentence Fluency

I've Got It!
- My sentences are well built and have varied beginnings.
- I've varied the length and structure of my sentences.
- My sentences read smoothly.
- I've tried to write using interjections or fragments to create variety.

On My Way
- My sentences are working pretty well.
- I've tried a couple of ways to begin my sentences differently, but could do
- When I read my piece aloud, there are a few places that need smoothing.
- I might put some sentences together or I could cut a few in two.

Just Starting
- My sentences aren't working well.
- The beginnings of my sentences sound the same.
- I'm having trouble reading my piece aloud.
- I've used words like *and* or *but* too many times.

Student-Friendly Scoring Guide
Conventions

I've Got It!
- My spelling is magnificent.
- I put capital letters in all the right places.
- I used punctuation correctly to make my writing easy to read.
- I used correct grammar and indented paragraphs where necessary.

On My Way
- Only my simpler words are spelled correctly.
- I used capital letters in easy spots.
- I have correct punctuation in some places but not in others.
- There are a few places where the grammar isn't quite right, and I've
  forgotten to indicate paragraphs except at the beginning.

Just Starting
- My words are hard to read and understand because of the spelling.
- I've not followed the rules for capitalization.
- My punctuation is missing or in the wrong places.
- The grammar needs a lot of work. I forgot about using paragraphs.

Student-Friendly Scoring Guide
Presentation

I've Got It!
- I've used my very best handwriting.
- My font choices are very readable.
- The margins on my paper are even and frame the writing.
- I used a heading and numbered pages or bulleted a list or fancy capital.

On My Way
- My handwriting is readable, but it's not my best.
- I picked one main font then added too many fancy fonts.
- I started out with even margins but they didn't end up that way.
- I put my name and date on my paper but I didn't try anything else.

Just Starting
- Yikes! I'm having a hard time reading my own handwriting.
- My fonts are distracting.
- I didn't use margins and my writing doesn't have white space.
- I forgot all about adding my name, the date, page numbers, and more.

Figure 4.3 - 4.9

Student-Friendly Scoring Guides for Ideas, Organization, Voice, Word Choice, Sentence Fluency, Conventions, and Presentation

Focus on Modes: What's What

As you help students learn how to write (traits), remember they are also learning what to write (modes). When students know the purpose for their writing, it is far easier for them to apply the traits appropriately. For example, if the writer tackles an expository piece on a topic that is technical or scientific, it's critical that he or she understand how to use words that are specific and accurate; a narrative piece might rely more on conversational language. Both modes of writing demand excellent word choice, but for different purposes. Expository writing also requires an organizational structure—such as compare and contrast, deductive logic, or point-by-point analysis—that best showcases the information. In narrative writing, organization is usually chronological. Again, both modes of writing need skillful organization, but for different purposes. Each trait adapts to the mode of the writing to optimize its power.

Students will appreciate having practical resources for narrative, expository, and persuasive writing. Figures 4.10 through 4.12 show thumbnails of the student-friendly mode scoring guides. These range in complexity and form so you can choose the ones that best fit the needs of your students. (Full-size versions are available in Appendix B and online.)

The student-friendly mode materials should be introduced in lessons that focus on the different purposes for writing and how to shape the use of each trait based on students' choices of mode and genre. Think of teaching the mode as the big picture of what the writer is trying to do. As you work with students to help them sort out the purpose of their writing, having a copy of the student-friendly mode scoring guide may help them understand that to write well, they need to clearly reveal the intent of the writing and at the same time draw the reader into the writing because it is well crafted. Traits and modes work hand in hand—craft and purpose.

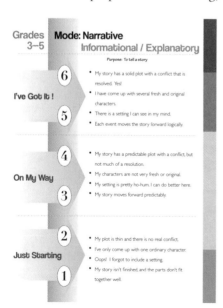

Figure 4.10 *Mode: Narrative–Informational/Explanatory*

TEACH WRITING WELL

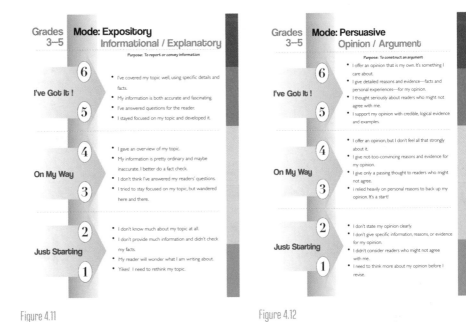

Figure 4.11

Mode: Expository–Informational / Explanatory

Figure 4.12

Mode: Persuasive–Opinion / Argument

Pause and Consider How will you choose which student-friendly scoring guides to give your students as a resource? Check them out in Appendix B and online at sten.pub/tww, and browse the options. Discuss which ones feel like the best match for the student-writing levels in your classrooms.

Focus on Key Qualities: Break Traits into Smaller Bites

The key qualities of each trait are how we break a huge writing concept down into smaller, more manageable pieces. Students will come to know these key qualities well through your lessons and their application of them to their writing this year. Over multiple years, they will deepen their understanding of what each one brings to writing as a whole.

Figure 4.13 *Key Quality Think Abouts*

Think About KEY QUALITY IDEAS

Think About Finding a Topic
- Have I chosen a topic that I really like?
- Do I have something new to say about this topic?
- Am I writing about what I know and care about?
- Have I gathered enough information about it so that I'm ready to write?

Think About Focusing the Topic
- Have I zeroed in on one small part of a bigger idea?
- Can I sum up my idea in a simple sentence?
- Have I chosen the information that best captures my idea?
- Have I thought deeply about what the reader will need to know?

Think About Developing the Topic
- Am I sure my information is right?
- Have I thought about what the reader needs to know to understand this idea?
- Do my ideas offer a new way of thinking about this topic?
- Have I included enough information to be credible?

Think About Using Details
- Did I create a picture in the reader's mind?
- Did I use details that draw upon the five senses? (sight, touch, taste, smell, hearing)
- Do my details stay on the main topic?
- Did I stretch for details beyond the obvious?

Think About KEY QUALITY ORGANIZATION

Think About Creating the Lead
- Did I give the reader something interesting to think about right from the start?
- Will the reader want to keep reading?
- Have I tried to get the reader's attention?
- Did I let the reader know what is coming?

Think About Using Sequence Words and Transition Words
- Have I used sequence words such as later, then, and meanwhile?
- Did I use a variety of transition words such as however, because, also, and for instance?
- Have I shown how ideas connect from sentence to sentence?
- Does my organization make sense from paragraph to paragraph?

Think About Structuring the Body
- Have I shown the reader where to slow down and where to speed up?
- Do all the details fit where they are placed?
- Will the reader find it easy to follow my ideas?
- Does the organization help the main idea stand out?

Think About Ending with a Sense of Resolution
- Have I wrapped up all the loose ends?
- Have I ended at the best place?
- Do I have an ending that makes my writing feel finished?
- Did I leave the reader with something important to think about?

Think About KEY QUALITY VOICE

Think About Establishing a Tone
- Can I name the primary feeling of my writing (e.g., happy, frustrated, knowledgeable, scared, convincing)?
- Have I varied the tone from the beginning to the end?
- Have I used expressive language?
- Did I show that I care about this topic?

Think About Conveying the Purpose
- Is the purpose of my writing clear?
- Does my point of view come through?
- Is this the right tone for this kind of writing?
- Have I used strong voice throughout this piece?

Think About Creating a Connection to the Audience
- Have I thought about the reader?
- Is this the right voice for the audience?
- Have I shown what matters most to me in this piece?
- Will the reader know how I think and feel about the topic?

Think About Taking Risks to Create Voice
- Have I used words that are not ordinary?
- Is my writing interesting, fresh, and original?
- Have I tried to make my writing sound like me?
- Have I tried something different from what I've done before?

Think About KEY QUALITY WORD CHOICE

Think About Applying Strong Verbs
- Have I used action words?
- Did I stretch to use a more specific word—for example, scurry rather than run?
- Do my verbs give my writing punch and pizzazz?
- Did I avoid is, are, was, were, be, being, and been wherever I could?

Think About Selecting Striking Words and Phrases
- Did I try to use words that sound just right?
- Did I try hyphenating several shorter words to make an interesting-sounding new word?
- Did I try putting words that have the same sound together?
- Did I read my piece aloud to find at least one or two moments I love?

Think About Using Specific and Accurate Words
- Have I used nouns and modifiers that help the reader see a picture?
- Did I try a new word and, if so, check to make sure I used it correctly?
- Are these the best words that can be used?

Think About Choosing Words That Deepen Meaning
- Did I choose words that show I really thought about them?
- Have I tried to use words without repeating myself?
- Do my words capture the reader's imagination?
- Have I found the best way to express myself?

Think About KEY QUALITY SENTENCE FLUENCY

Think About Crafting Well-Built Sentences
- Do my sentences begin in different ways?
- Are my sentences different lengths?
- Are my sentences grammatically correct unless constructed creatively for impact?
- Have I used conjunctions such as and, but, and to to connect parts of sentences?

Think About Varying Sentence Types
- Do I use different kinds of sentences?
- Are some of my sentences complex?
- Are some of my sentences simple?
- Did I intermingle sentence types from one to the next?

Think About Capturing Smooth and Rhythmic Flow
- Is it easy to read the entire piece aloud?
- Do my sentences flow from one to the next?
- Do individual passages sound smooth when I read them aloud?
- Did I thoughtfully use different sentence types to enhance the main idea?

Think About Breaking the "Rules" to Create Fluency
- Did I use fragments with style and purpose?
- Did I begin a sentence informally to create a conversational tone?
- Does my dialogue sound authentic?
- Did I try weaving in exclamations and single words to add emphasis?

Think About KEY QUALITY CONVENTIONS

Think About Checking Spelling
- Have I used standard English spelling, unless I chose not to for a good reason?
- Have I checked words that don't look right to me?
- Have I used the resources in the room (e.g., charts, word walls, word lists) to help with spelling?
- Have I checked my work for words I have trouble spelling?

Think About Punctuating Effectively
- Did I place quotation marks around dialogue and direct quotes?
- Did I punctuate complex sentences correctly?
- Did I use apostrophes to show possessives and contractions?
- Did I begin new paragraphs in the appropriate places?

Think About Capitalizing Correctly
- Did I capitalize proper nouns for people, places, and things?
- Did I capitalize dialogue correctly?
- Did I capitalize abbreviations, acronyms, and people's titles correctly?
- Did I capitalize the title and/or other headings?

Think About Applying Grammar and Usage
- Did I use special words such as homophones, synonyms, and antonyms correctly?
- Did I check my sentences for subject-verb agreement?
- Did I use verb tenses (past, present, future) consistently throughout my piece?
- Did I make sure pronouns and their antecedents (the word they stand for) agree?

Think About KEY QUALITY PRESENTATION

Think About Applying Handwriting Skills
- Is my handwriting neat and legible?
- Did I take time to form each letter clearly?
- Do my letters slant evenly throughout?
- Did I leave space between words to enhance readability?

Think About Using Word Processing Effectively
- Is my choice of font easy to read and appropriate for the audience?
- Is the font size appropriate?
- Did I use formatting such as boldfacing, underlining, and italicizing effectively?
- Does color enhance the look and feel of my piece, or does it weaken them?

Think About Making Good Use of White Space
- Do my margins frame the text evenly on all four sides?
- Did I leave enough white space between letters, words, and lines to make the piece easy to read?
- Did I avoid cross-outs, smudges, and tears?
- Did I create a nice balance of text, text features, illustrations, photographs, and white space?

Think About Refining Text Features
- Do my illustrations and photographs help to make the piece easy to understand?
- Did I include my name, date, title, page numbers, and other headers and footers?
- Are text features such as bulleted lists, sidebars, and time lines clear, well positioned, and effective in guiding the reader and enhancing meaning?
- Are charts, graphs, and tables easy to read and understand?

Students will appreciate having key quality think abouts as a resource as they write and revise (see Figure 4.13; full-page versions are available in Appendix B and online). Think abouts provide questions for writers about one key quality at a time, giving them something concrete to consider while revising with each trait and key quality in mind. These think abouts also provide a nice jumping-off point for conferences, either teacher-to-student or student-to-student.

Writer's Tools for All

The secret to teaching writing well turns out to be breaking the writing process and the traits into smaller, more manageable parts so students learn to read their writing and determine what needs to happen next—for themselves. You'll read a lot more about this in the second half of this book, where I share strategies for teaching using this mind-set.

Here you have been provided four sets of resources: think abouts for writing process, student-friendly scoring guides for traits, student-friendly scoring guides for modes, and think abouts for key qualities. Use them so students develop their own way of understanding writing process, writing traits and their key qualities, and modes of writing. These tools can be shared with parents, too, when they ask for ways to help students at home. The tools in this chapter can be a bridge for students, parents, and teachers who all want the same thing: strong student writers. I firmly believe the more user-friendly resources we have for the learner and the learner's support team, the better.

Now let's address another way to support young writers: conferring and talking with students about their writing. We can take the information from these student-friendly resources and help our writers apply it to their work in a way that is respectful, constructive, and manageable.

Conversations That Move Writing Forward

Learning to read student writing to discover its riches and teaching students to do the same is at the core of our writing conversations with students. Once you both become familiar with the traits and their key qualities, you have the ideal entry point into discussions about what is working and where the writing could go next. This is a big part of a successful student conference: the content.

There are other issues to consider, as well, such as the structure and timing of the conference. To dive deeply into techniques for conferring with young writers, I refer you to Carl Anderson's work. He's published several outstanding books that deal exclusively with conferring, including *How's It Going? A Practical Guide to Conferring with Student Writers* (2000) and *Strategic Writing Conferences: Smart Conversations That Move Young Writers Forward, Grades 3–6* (2008).

I'd like to share some thoughts about what I've found works in the busy writing classroom for teachers and students alike. Simply put, I've found success with two kinds of conferences: 1) over-the-shoulder comments and 2) eye-to-eye conversations.

Over-the-Shoulder Comments

Over-the-shoulder comments are quick, focused, and happen on the fly. As students write, teachers circulate the room looking over kids' shoulders to glimpse writers in action, encourage them, and nudge writing forward. You can make over-the-shoulder comments even if you have not read and thought about the piece the student is working on yet, or they can be made after you've read a draft and know where the writer is heading with the piece.

Over-the-shoulder comments happen one at a time and with individual students in the class, based on the writing and the writing behavior the teacher observes. Fortunately, because of the key qualities, you can dive easily into the writing content for your comments in one of twenty-eight places at any time. You may want to deal specifically with what was taught most recently, but you should feel free to discuss any key quality and trait that benefits the writer, regardless of how much you have worked on it as a class. The key to success with over-the-shoulder comments is that they be fast, focused, and friendly. Here are some examples.

The Walk-By

All writers need to know they are on the right track. As you walk by a student, try to notice a behavior or a particular skill that is going well or perhaps leave a quick sticky note about something you'd like the writer to consider. *"Albina, it looks like you are reworking the introduction. I am excited that you are focusing on how to entice the reader with your lead."* Or, *"Jason, you are really on fire today. I don't want to interrupt your flow, but remember how we talked about adding interesting verbs? Keep that in mind as you continue to blaze forward."*

The Stop and Go

Sometimes a little nudge is all the writer needs to move forward. Here you can do a quick over-the-shoulder read of part of the writing and then make a suggestion about what to try next. *"Mia, I've just scanned a little of your paper, and I notice that a lot of your sentences begin with 'I.' Can you rework one or two for variety and to make the writing flow more smoothly, like we did in our group-write earlier today? Maybe you and Kaitlin can work together on sentence beginnings, too."* Or, *"Dusty, you've been up and down looking up information quite a bit today. Can I help you zero in on a resource that might help you find what you are looking for?"*

The Stop and Stay

A few students will get stuck. Perhaps it is hard for one writer to self-start, or maybe another one is mired in a particular issue. These students will need more time and support, so pull up a chair and plan to stay a minute or two. Even though you'll want to keep an eye on the clock so you can meet with other students too, try to help a stuck writer form a plan to move his or her writing forward in one particular way that feels doable. For instance, *"Javier, let's figure out together what you want to do next on your writing. Tell me your idea, and let's make a plan."* Or, *"Cassie, since you left your paper at home, let's work on something else so you are using this time well. Pick a piece from your Writing Wallet and let's explore your use of details, since we just talked about them together as a class."*

Pause and Consider Imagine a classroom where students are working on a piece of writing. How do over-the-shoulder comments look and feel? Role-play these three levels of over-the-shoulder comments with other teachers in your study group. Which comments come the easiest? Which are trickier to carry out?

Eye-to-Eye Conferences

The eye-to-eye individual or small-group conference is much different from the over-the-shoulder conference because it is planned and scheduled. To make eye-to-eye conferences productive, establish a routine for conference time so students know what to expect and can actively participate, regardless of their writing skills. The conference should focus on the writer's needs and how the writing is progressing. The teacher's job for eye-to-eye conferences is to steer the discussion in a positive direction; make sure the conversation includes helpful, specific feedback; and model for and support students as they learn to use the language of writers to improve their own work. Using the common language of traits and key qualities can help students note strengths in their writing and nudge them toward a change, an addition, a deletion, or some other revision.

I appreciate Carl Anderson's wise conferring advice, adapted here from *How's It Going?* (2000). He asserts the following:

- A writing conference is a conversation.

- The point of a writing conference is to help students become better writers.

- Writing conferences have a predictable structure.

- In conferences, teachers and students have predictable roles.

- It's important to communicate to students in conferences that we care about them as people and writers.

There is a strong affective quality in an eye-to-eye conference. Not only should students walk away from this conference with a clear sense of how they are doing and what to do next, but they also should know that their efforts are paying off and they are valued as writers. They should look forward to the eye-to-eye conference as an opportunity to be validated and supported, not judged.

Eye-to-eye conferences can happen in small groups or with individuals. They require planning and organization of both content and structure. Here are some general "rules" I like to follow when talking in-depth with one or more writers. I also try to use these tips when I write comments on student work.

- Name the trait and key quality you are addressing. Refer to language in the scoring guide to teach more about the trait while guiding the student to strengthen that key quality or trait.

- Skip superficial responses, such as *"nice job"* or *"good work."*

- Begin with a positive comment. Notice something the student can do or that is working well. Follow up with a specific, purposeful suggestion that the student can use to improve in one small way.

- Try not to use the word *but* in comments. Instead use *and, next, now,* and other process-driven words. For example, *"Your bold beginning draws me in; now let's look at your transition to the body of the piece and make it just as strong in organization."*

- Look for early indicators of success. Notice what students are trying to do and praise it by naming it.

Whenever I bring up the eye-to-eye conference to teachers, one question always arises: "What are the other kids doing while you are conferring with one writer or a small group of writers?" Ah, this is the jackpot question. The answer lies in classroom routines that help students learn to self-manage. Remember the student-friendly guides and think abouts? Once students are familiar with them, they can be used at any time to help students stay on track and move forward.

Once you've established a routine of pulling individuals or small groups of students to confer about their writing on a regular basis, the rest of the students need to know what is expected of them while you are otherwise engaged. They can do one of two things:

Remember that writers learn about writing from reading— so let them read.

1. Write

2. Read

That may seem like an oversimplified answer, but everything boils down to reading and writing. We can't do enough to help students with both. So, when you are busy with other students, the rest of the class should have a clear understanding of what they can and cannot do. Please don't give them worksheets just to keep them occupied. Let them work on their writing and encourage them to leave notes for themselves about where they have questions for when it's their turn to confer with you. Teach students how to help each other, one key quality at a time, by working with a partner. Show them the resources in the room to turn to if they have questions. And explain that if they hit a major stumbling block in their writing, they can pull out a book of their choice and read. Remember that writers learn about writing from reading—so let them read.

The writers you are conferring with need your undivided attention. I am fully aware that teachers have eyes on all sides of their heads, but do not stop the conference to redirect other students. This is sacred time, and all students must learn to respect it.

Make a note of any distractions and, when the conference is over, talk to the student in question about his or her choices and what your expectations are—again. Is there blood? Fire? If not, it can wait. It's a matter of being clear and consistent. Writers will appreciate their time with you so much, they ideally will respect your time with others too. Some students are challenged by this notion, I understand. But clear guidelines (and peer pressure) can be positive and powerful. A look, a glance, and a respectful "shh" from other students can go a long way.

If this soft but unyielding approach to managing the classroom doesn't work for a few students, chances are it's not just a writing issue. Students who don't conform to the norms of the classroom are often unsettled in all areas of

How are over-the-shoulder comments like eye-to-eye conferences? How are they different? What is the purpose of each? When would you use both strategies? How long should each last? What are the promises and pitfalls of students' conferences?

learning. It's best to address that concern with your team, the family, and the student to implement plans to help him or her with self-regulation and classroom expectations.

The Proof Is in the Writing

Having the right tools and time for talking about writing is important to help students zero in on different qualities of their writing. Tools provide you with the common language necessary to talk about what you notice in students' work and to nudge them in the right direction as they revise. Teaching students to have constructive conversations about writing makes all the difference in how they learn about what is working and what to try next.

What is more convincing than watching students' writing improve right in front of your eyes? Meet Allia. At the beginning of fourth grade, Allia's teacher asked her to write a benchmark piece to document her writing skills under the following circumstances:

- There was a prompt: "What I Like Most of All."
- There was no interaction with the teacher or peers.
- There were no tools offered to guide the writing process.
- There was a specific amount of time to write: twenty minutes.
- There was no time allowed to revise or edit.

Teaching students to have constructive conversations about writing makes all the difference.

What I Like Most of All

What I like most of all is horse back riding. I've like them since I was about say last January because thats when I started hores back riding. The first hores I rode was Herby his one of my favorite horses and theirs one hores that I really like too and his name is Sherman but he got retird because he was blind in one eye. So know their's only Jane, Herby, Flint, Fielx, Allis, and Rino. And Rino is the only pony I can ride and ther is something bad that happened one of my dads Busness people got throne off Flint. Because they say that Flint doesn't like on him.

When you use the scoring guide tools to assess this piece, you'll notice what's going relatively well and where to dive in for more work with this student. Here are the scores I'd give this piece of writing, however, so I can make my bigger point:

Remember, this was a beginning-of-the-year piece of writing. The purpose was to get a sense of Allia's confidence and capability as a writer. As you can see, she's not showing strengths in any of the traits at this point, and she hasn't had much support or guidance.

Ideas: 2

Organization: 1

Voice: 2

Word Choice: 2

Sentence Fluency: 1

Conventions: 1

Rather than swamping Allia with comments and suggestions about what to do to improve the piece on every trait, her teacher decided to center comments on the ideas trait because Allia seems to be having trouble focusing the topic. Writing begins, first and foremost, with having something to say, and this writer is not sure about what her topic should be and how to develop it. Here is the teacher's comment to Allia to nudge her forward in the ideas trait on the next draft:

> *There are several great ideas in here worth writing about more: When you learned to horseback ride; why Herby is your favorite horse; what happened to Sherman; why Rino is the only pony you can ride; what happened the day your dad's business associates came to ride. You pick!*

This wise advice will guide Allia to draft a more focused piece using the ideas trait on the next go-round. There is more to do after that, of course, but a specifically defined idea is the perfect place to start. Allia may decide to do more with this piece, or she may decide that working on it for a specific purpose was enough for now and turn to a different piece for further work—applying this new knowledge about choosing a topic to that writing as well. The teacher would confer with Allia to help her make this determination based on Allia's desire to stick with this piece or move along.

So it went for Allia and all the other students in this fourth-grade classroom. They worked on one trait, one key quality at a time, over time. Their teacher introduced them to student-friendly guides and think abouts. They worked on pieces for specific skills and watched their writing improve with their efforts. They met with the teacher in eye-to-eye conferences and learned from one another.

By the end of the year, Allia crafted the following piece of writing under different circumstances:

- There was no prompt; Allia picked her own topic.

- There was constant and thoughtful interaction with the teacher and peers about how to improve the writing from draft to draft.

- There were many revisions to the writing over time.

- There were tools and resources galore to support Allia's writing.

- There was an extended period of time to draft, revise, and edit.

Unlike the beginning-of-the-year piece, this one went through the entire writing process. It's hard to believe this is the same writer who drafted the previous piece. After many months of lessons, interactions, suggestions, and positive collaboration with other writers in the classroom, Allia was able to move from muddled to majestic writing.

Trouble

Boy, do we have trouble! I don't mean the normal kind of trouble. I'm talking about a mischievous little kitten named Trouble.

Trouble is the darkest one in his family with white markings around his eyes and grey and black stripes on the rest of his body. His fur is fluffy and wild, which matches his personality perfectly.

Trouble likes to climb to the top of the scratching post and knock down his brothers and sisters when they try to join him. He is a good kind of trouble, though, because he's always willing to snuggle and play with his family.

We got Trouble when my mom became a foster parent though the S.P.C.A. Although we won't be able to keep him much longer, I will never forget our little king of trouble and all the joy he brought to us this last summer.

And here are the traits-based scores, as I assessed them.

Even when students write exemplary pieces such as this one, it's helpful to tell them exactly what was done well (so they can do it again) and to share any suggestions you may have. In this case, I'd make a comment such as this one, but I would not ask the student to rewrite the paper. The suggestion is just food for thought, something to consider the next time the writer tackles a new piece.

Ideas: 6

Organization: 6

Voice: 5

Word Choice: 5

Sentence Fluency: 5

Conventions: 6

You've grown so much as a writer. Your idea is well developed and logically organized from beginning to end. Your use of conventions is stunning! Here is something to think about: would you consider adding a few more details about something Trouble did to add to the voice of the piece?

My take-away from this pair of papers is that students can and do improve when they have the right support. The teacher conferred with Allia, and Allia sought the advice of peers. She was given the time she needed to develop and revise the piece. Student-friendly tools were available to help her take small steps from beginning to end. Allia and countless other students have proved that once young writers see what they can do, they're eager to dig into another piece to revise it thoroughly as well. Success breeds success.

Pause and Consider Discuss with colleagues the difference between what this writer knows how to do in the first piece and in the second piece. Examine the comments provided; how do they help the student revise in the ideas trait and the key qualities? Talk about how important it is to have an open and supportive classroom environment. Then take a close look at the think abouts and imagine how you can use them to support student writers through the revision and editing process.

Putting It All Together

This first half of the book has been devoted to reading student writing as formative assessment and learning how to put tools and talk in the hands of student writers so they are engaged and focused on how to make their writing stronger. In other words, teachers assess so students can revise.

The second part of the book shifts from how to read the writing to how to teach the writers based on what you and they have learned from formative assessment. Now would be a good time to look back through the first half of this text if you need to review and synthesize your thoughts about the traits and key qualities; this will help guide your thinking in the second half of the book as well. Here we go!

PART II

Teach the Writer

Some of the most deeply embedded methods of teaching writing—worksheets, canned prompts, and formulas, for example—drain all of the energy and desire required to write well. Our classrooms should be places of inquiry, joy, trial and error, exploration, success and failure, and fascinations revealed—where the process of discovery matters as much as (if not more than) the destination. They must be places where writers are supported and encouraged every day. Students should feel this sentiment fully: because you thought I could, I dared to try.

To teach writing well requires a two-step process: first you find out what students know and can do (assessment); then you teach them what they still need to learn (instruction). Read the writing, teach the writer. Sounds simple enough, right? Of course, we know it is not simple at all! But it is doable, and it's easier than you think. With a game plan that is designed to help you reach many students who have different needs at the same time, you can take your students farther along their exciting journey of learning to write.

Children don't hate to write; they hate how we teach writing.

In Part 1, we explored how writing traits and modes provide clear and common language that you can use to read students' writing, discover how they are progressing, and talk with them about how to move their writing forward. You and your students now have a number of tools at your fingertips that will be extremely helpful in these efforts. You also have a solid rationale for why and how they work.

In Part 2, we'll shift our focus to how to apply smart writing instruction every day in the writing classroom. I'll help you construct solid lessons so your students have choice and voice in their writing lives.

The goal throughout both parts of this book is to demystify how to teach revision, which is arguably the trickiest part of being a writing teacher. I've focused on what we do to invite revision and make it doable for students and teachers alike—from detailed and on-the-spot assessment to purposeful, meaningful instruction. The process of moving from a draft to a more thoughtful, polished copy is where writing transformation occurs—and this is also where we stumble. Students are not excited about rewriting, and we've not been as effective as we'd like at helping them through this critical stage. Remember, think of the writing process this way: the draft is the rehearsal; the first revision is the dress rehearsal; and the final copy (regardless of how badly that dress rehearsal may have gone) is the performance—a joyful performance in which doing what was once considered impossible becomes possible.

To that end, in Chapter 5 we'll revisit the writing process with an eye toward revision, acknowledging that it has always been a wall we hit over and over in the writing process. Chapter 6 explores the construction of highly effective lesson design and how to focus on a landing place—the central point of the lesson. I'll share thoughts about "scaling up" and making sure every grade moves forward with new knowledge and skills. Chapter 7 is devoted to using mentor texts to teach writing by taking close, focused looks at pieces from published authors. New books and resources will be shared to help you discover your inner "writing thief."

If it seems ambitious to cover everything listed here, it is. But in the forty years I've been doing this work with my own students, and now with teachers in every single state, I've learned a great deal that I really want to share with you. What better place than in the second half of this book that challenges you in a new way to teach writing well?

☀

5

Rethinking Revision: The Real Work of Writing

Revision looms large and treacherous in the writing process—the Mount Everest of writing instruction. As a profession, we've yet to figure out how to scale it. In fact, most teachers struggle with how to teach it, and most students struggle with how to do it.

I've found, in fact, that most students view revision as editing: cleaning up the spelling, capitalization, punctuation, and grammar. These mechanical writing skills are taught and emphasized in their classrooms, so it's easy to understand why they gravitate toward them. But revision is much more than mechanical corrections; it's about clarity and coherence. It's the ultimate power position in the writing process. Revision is where the real work of writing happens, where the writer starts to transform mere words into tight descriptions, scintillating action, and transparent thinking.

Yet in too many classrooms, revision has not been taught. It has not been modeled. It has not been given enough time. Students instinctively sense that revision is supremely challenging and actively seek ways to avoid the deep thinking and reflection needed to do it right. They avoid revision like the plague. Although the phases of the writing process are prewriting, drafting, revising, editing, and publication, too often here's what we see in classrooms:

Student version of the writing process: prewrite, draft, "I'm done."

Teacher version of the writing process: prewrite, draft, "Now let's think about revision. We just worked on strong endings to support the organization of your piece. Can you choose one of the strategies we identified and try it as you revise your ending?"

What writing teachers know and what students must ultimately embrace is that revision is the stage where writing improves. It's evident in the word itself: *re-* means "again" and *vision* means "see." See it again. Seeing the writing again with critical eyes is essential for clarifying thinking and moving writing from a rough draft to a polished expression of thought. Let's be honest: most students don't want to see their writing again. Period. That might be why writing progress stalls for many students, or why students lack confidence with writing. It's our job to show them how to make their writing clearer by revising in a way that is helpful, doable, and immediately reinforcing that the work is worth it. Our students need to see that revision actually improves their writing, because—let's face it—we'll never persuade them to take on this hard work if they don't.

Revision Matters

Writing is thinking aloud on paper. In the same way we continue to clarify our thinking as we read, speak, and listen to others, we need to make sure our writing reflects our best, most thoughtful selves as we rework it through multiple drafts. Writing is a highly creative process that requires time, effort, and trial-and-error decisions. Revision requires exploring new techniques, incorporating changes, and moving forward—always pushing toward clarity and the strongest piece possible.

No one writes their best, most coherent thoughts in a first draft—no one. Yet often our students seem to be content with that first draft; the words "I'm done" indicate that students see writing as a finite task and not a process. So, our first job is to clarify that writing continues to evolve. The writing process is not a step-by-step march—sometimes steps need to be repeated or rethought. Revision may happen more than once between prewriting and final publication. Our second job, then, is to provide our students with the time, space, and tools to tackle this pivotal stage of the writing process.

If, for example, writing is always task focused, there is little to no incentive for students to revise. Why take on the challenge of revision when writing is focused on answering a question, following the prompt, or simply doing the assignment? There is no payoff for students— no evolution of expression—when writing is just about following directions to get it done. It's also likely, in task-focused classrooms, that little time is provided for revision. Writing is seen as another box to check on the to-do list of everyday school.

On the other hand, if writing is process focused, teachers can offer students opportunities to explore what they want to write about: what excites them, what interests them, what fascinates them. As a result, students

Figure 5.1

A writer uses a picture for inspiration.

Figure 5.2

This writer fact checks a geography detail.

TEACH WRITING WELL

engage in writing with more energy and ownership—and more willingness to make substantive changes. Look at how one student uses a photograph to generate an idea and make it her own (Figure 5.1) and how another student refers to a globe to check her geography and make sure it is right (Figure 5.2)! They choose their own topics and rework their papers over time to create publishable books. They learn to see revision as necessary and important because it matters to them that their writing showcases their best thinking. Anne Lamott explains an organic need to revise this way: "Very few writers know what they are doing until they've done it" (1994, 22).

Take a look at Figure 5.3, which shows an example of famous writing in the midst of the revision process: the speech Franklin Delano Roosevelt gave on December 8, 1941, the day after the attack on Pearl Harbor. Notice how his first draft began, "Yesterday, December 7, 1941, a date which will live in world history" but then was revised to "Yesterday, December 7, 1941, a date which will live in infamy." This is a much more powerful word choice—so powerful, in fact, that it has been called FDR's most memorable line from any of his fine speeches. The second line shows a tightening of language, too: *simultaneously* was revised to *suddenly.* Notice the change in connotation. And in the final line of the first paragraph, he added *without warning,* then thought better of it and cut those words, perhaps in conjunction with the decision to use *suddenly* in the sentence. This revision makes the sentence more concise and direct.

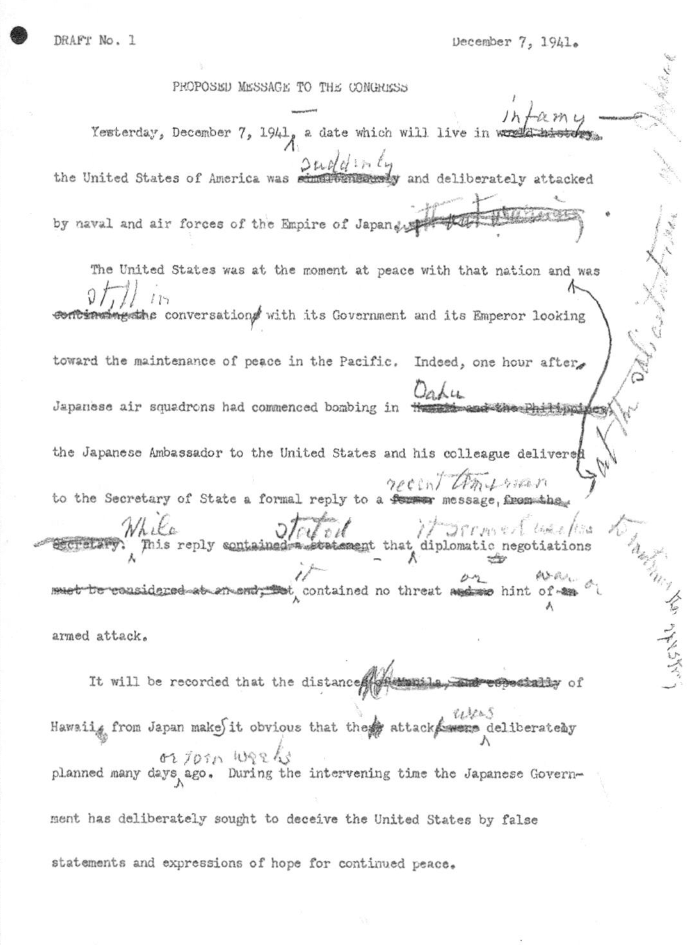

DRAFT No. 1 December 7, 1941.

PROPOSED MESSAGE TO THE CONGRESS

Yesterday, December 7, 1941, a date which will live in world history, the United States of America was simultaneously and deliberately attacked by naval and air forces of the Empire of Japan.

The United States was at the moment at peace with that nation and was continuing the conversations with its Government and its Emperor looking toward the maintenance of peace in the Pacific. Indeed, one hour after Japanese air squadrons had commenced bombing in Hawaii and the Philippines the Japanese Ambassador to the United States and his colleague delivered to the Secretary of State a formal reply to a former message, from the Secretary. This reply contained a statement that diplomatic negotiations must be considered at an end, but contained no threat and no hint of an armed attack.

It will be recorded that the distance of Manila, and especially of Hawaii, from Japan makes it obvious that the attacks were deliberately planned many days ago. During the intervening time the Japanese Government has deliberately sought to deceive the United States by false statements and expressions of hope for continued peace.

Figure 5.3 *FDR's message to Congress shows the effects of revision.*

As you search the Internet, you'll find more examples like FDR's, created in the writer's own handwriting. Each example is a fascinating look at the thinking the author did as he or she revised. I especially love this July 14, 2015, post from Kate DiCamillo on Facebook:

> I usually rewrite a book a total of eight or nine times. Sometimes more. When I'm done, I take all of those drafts and I pile them up and put them in a box and I take them to the Kerlan Collection at the University of Minnesota. They archive the drafts. They make them available for people to look at, to study, to puzzle over. The drafts are meandering, desperate, coffee-stained, confused, hopeful. They're a mess.
>
> You can see just how hard writing is for me. So when I take the manuscripts in, I think: man, I don't want anybody to see this. It's too embarrassing.
>
> But.
>
> I talked with someone once who visited the Kerlan and looked at the first draft of *Because of Winn-Dixie*. She said, "It was terrible. I was horrified. But I looked at it and I thought 'If you're allowed to start a novel this way, then I can start a novel.'"
>
> She did start a novel.
>
> She got it published.
>
> And that's why I take the drafts in.

Pause and Consider

Discuss the impact of the revision President Roosevelt made to his original speech and the choices he made. Which traits did he employ, and did his revisions succeed in clarifying his message and strengthening his voice? Read through the second paragraph in Figure 5.3 to see further revisions. Then talk about Kate DiCamillo's courage to expose her writing process to the public. How might students react to knowing that their favorite authors revise over and over again?

Entering the Revision Zone: How the Traits and Writing Process Work Together

It's important to clarify for students the difference between revision and editing. They are discrete phases of the writing process. As Donald Murray wrote in *The Craft of Revision*, "We have not been taught how to rewrite. We confuse revision, which is re-seeing, re-thinking, re-saying, with editing, which is making sure the facts are accurate, the words are spelled correctly, the rules of grammar and punctuation are followed" (2013, 2). When students embrace the revision process, they need to understand that they make choices when they prewrite, draft, get feedback, revise, edit, and publish. We must show and model for students the different options they have not for just writing, but for writing well.

Figure 5.4 illustrates the different steps in the writing process and shows how they align to each of the traits. Notice that revision is greedy—five traits (ideas, organization, voice, word choice, sentence fluency) out of seven align with this stage of writing. Conventions (spelling, capitalization, punctuation, grammar) and presentation (appearance) are editing skills that require different thinking and teaching than their revision-oriented sister traits. (Convention skills, by the way, are grade-level specific in most state standards documents, introducing new editing tasks every year for students to learn and apply in a cumulative fashion.)

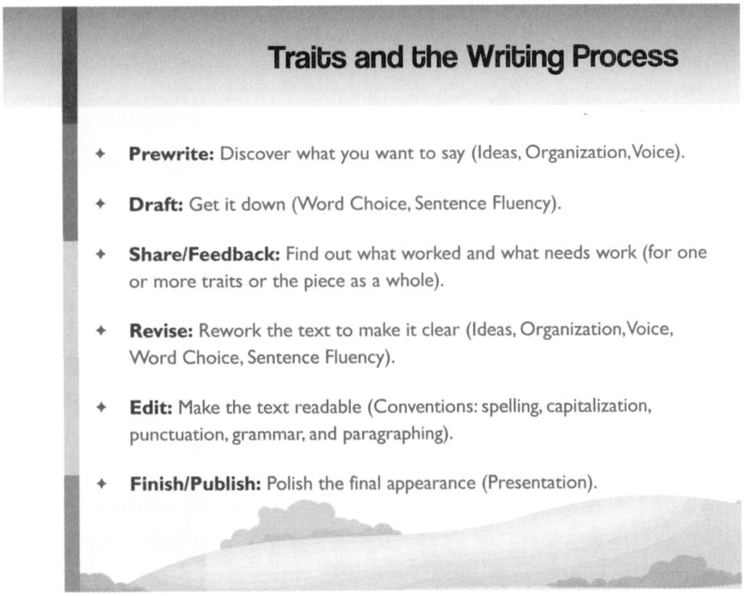

Traits and the Writing Process

+ **Prewrite:** Discover what you want to say (Ideas, Organization, Voice).

+ **Draft:** Get it down (Word Choice, Sentence Fluency).

+ **Share/Feedback:** Find out what worked and what needs work (for one or more traits or the piece as a whole).

+ **Revise:** Rework the text to make it clear (Ideas, Organization, Voice, Word Choice, Sentence Fluency).

+ **Edit:** Make the text readable (Conventions: spelling, capitalization, punctuation, grammar, and paragraphing).

+ **Finish/Publish:** Polish the final appearance (Presentation).

Figure 5.4 *Traits and the Writing Process*

Let's quickly recap the traits, noting that the first five are used in revision and the last two are applied during editing:

- **Ideas:** the content of the writing—its central message and the details that support that message

- **Organization:** the internal structure of the piece—the thread of logic, the pattern of meaning

- **Voice:** the tone of the piece—the personal stamp, which is achieved through an understanding of purpose and audience

- **Word Choice:** the precise vocabulary used to convey meaning and enlighten the reader; this contributes to a stronger voice, too

- **Sentence Fluency:** the way the words sound as they flow through the writing

- **Conventions:** the mechanical correctness of a piece of writing; this guides the reader through the text

- **Presentation:** the physical appearance of the final piece of writing—a visually appealing text provides a welcome mat and invites the reader in

If the traits are the specific skills writers need to strengthen their writing and drive it forward during revision, then the traits and revision are inextricably linked. But even if students are fortunate enough to be in a classroom that uses the trait language, they need guidance on how to use traits to drive the revision process. Should they dive into ideas first, or organization, voice, word choice, or sentence fluency? Or combinations of these traits? How do they know what to tackle first? What are they supposed to do that they haven't tried already? It can be an overwhelming prospect for teachers and students alike. The question becomes how to make revision doable for students (and teachers) using what they have learned about each of the traits and its key qualities.

Begin by differentiating between revision traits and editing traits. Using the terms *revision* and *editing* differently and specifically will make it clear which part of the writing process you want students to focus on as they massage their drafts. This will be a big step toward clarity on its own. However, it takes more than a general understanding; students need to refine skills in both areas, one year to the next in a spiraling curriculum, so their writing deepens and shows more complexity as it matures.

Teachers have made this notion concrete by using inexpensive visors or simple hats and writing "Editor" on the top, for the kids to decorate. As students move into the editing phase of writing, they put on the visor or hat to indicate they are now checking spelling, grammar, punctuation, and capitalization (Figure 5.5a and 5.5b). It helps them make the switch from revision to editing and lets the teacher know what stage they are in as well.

Figure 5.5a and 5.5b *Writers in editing mode*

If your goal is only to make the writing look correct, you can edit the writing to mind the manners of the English language (conventions). But good writing—and good writing instruction—is about more than just fixing. It's about making the message clear and knowing how to move the piece of writing forward by revising it first, then editing for correctness. Each part has its place in the writing process. And remember: a writer does not have to revise or edit every aspect of a piece all at once, which means you don't have to suggest revisions and edits on every trait at the same time. Read on to explore how the revision and editing processes become manageable when we zero in on what matters, one key quality at a time.

Squeeze It Once and Let It Go

From Chapter 1, we know that each trait has four key qualities that break it down into smaller, more tangible and teachable components. In Chapter 2 we practiced assessing for each trait, one at a time, then in Chapter 3 we walked through some of the major challenges students face when writing in each specific mode. Chapter 4 focused on the tools students can use to read, talk about, and revise their own writing. So now try this as you roll up your sleeves and get into teaching the hard work of revision: focus on one and only one key quality at a time, providing tips and skills to help students as they revise. When the focus is smaller, it's more doable for both you and your student writers. Let's call this approach "Squeeze it once and let it go." In other words, if you are teaching students how to write using strong verbs—a key quality of the word choice trait—then using strong verbs becomes the focus of instruction and application for a short period of time (about a week). You model, you share craft knowledge in focus lessons, you use mentor texts to show strong verbs in action, and, when providing feedback on student writing, you focus on writing with strong verbs. You leave other key qualities in word choice and other traits for a future time.

Of course, as you read students' work, you'll notice how much the other issues need attention too, but for now, squeeze it once and let it go. It may take some time and practice to let go of other concerns about the writing, but focusing on one at a time is a big part of teaching writing well. Keep in mind that all those writing issues you are not addressing on this draft will show up in the next draft or piece students write, so you can tackle those issues then. If, for instance, a student is learning about strong verbs and focusing her revision on improvements in this area, you might also notice that her sentences need work. You may be tempted to fold in notes and comments about the sentences because they need it. Don't. Save that for next time. Remember: the person holding the pen is the one doing the learning. Focus on one key quality at a time, and allow students to make the appropriate revisions. Squeeze it once and let it go. It works.

Here is an example of a fourth grader who worked on adding details to her writing, one of the key qualities of the ideas trait. The teacher read aloud *Old Henry* by Joan W. Blos; this book ends without a clear resolution to a problem in the story, so it makes a fine mentor text to show students how endings work.

After reading the book aloud, the class discussed their opinions about how to resolve the story's problem: should Old Henry be invited back or not? They also talked about what makes a good conclusion and how to wrap up the details in the piece so the writing feels finished. The teacher challenged students to write an ending to *Old Henry* in which they addressed their opinions about how the story should end to the mayor in the book. This part of the lesson focused on the key quality of ending with a sense of resolution. Figure 5.6 shows a first draft of Hannah's response.

Oh! So much great and not-so-great in this piece. It is ideal fodder for the Writing Wallet (which we'll discuss in more detail later in this chapter) so Hannah can come back to it and revise it one key quality at a time. Let's take a look at what's successful in Hannah's piece and what Hannah needs to revise:

Figure 5.6 *Hannah's draft*

What Hannah has done well	What Hannah needs to work on further
Organization: A successful conclusion to the story that wraps up the loose ends	Conventions: spelling and punctuation
Ideas: Uses a few examples from the text to make her case stronger	Ideas: adding more specific details and reasons why those details strengthen her case

Hannah put this piece in her Writing Wallet and, a week or so later, when the class worked on using details (a key quality of the ideas trait), she returned to it and added a detail that showed she understood the point of the lesson. Figure 5.7 shows her revision. Notice that Hannah doesn't copy her piece over; she just adds the new detail to the page. If at some point the paper is completely revised, she'll include this detail in her new copy.

Hannah's new detail is *"You should shovel your walk because you would have less risk of getting a concussion."* Notice that Hannah self-corrected her word choice from *higher* to *less* as she worked, choosing a word that made better sense. She's shown us three things in this simple exercise: 1) she's able to write an opinion conclusion, 2) she's able to add a meaningful detail that shows cause and effect, and 3) she can self-correct for other traits and key qualities because she's been working on them over time, too. Sweet success.

Hannah was not alone in her accomplishments. Notice how much thinking went on in this multiage special education classroom as students made meaty revisions to their *Old Henry* conclusions:

Zachariia: "He could fall because he doesn't know what's hidden in the grass."

Nolan: "Bricks hitting him on the head is really important!"

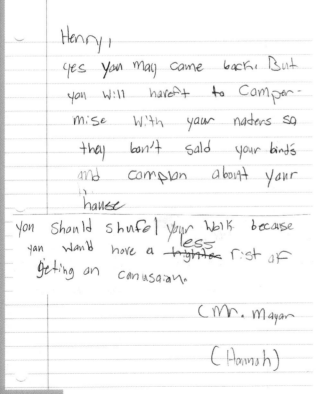

Figure 5.7 *Hannah's revised piece*

Gei: "He could control his bird so it doesn't bother people by flying around them."

Hannah: "Maybe now he'll understand why he should shovel his walk to be safe and have less risk of getting a concussion."

William: "If the grass goes too high, people might forget about him. He might not have any friends! I would be lonely and sad, if it was me."

The key qualities of the traits make the perfect framework to organize your revision-driven writing instruction during the school year. I recommend you spend about a week on each, knowing full well that each element of writing will not be mastered. Rather, your goal should be for every student to know more about that particular key quality than before. Plan to spiral through all of the key qualities, one at a time, over the course of the year. Focus on one teachable skill at a time, and it's more likely that students will be able to handle that skill with confidence on their own. Remember also that the traits are interconnected: by working with one key detail, such as strong verbs, you may find that sentence fluency and voice improve, too.

Another benefit of my "squeeze it once and let it go" approach is that students can help each other. So often, when students work with peers, we don't see successful outcomes. They tell each other their work is "good" or "fine" and then sit, fidget, or talk about something else the rest of the time. Imagine, instead, that your students just experienced a lesson or two about one of the key qualities, such as strong leads, and then were asked to work with a partner to revise only that part of the writing. Totally doable, right? Your job as the teacher, then, is to circulate around the room to make sure everyone is having constructive conversations; you can inject ideas, compliment changes, and note what students are doing. This will help you modify and adjust your lessons according to what your students need.

At this point, you may start to notice what this approach to teaching and learning does to your paperwork load. It goes way down, because you are no longer the only person capable of offering revision advice to students—they can help each other. And now, when you decide to collect a set of papers and look at them on your own, you can focus on making comments and suggestions on one key quality instead of all of them. That's a lot less work. Remember what happens when you try to respond to everything in the student's writing at once? You end up with all twenty-eight key qualities to cover in your comments and corrections. Or, if you are focusing on just one trait at a time, you'd still be looking at four different key qualities. "Squeeze it once and let it go" removes the overwhelmed feelings that writing invokes for both teachers and students.

Consider the benefit of setting your teaching sights on one key quality at a time, going as deep as you can with new information that builds from one year to the next. No one learns to write in one year, so no matter what your writing curriculum looks like and what specific materials you use, it helps to realize that the key qualities can spread out across this year and every year that follows, building confidence and competence in your students. Traits and key qualities fit within any curriculum. Imagine how much students would learn about writing in a school where this approach happens over time. Mind-boggling, right?

Figure 5.8 shows what it might look like if you spend about a week focusing on one key quality at a time over the course of the year. The revision key qualities spiral in an order that follows the scoring guide, but if you wish to move any of them around, you certainly could. Just make sure each is the focus of dedicated instruction for a week or so every year.

Figure 5.8 *Spiraled curriculum*

Notice this spiral focuses on the revision traits (as does this chapter). But, editing key qualities—spelling, punctuation, grammar, capitalization—must be the focal point for instruction, too. Because editing skills tend to be grade specific, consult your district and state's list of what should be taught and when.

I recommend this: each week, focus on one key quality for revision and one key quality for editing. That way, you can make sure both editing and revision skills are taught, practiced, and learned. You'll want lessons for every single key quality at your grade levels, right? Don't worry. Chapter 6 will help you out with that very issue.

Pause and Consider

Refer to state and district documents that list the conventions to be taught by grade level and pair them with the revision key qualities so you have a list of the editing skills you will teach—and when.

The bottom line is that it will take the whole school year to teach and practice each of the key qualities of the traits. But consider what you have in your hands: a road map for teaching revision (and editing). Will students learn everything there is to know about each of the key qualities during their time with you? Certainly not. But if you provide modeling, creative instruction (no worksheets!), and time to apply new skills—one at a time, over time—in a positive, process-inspired environment, imagine how much your students will understand about revision by the end of the school year. Think of the writing stamina they will develop as they learn the value of working and reworking a piece for each key quality over time. Then imagine what they will know about writing and how it works if this process is repeated year after year. No more "I'm done," because they will know that writing is never really done—it's not like baking cookies. Writing is meandering, complicated, and exasperating but also a satisfying, rewarding, never-ending process that students will come to understand and appreciate.

Consider what you have in your hands: a road map for teaching revision (and editing).

If the traits and their key qualities make sense to you as a way to crack the nut of revision, you'll likely be looking for teaching ideas about how to make them clear to students each day. Ideas that do not include worksheets. Let me start by sharing an idea that works beautifully to lead students into revision as a classroom routine: the Writing Wallet.

The Elegant Simplicity of the Writing Wallet

Wallets are a commonplace item. But even though the contents may be similar among individuals—credit cards, IDs, cash, photos—the particulars will vary. I have a driver's license from Oregon, for instance, and you likely have one from another state—but we both have driver's licenses. Wallets are handy for storing things you need to make a purchase, board a plane, show a picture of a grandchild, share insurance information, and so on.

I propose that you have students create a Writing Wallet for the same purpose: as a simple storage place where they can hold a small set of rough-draft writing pieces until they need them. No two students will have exactly the same papers, because each composes differently, but they will collect a similar set of papers to store. These papers become practice pieces they can revise for one key quality at a time as you conduct specific focus lessons on writing craft.

The benefits of the Writing Wallet are simple. Instead of using worksheets or prepackaged materials, students apply what they are learning to their own writing in guided practice. Each student has a personal portfolio of work that reflects his or her current level of writing skill. If a student is struggling to form a sentence, for instance, his pieces in the Writing Wallet will reflect that. And if another student is writing fluently and with skill, her pieces will reflect her ability as well. Both students will need to revise but at different levels.

In the Writing Wallet, students are working on pieces that reflect what they know and writing about topics that they've chosen and are interested in; no other tests or placement decisions are needed. They have their own personalized, differentiated works in progress, just waiting to be called into revision service. The pieces can be worked on again and again, giving the student an insider's view of what revision should really look and feel like.

> **Using a Writing Wallet for writing practice is a simple, straightforward way to engage students in revision.**

Before we get into the specifics of how to create and nurture a Writing Wallet, I want to take a minute to remind you how ineffective traditional worksheets are when it comes to teaching writing. There is plenty of scholarly evidence about writing instruction that backs up my position. Consider, for example, Marilee Ransom and Maryann Manning's conclusion from their research on the way students learn: *"We believe that consistent use of worksheets is counterproductive for student learning"* (2013, 188). They define a worksheet as *"a piece of paper, a computer screen, or a projection that contains problems. These problems have right and wrong answers, and there is generally only one way to complete the problem"* (188). They go on to recommend better ways to actively engage young minds and open the door to learning through discussion, deliberation, and project-based learning.

Another of my favorite sources on this topic is Marcia L. Tate. In her book *Worksheets Don't Grow Dendrites* (2015), she offers practical strategies that should take the place of worksheets to maximize learning, such as brainstorming, discussion, drawing, artwork, writing, field trips, project-based learning, visuals, manipulatives, games, technology, and humor.

But in the end, isn't it obvious that worksheets don't work? When only 27 percent of eighth- and twelfth-grade students are proficient in writing, according to the National Center for Educational Statistics (2012), and when we know that many if not most of those students were fed a steady diet of worksheets during writing instruction, we can logically conclude that worksheets don't create skilled, confident writers. What researchers and our own observations have shown about why worksheets don't work can be summed up pretty quickly. Worksheets are ineffective because they

- make lessons task-oriented rather than learning-oriented;

- emphasize quantity over quality as a measure of success;

- are intrinsically unchallenging, passive-versus-active learning;

- invite uniformity and discourage collaboration;

- prevent students from devising their own ways of documenting understanding;

- create more work for teachers;

- waste paper, money, and precious instructional time; and

- create dependence, not independence.

So why, then, given what we know from experience and research about traditional worksheets, do they still flood writing classrooms across the United States? Why does it feel as though we have a de facto writing curriculum from online sources such as Pinterest and Teachers Pay Teachers? Because well-intentioned teachers know three things: 1) you have to teach skills to students, 2) students have to practice those skills, and 3) students have to apply those skills. This presents a conundrum—how else can we practice writing skills other than with traditional worksheets?

Enter the Writing Wallet.

Here's what I've found that makes Writing Wallets so successful:

- Students work at their own levels.

- Students make choices and apply new skills on their own.

- Little to no management or grading is necessary.

- The teacher has a natural place to model writing skills—this is essential for all writing classrooms.

- Students make writing decisions that become more complex over time.

- The teacher helps by nudging students forward in brief, nonthreatening interactions.

- Collaboration among peers and with the teacher is encouraged.

- Revision and editing become manageable processes.

- Skills are transferred to independent writing through meaningful practice.

Using a Writing Wallet for writing practice is a simple, straightforward way to engage students in revision using their own work as the resource for their practice. The student's writing becomes the heart of instruction and learning as you fold it into the recursive nature of the writing-to-assessment-to-instruction-to-revision-to-learning process.

The stated policy of the National Council of Teachers of English for many years has been that "each teacher must be knowledgeable enough about the entire landscape of writing instruction to guide particular students toward a goal, including increasing fluency in new contexts, mastering conventions, and perhaps most important, developing rhetorical sophistication and appropriateness—all of which work together" (2016). The Writing Wallet supports this important thinking. In other words, to teach writing well, we must discard practices that don't work in favor of those that do. The Writing Wallet is a simple, interactive tool that allows students to succeed where worksheets have failed.

Pause and Consider Discuss the use of worksheets for writing practice. What is the difference between a worksheet and a graphic organizer, a visual map, or other methods designed for long-term retention of information? Why would a Writing Wallet be a more logical way to invite revision than worksheets? How important will modeling be as you implement a Writing Wallet?

Getting Started with Writing Wallets

The Writing Wallet requires a dedicated space, so if you already have writing folders, notebooks, journals, and so on, separate them from the Writing Wallet. If you are a teacher who has embraced technology, I'm sure you can find a way to make the Writing Wallet work in digital spaces. But for the purposes of describing the process, I'm going to stick to physical, hold-in-your-hand Writing Wallets. They work well when they are paper because notes can be added easily and students literally have something in their hands to revise. You can create a digital version of the Writing Wallet, but I prefer the paper version; there is just something about the medium that works. Keep in mind that the benefit of the Writing Wallet is not the physical container but how you use the contents to guide revision so students learn to think more clearly and thoughtfully about their work.

Starting Writing Wallets in your classroom is simple. In fact, you can start tomorrow, regardless of where you are in your curriculum or instructional goals. Here's an overview of how to launch a Writing Wallet:

1. Give a manila folder to every student and have them label it "Writing Wallet." Let them decorate it if you wish, but resist the temptation to invest in folders that have pockets or other bells and whistles. It's just a receptacle. Don't complicate it.

2. Put two to four pieces of the student's writing in the Writing Wallet. (Keep reading to learn some ways to determine which pieces go into the Writing Wallet.) These pieces may be quick-writes, responses to literature, self-reflections at the start of writing activities, warm-ups, journal ideas, short answers to essays, or any other writing students do during the day. Each piece should be short (less than a page) and raw. No corrections or revisions should be evident—yet.

3. Create a Writing Wallet for yourself (Figure 5.9). Generate two to four pieces of paragraph-length writing on topics of your choice and use them to model how to revise for each key quality as your instruction unfolds. Modeling is critical for students to see and hear how you make revision decisions for your writing, one key quality at a time.

> *To teach writing well, we must discard practices that don't work in favor of those that do.*

Figure 5.9 *A teacher's Writing Wallet*

Picking the "Right" Papers for the Writing Wallet

There are three ways that pieces can be selected for the Writing Wallet:

1. If you'd prefer a more structured process, you could assign a piece for the express purpose of having a writing draft to put into the folder.

2. Another approach is to add pieces as you and the student discover them together, perhaps during a conference: "Jayden, I noticed this piece is giving you trouble today. Maybe it would be a good one to put in your Writing Wallet so we can work on it more over time."

3. The third approach is a hybrid of teacher choice and student choice: you pick, they pick. How you determine which pieces ultimately make it into the Writing Wallet will depend on how much control you want to have over their contents.

Ultimately, it doesn't really matter which pieces are in the Writing Wallet as long as they are the student's authentic work. It helps, however, if each piece holds the student's interest and is a piece he or she cares about.

Managing the Writing Wallet

Organization is one of the most important skills a teacher must develop. We all know what it's like when you can't locate a key resource when it's needed or when some students have what they need and others don't. In that spirit, I offer these suggestions to keep the Writing Wallet organized and accessible:

Writing Wallets should stay in your classroom so they don't disappear into backpacks or lockers. Store the Writing Wallets on a shelf, in a hanging file system, or in a box after they've been used for the day.

The Writing Wallet should not be the place where tip sheets and other pieces of writing-in-process are stored. A traditional writing folder or notebook can typically be used to keep multiple drafts of a longer piece, ideas that you share with students as reference pages, and any notes they are using in their work. Use the Writing Wallet as a dedicated place to practice revising and editing, one key quality at a time.

I recommend keeping two to four writing pieces in the Writing Wallet at all times so students have a choice about which piece to revise. Choice is important; even if it's only between paper A and paper B, students feel more control when they can make that decision for themselves. More than four pieces creates a different sort of problem: the short time that is set aside to revise or edit one piece will be spent rereading all the papers and choosing one—that's counterproductive. It actually doesn't matter which piece they select. They need to choose one and get to work. The entire process of choosing and revising or editing a piece should last five to ten minutes at most.

How Instruction and Revision with the Writing Wallet Unfold

Consider the role of the Writing Wallet in the ongoing instructional process (Figure 5.10), described in these three steps:

1. Trait-based focus lesson: You conduct a large-group focus lesson on one of the key qualities of a trait. (10–15 minutes)

2. Writing Wallet: You model using a piece from your personal Writing Wallet to show students the revision decisions you make based on the focus lesson and how you apply them to your writing. Then students try using the new skill on a piece of their work and revise it. (5–10 minutes)

3. Independent writing: Students return to their longer, ongoing piece of writing from writing workshop, and continue writing and revising with new knowledge about a writing skill firmly in mind. This piece is often mode specific and works through the entire writing process over time. (20 minutes or more)

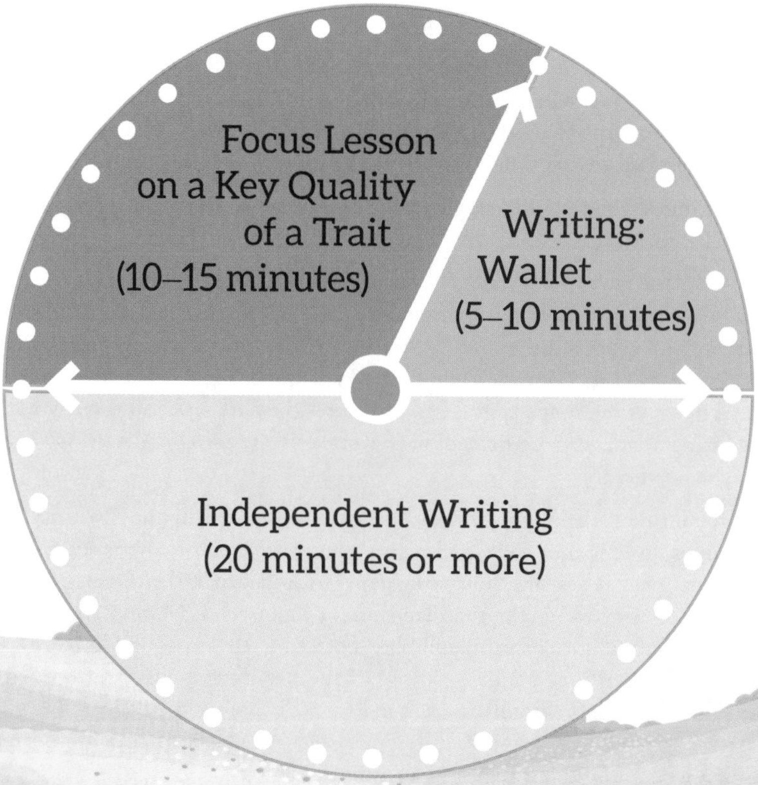

Figure 5.10 - *The instructional process*

Lather, rinse, repeat. Every time a new skill or understanding about writing is introduced to students, usually twice a week (once for a revision skill and once for an editing skill), they apply it to the pieces in their Writing Wallets. But they don't revise the whole piece each time, nor do they rewrite. Students make the revisions they feel are appropriate based on the lesson modeled and then put their Writing Wallets away. They cross out, revise, add on, attach—whatever is needed to make the piece work better in one specific way—but they don't recopy. This way the odious task of recopying is avoided, and less time is needed to complete the teaching and guided practice part of the lesson.

Most focus lessons last less than fifteen minutes; the writing wallet should take five to ten minutes. Then you can move quickly to the longer, more independent writing that students are doing for the rest of the writing time. Please note, too, that this process does not create a stack of worksheets to correct or grade. Your valuable time is spent working with students, circulating around the room, and helping them with their writing, not correcting superficial worksheets.

How to Sustain the Writing Wallet

The Writing Wallet becomes the students' practice, their personalization of what is being taught, their way to show what they are learning in small increments over time. Remember: squeeze it once and let it go. These small, focused moments of understanding and application add up until students actually know what it means to revise and why it is so important. They see, firsthand, how revising their work for one trait or quality at a time makes a big difference over time.

> They see how revising their work for one trait or quality at a time makes a big difference over time.

After five or more dips into the Writing Wallet, a student may ask, "Are we ever going to do anything with these papers? They are getting very messy with all the changes and corrections we're making." Ah, music to our ears. No longer reluctant to revise, this student is now asking to revise. A comment like this is an indication that it's time to stop making changes on the pieces in the Writing Wallet and transfer the changes to a new copy, clean it up, and finalize it.

Perhaps you'll decide for other reasons when the time has come to stop working on the current pieces in the Writing Wallet. Either way, you'll want to pause periodically, have students revise and edit one of the papers, and turn it in. Clear out the old and pick new papers for the next round of the Writing Wallet. Then you begin again. Occasionally, a student will want to keep one of the pieces to continue revising rather than replacing it with something new. It's your choice, of course, but I would encourage this. It shows ownership and understanding of the role the Writing Wallet plays in the revision process.

It's a good day when students ask to transfer the changes they have made to a more polished copy of their original rough draft. No, they won't have revised it for every trait and all the key qualities in just a few weeks, but one of the best things about using the traits is realizing how they overlap and support one another. For instance, you may have taught a lesson about using details from the ideas trait but you notice that voice has also improved as a result. Or you might have spent time on using sequence words and transition words from the organization trait and you note that sentence fluency has improved as well. Victory!

We're teaching students to write, not to trait, so when they begin to see the interconnectedness of different elements, it's a breakthrough in understanding and owning the revision process for themselves. We use traits as the structure to make knowledge about writing and specific writing skills accessible and doable for students; we use the Writing Wallet to make revision tangible. We put it all in a big pot and stir until it's just the right consistency.

Writing Wallet Basics

- Start with a simple folder or a folded sheet of construction paper.

- Include two to four pieces of the student's own work.

- Keep Writing Wallets in the classroom.

- Practice on the pieces in the Writing Wallet, not worksheets.

- Maintain a Writing Wallet of your own to model and demonstrate.

- Finalize a piece periodically (every three to four weeks or so).

- Clear out the contents and begin again by adding new practice papers.

Try It! "Little Red Riding Hood" Interview

Let's walk through a lesson designed to give students hands-on practice with one of the key qualities of the organization trait: structuring the body. As you launch the lesson, discuss the key quality with students and refer to their student-friendly guides (see Chapter 4). When they dig into their Writing Wallets, they'll be on the lookout for issues in their writing that may be problematic for the body of their papers. Maybe they have extraneous information in the body; maybe they have jumped too quickly (or slowly) from one idea to the next; maybe they have left out something that is critical to understand so the order of ideas makes sense. In my experience, I've found this to be one of the more challenging aspects of teaching writing and worth the extra time an extended lesson will take.

One of the best things about using the traits is realizing how they overlap and support one another.

In this lesson, students will interview the Big Bad Wolf, asking him to answer questions about Little Red Riding Hood's tale. The emphasis will be on putting statements and questions in an order that makes sense and shows logic and reason—in other words, structuring the body.

After you've completed an introduction to the key quality, make sure all students are familiar with the "Little Red Riding Hood" story; you may want to factor in some time to read or retell it. Then put students into pairs and give them a set of the interview questions on cards that you've prepared ahead of time.

Read aloud the introduction in Figure 5.11 and have students put their cards in the order that makes sense for the interview, encouraging them to remove questions completely if they don't believe they belong. Have a set of blank cards available if students wish to add questions as well.

Once they have put their questions in order, each pair of students should compare their results with another pair and make revisions as they wish. You can share the order you feel makes the most sense, but leave room for different defensible answers. Doing this exercise gives students practice with the thread logic that good organization requires. Putting the questions in order and then deciding which are needed and which aren't requires writers to think carefully and with attention to how all the details fit together to create meaning—an excellent skill for all writers to develop.

After the questions are ordered and selected, the really fun part begins: students role-play the interview. One student will be the interviewer and one will take on the role of the wolf. Ask for volunteers to act out their interviews for the class. Comment on the different ways the interviews developed because pairs ordered their questions—and therefore structured the body—slightly differently. This part of the activity will require even more time, of course, but it is time well spent when students can enjoy the fruits of their labors.

When students complete the interview and discussion, invite them to select a piece in their Writing Wallets and focus some revision on crafting a clear and coherent structure in the body. Remind them to be on the lookout for places to cut, move, or revise in other ways, just as they did in the "Little Red Riding Hood" lesson. This focus lesson will help students pinpoint issues in their own writing, and it gives them a creative and imaginative experience along the way.

"Little Red Riding Hood" Activity Introduction

You are the moderator for a weekly news interview program on a major television network. You've planned your questions for this week's guest, the wolf from "Little Red Riding Hood" (LRRH), but you accidentally drop the cards so they fall out of order and get mixed in with some questions you've already decided not to ask. Put the questions back into an order that makes sense before the cameras start to roll. Feel free to discard questions that you feel are irrelevant and don't make the interview stronger.

Interview Questions

"Little Red Riding Hood" Activity

Do you have any regrets?

Tell us what happened from your point of view so the viewing audience is up to speed on the most current version of this story.

No offense, Mr. Wolf, but you aren't well known for being honest and trustworthy. What did you do to win LRRH's trust?

Thanks for coming in today and clarifying this rather grisly episode, Mr. Wolf. Do you have plans for what you will do next, after you recover?

So, are you saying that you ate LRRH's grandmother? Explain why you thought that was okay.

What was the weather like?

Who is your biggest enemy?

Figure 5.11 *Structuring the body: "Little Red Riding Hood" interview activity—introduction and interview questions*

How did you disguise yourself so LRRH didn't realize you were not her grandmother?

I imagine you were looking forward to LRRH's visit. Did you do anything special to prepare?

Welcome. Thanks for coming today. Let's get right to it. What's the hardest thing about being a wolf in a fairy tale?

How old are you?

What's your favorite television show?

Describe how you felt that day, when you saw LRRH coming down the road.

How long have you lived in the woods?

Have you ever had any problems with the Woodsman before?

Did anything happen during this whole course of events that surprised you?

Take a minute and tell us what this experience meant to you and what you have learned as a result.

Figure 5.11 cont. *Structuring the body: "Little Red Riding Hood" interview activity—introduction and interview questions*

Suggested Order of Final Questions

Note: There will be other variations that work well to structure the body, too; just be sure there is logic behind student responses.

Q1: *Welcome. Thanks for coming today. Let's get right to it. What's the hardest thing about being a wolf in a fairy tale?*

Q2: *Tell us what happened from your point of view so the viewing audience is up to speed on the most current version of this story.*

Q3: *So, are you saying that you ate LRRH's grandmother? Explain why you thought that was okay.*

Q4: *I imagine you were looking forward to LRRH's visit. Did you do anything special to prepare?*

Q5: *How did you disguise yourself so LRRH didn't realize you were not her grandmother?*

Q6: *Describe how you felt that day, when you saw LRRH coming down the road.*

Q7: *No offense, Mr. Wolf, but you aren't well known for being honest and trustworthy. What did you do to win LLRH's trust?*

Q8: *Did anything happen during this whole course of events that surprised you?*

Q9: *Do you have any regrets?*

Q10: *Take a minute and tell us what this experience meant to you and what you have learned as a result.*

Q11: *Thanks for coming in today and clarifying this rather grisly episode, Mr. Wolf. Do you have plans for what you will do next, after you recover?*

Wrap-Up

The purpose of the Writing Wallet is to help students learn to revise and feel that they can face writing challenges with skill, knowledge, and confidence. As their teachers, we understand that they will apply the traits to pieces in the Writing Wallet, one element at a time, in authentic writing contexts. Once students embrace the value of revision, they need our help to figure out how to do it well. Writing Wallets make the elusive revision process possible.

The next chapters will help you find and design lessons that focus on the knowledge and skills students need to tackle so they can apply them to their pieces in the Writing Wallet and beyond.

6

Invigorate Writing Instruction

Enter Goldilocks. She checks out each of the three bears' beds and discovers one is too soft, one is too hard, and one is just right. How does she reach this conclusion? Formative assessment. She sits on the beds and tries each for comfort. Her ability to find the one that is "just right" depends on her experience and knowledge of what works best for her.

In much the same way, we create and modify the instructional writing lessons we plan for students. It's differentiation. Just knowing, for instance, that we need a lesson on developing skills in word choice to enhance the key quality of using specific and accurate words is not enough. Remember: Goldilocks knew she needed a bed, but not just any bed. It had to be "just right." We also need our lessons to be "just right" to fit the needs of our students and their abilities to learn each key quality. Some students will be quite far along, others will be just beginning, and some will be just where we would expect for their grade level. So, what makes a writing lesson "just right"? It's designed so all students can benefit from it, regardless of their skill or ability in the targeted area.

Start with the Whole Class

Ironically, the way to begin lesson planning for individuals is to think about the whole class first. Let's get real: it's not possible to plan and implement individual lessons for each writer in your class every single day, nor is it necessary. True individualized instruction occurs in conferences and small-group instruction. Large-group instruction gets everyone moving in the right direction and lays the groundwork for individual work to follow.

Many teachers I know confide that they feel inadequate because they don't individualize for each of their students every day, in every lesson. They feel guilty because they know how important it is to differentiate but realize what a daunting (if not impossible) task it would be. Perhaps you feel the same way. My advice? Stop beating yourself up. You will exhaust and frustrate yourself with this expectation. It's unfeasible and, frankly, unnecessary to create unique lessons for every student all the time. Breathe. You can create plans to meet your goals for student writers that will allow for balance: whole-group, small-group, and individual work. And you can do it relatively easily.

Begin with a well-designed lesson and share it with the entire class—you may be surprised by how many students find it to be "just right." For those who don't, create places in the lesson where you can circle back and reinforce the main concepts in fresh new ways in small groups or one-on-one. In other words, differentiate after you present a whole-group focus lesson; determine which students need more work in a specific area and who needs to be challenged further.

If you have designed your writing curriculum around spiraling key qualities of the traits, as suggested in Chapter 5, the primary goal of the lesson should be fairly easy to determine. The questions to ask yourself as you create lessons on key qualities are, *How will I know students have gained skill in this area? What will I accept as evidence of this learning? What else can I plan for students who need more work or an extension in this area?*

Remember, you'll want to spend about one week on each key quality, which you'll introduce as a revision-related skill, and one editing skill. Regardless of the writing abilities of your students, focus on these two skills to keep moving forward. Students apply what they have learned to the pieces in their Writing Wallets; ultimately, the lesson is differentiated by students' application of the skill in the context of their own work and your observation of who got it, who didn't, and who needs an even more advanced path. No one learns everything about a quality of writing in just one week. But regardless of where each student begins, a little knowledge that builds on the previous skill and goes deeper and deeper each year is, well, priceless.

Whole-class instruction consists of a fifteen-minute focus lesson—give or take five minutes, depending on the age and attention span of your students and the concept you're teaching. I use the term *focus lesson* here rather than *mini-lesson* because I think it better represents what we are shooting for: a short instructional burst on a specific topic. Design the focus lesson to help all students understand more about a writing skill that makes a difference in the quality of their work. Deliver it to the whole class to maximize your instruction time.

Some common concerns about focus lessons, and suggested solutions, follow:

1. **They last too long.**

   Stop talking. Every teacher knows much more than their students, so it's easy to just keep explaining and elaborating. Streamline your lessons: you talk, they talk, we write.

2. **They cover too much.**

   Have a landing point in mind. That means focusing on one writing issue at a time and sticking to it. Remember "squeeze it once and let it go"? It applies here, too. Focus, focus, focus.

3. **They have to be finished to be successful.**

   Finishing is not the goal; learning is the goal. If you teach and students practice during the focus lesson, you don't always need to finish. (Heresy!) Practice is where the learning takes place. You can always add unfinished pieces to the Writing Wallet to complete later if more time is wanted or needed.

4. **They are too teacher-driven.**

   Put yourself in your students' shoes. Is this lesson appropriate for their ages and abilities? Is there something in the lesson that will make them sit up and take notice—an element of inspiration or fun? The person holding the pen is doing the learning . . . so was this lesson designed for them or for you? (Hint: the right answer is "for them"!)

5. **They presume all students will "get it."**

   All students won't. Learning to write is a process of trial and error, accumulation of skills, and trying out those skills in new writing pieces over time. Mastering a complex skill requires multiple attempts. Expect failure as much as success. It's a key ingredient of good writing instruction.

Plan time for small-group and individual work as a follow-up to the large-group focus lesson. We can safely assume that one large-group lesson will not solidify a concept for every student. Some will get it—some won't. Teaching in small groups allows you to revisit a writing skill with a different approach. After all, the first run at it didn't work for these students, so you need to change it up. Some students probably will continue to struggle after a second or third pass at a skill. That's when you pull up a chair and do some carefully targeted one-on-one instruction. And if you still don't have that "breakthrough moment," take heart—students will receive more instruction on this writing key quality next year, or they'll continue to pick it up through practice and by learning other key qualities. (Revisit Chapter 4 for more on student tools for writing and revision, as well as tips for how to confer with students at all levels of accomplishment.)

Discuss the role of large, small, and individual instruction **Pause and Consider** in the writing classroom. How would you use formative assessment to pinpoint those who might benefit from follow-up work? Are there ways you can work check-ins into a lesson? How is the writing classroom organized so whole-class, small-group, and individual time can be facilitated?

Weekly Writing Routines

Your schedule is your own, of course, but in any given week, you should have two specific goals to accomplish in writing: one for revision, one for editing. Between the key qualities spiraling set of revision skills and your state standards list for conventions, you'll have a guide for what those should be.

Here is how you might plan your week:

- One focus lesson on the key quality for revision (15 minutes)

- One focus lesson on the convention chosen as an editing skill (15 minutes)

- One focus lesson on the mode (narrative, informational, opinion/argument) (15 minutes)

- Two Writing Wallet follow-ups, one after each trait focus lesson (5–10 minutes each)

- Five open writing opportunities for work on the independent, mode-specific writing that extends over one, two, or three weeks, depending on the goal of the project (minimum of 20 minutes per day; longer when possible)

For example, your week might look like Figure 6.1:

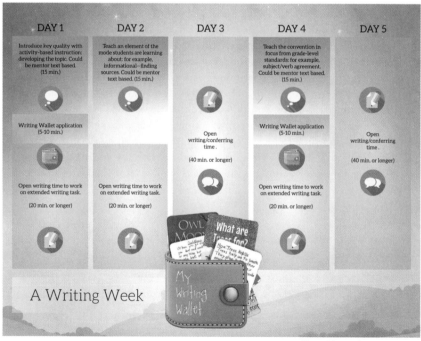

Figure 6.1 *A Writing Week*

TEACH WRITING WELL

Remember that after a week or so, you'll move on to a different revision key quality and editing skill, even if students have not mastered the current ones. Your main goal is for students to know more about those key qualities at the end of the week than they did at the beginning.

I can't stress enough how important it is to adapt these ideas to your unique schedule so it works for you within the parameters of your school or classroom. You can carve out time to work on the extended writing task at any time during the day, for instance. Or, maybe the writing is centered on science or social studies content and can be done during that part of the day. Do whatever works so students have explicit instruction and as much time as possible to write, talk, revise, edit, and learn.

Can you . . .

- change the order of focus lessons and mentor text lessons? YES

- skip a day? YES

- spend more time than usual teaching and writing? YES

- let student interest guide how long lessons last? YES

- end the focus lesson before everyone has finished practice work? YES

- spend more time on a key quality that is particularly difficult? YES

- spend less time on a key quality that is easier? YES

You get the picture. Flexibility, creativity, imagination, and engagement matter more than what's included in a scheduled lesson plan.

How to Create a Great Writing Lesson

Please keep this in mind: there is no ironclad recipe for a strong writing lesson, but there are essential ingredients. The best cooks I know assemble the makings and use their experience and judgment as they go rather than measuring every item with precision. That means that each time the cook prepares the dish it is slightly different—but consistently delicious.

Effective large-group writing lessons include the following ingredients:

- A landing point and going deeper

- An element of energy and interest

- Modeling and resources

- Flexibility and room for adjustment

There is no ironclad recipe for a strong writing lesson, but there are essential ingredients.

Each lesson should contain identifiable ingredients that make it appetizing for students while also accomplishing your instructional goals. The basics of what goes into a writing lesson don't change, but how much of, and how long you spend with, each element is where your teacher judgment comes in. Teaching writing is part logic and part instinct. You need to have clear goals and bring creativity and innovation to lessons and activities to achieve buy-in from students so they make the progress you have in mind.

A Landing Point and Going Deeper

To create a strong writing lesson, it's critical to have a landing point: the focus of the lesson that reflects a crystal-clear understanding of the learning target. You're in luck! A list of landing points for lesson design already exists in the key qualities of each trait. Over the course of the year, you should plan to spend about a week focusing on each key quality in pairs: one from a revision trait and one from an editing trait. Revisit Chapter 5 for further details about how to spiral the key qualities across the year.

Going deeper, or repeating concepts with an increased level of detail across every grade, is just as important. In a perfect scenario, you will be adding information to what students already know about each key quality from previous grades. For instance, if you teach fourth grade and the third-grade teacher is using the same spiraling approach, you'll not be the first person to share ideas about how to vary sentence types. That topic will have been worked on the previous year, and you can refresh and build on what is already known.

Moving forward at different levels of skill with the same landing points each year is critical to writing progress. Think about it. We have to go deeper each year to reach our goal: strong, independent writers.

I've been fortunate to work with a few forward-thinking school districts over time as they revamped writing assessment and instruction. One Midwest district I've had the pleasure of working with saw the wisdom of a spiraling curriculum and embraced the idea completely. We worked hand in hand to provide extensive professional development to assist teachers as they implemented this different vision of teaching writing. Almost immediately they saw growth in writing scores (not the only measure of success, but certainly worth noting) at all grade levels, but after several years of steady gains, the scores plateaued.

When the administrators, literacy coaches, and I met to discuss these results, we considered several possible reasons for the plateau:

1. Students had reached the limit of how well they could reasonably do in writing. This was improbable, because we believe there is no limit to writing success.

2. Some teachers may have strayed from the spiraling model. This could be rectified with additional professional development and coaching.

3. The lessons didn't increase in difficulty across the grades. This was examined more thoroughly as the possible missing piece of their writing curriculum reform.

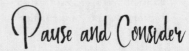

Which of these issues do you and your colleagues have a plan to address in your schools? Do you have a belief system that every child can learn more than we dare to dream? Do you have ongoing professional development for teachers who need a refresher, are new to the school or grade level, or have new ideas to share and refinements to suggest to the curriculum? How do you account for going deeper across the grades to make sure lessons and expectations become more complex over time?

We decided to conduct an experiment to validate our hunch that lessons not increasing in difficulty across grades might have led to the writing plateau. Teacher representatives for grades K–8 were invited to a professional development session to participate in our investigation. Before the meeting, the district coordinator gathered an example of a focus lesson from each grade for one of the key qualities of the ideas trait: using details. We assumed this key quality was familiar to most teachers and that there would be splendid examples of lesson ideas from every grade. We typed up the lessons using a simple-to-follow format and removed the teacher's name and grade level, making the lessons anonymous.

Once we had formatted lesson examples from all nine grades, we copied a set for each participant. At the professional development session, we challenged teachers to rank the lessons in order, from the least difficult to the most difficult. The district coordinator and I watched and listened as they worked. We made notes and talked about what teachers commented on as they worked: What made a lesson challenging or easy? How much prior knowledge was needed? How complex was the task? Once the teachers reached a general consensus about the order of difficulty of the lessons, we revealed the original grade levels. The fifth-grade lesson was deemed the most difficult by the majority of the group. The second-grade lesson was ranked the easiest. That meant other grades were out of sequence as well. The group also considered three grades to have the same degree of difficulty.

I found the whole process revealing and fascinating—as did the teacher participants. We had worked hard as a team to unify their teaching approaches and spiral the writing curriculum, but the actual grade-level lessons were left to individual teachers to design. Turns out that, to have a robust writing curriculum that continues to meet students' needs over the years, factoring in the degree of difficulty is very important. Following this activity, the district held many cross-grade-level meetings in which teachers worked together to establish a smooth and continuous arc of learning. Student writing scores took off again.

Two things made an appreciable difference in this district's writing success: 1) every lesson had a clear landing point with touch points to other subjects and content whenever possible, and 2) every year students were asked to do more, and they were successful because of the spiraling curriculum and lessons with differing degrees of difficulty.

An Element of Energy and Interest

Shouldn't everything we do be aimed at firing up our students' desire to learn? That means teaching so they are inspired, not bored. Every single lesson you create should focus on how to light up students' excitement about learning. I'm certain we're not doing that consistently—especially when so many schools and classrooms are worksheet driven for writing instruction (and other subjects as well).

If you want students to write better, they have to write. If you want them more engaged in learning skills that relate to writing, they have to find writing useful, interesting, and—dare I say it—fun. Every lesson should seek to captivate and fascinate. Remember what Mary Poppins, the world's most beloved authority on children, reminds us about a spoonful of sugar.

Shouldn't everything we do be aimed at firing up our students' desire to learn?

Engagement adds to everything we hope will happen for writers. They work harder when they are genuinely interested; they build stamina for writing longer; they collaborate and push each other's ideas to new heights; they enjoy what they are doing; they ask questions that show how much they are thinking; they consider better ways to express themselves in writing; they use their time effectively; and they experience the success that hard work brings to the writing process.

All of this happens when students are intrigued, fascinated, absorbed, and engaged in the lessons you present and apply them to their writing. I've never met a worksheet, by the way, that could accomplish any of these things. And simply adding a bit of technology or gamifying a canned lesson doesn't automatically make it engaging. Kids need to get out of their seats, be interactive, and solve problems to get truly involved.

The amount of time needed for interactive learning varies. For example, the lesson plan shared later in this chapter, "Sentences Alive," can be completed in about ten minutes, or it can take much longer, depending on the word list and the energy and understanding of your students on a particular day. There's no telling until you get into it—which is one of the things that makes it work so well. Students won't forget "Sentences Alive," because it is interactive and doesn't have one simple solution. It's designed for long-term, process-driven learning. Later, you can remind struggling writers about what they learned from "Sentences Alive," and that simple nudge may be all that's needed to help them out of their immediate sentence trouble. I love watching students (and teachers at workshops) engage in the process of solving problems in interactive activities. It's some of the best teaching we do.

Modeling and Resources

When I address the topic of modeling writing for students in professional development workshops, I see two different sets of body language from teachers: some look up, eager for validation and refinement of what they are already doing, and some look down, hoping that this part of the workshop will pass quickly. They may even make a beeline to the restroom or step out to return calls so they miss the whole topic.

As I see it, modeling doesn't have to cause heartburn. There are numerous ways to model revision that are painless and actually quite enjoyable. And think of the benefits! Students

> Modeling is essential to the teaching of writing.

can learn by example what the writer's internal dialogue sounds like during revision. Students learn what published authors do successfully and give it a try themselves. Students see firsthand the benefit of revising and notice how the writing improves over time with strategic revision.

Modeling your own writing and revision

I know it can seem intimidating and uncomfortable to model writing for your students. I'm not sure many teachers have a clear picture in their minds about what modeling could look like, and, coupled with reluctance to publicly display their own writing, many don't go down this road at all. That's a mistake. Modeling is essential to the teaching of writing. Students desperately need to know what is going on in the head of a writer as the composition process unfolds. They need to know that writing does not start out great. It begins, as Anne Lamott says, with a "shitty first draft" (1994, 21). Of course, you may not want to use these exact words with third graders, but every writer has learned this the hard way. We all stumble through the writing process from the earliest rough draft to the smoothed-out and clarified final draft.

I learned something vital when I went through the Montana Writing Project many years ago: a writing teacher has to write in order to understand the challenges that face student writers. By being a writer yourself, you get it—you understand that sometimes the words don't flow, that the image you want to create still seems foggy, that your idea is not well supported, that the language sounds stilted, or that the grammar is off in places. These struggles are real no matter how experienced you are as a writer.

Who better to teach young writers about writing than someone who understands this from personal experience? You are the very person to empathize with the challenges of the writing process. By sharing your writing with students, they learn that writers don't just get up in the morning and write brilliant prose—the type they are used to reading in books. They learn that writing is more than a process written on an anchor chart or a handout. It's a real, breathing organism—something that takes nurturing to grow and flourish. And it's okay to start with a shitty first draft. In fact, it's pretty much guaranteed.

Embrace the process.

Embrace the process. Share with students a rough draft of your own that will likely find its way into your Writing Wallet.

1. Create a piece of writing on a topic of your choice. It can be related to something you and the class are working on or simply something that interests you.

2. Keep it short. A paragraph is enough to get started. (You're feeling better already, right?)

3. Make sure the piece is flawed in the key quality you are studying. For example, if your revision landing point for the week is using active verbs, make sure your piece doesn't have many. Give students several places to note where the convention you are studying is used incorrectly, too.

4. Project the writing and ask students to help you improve the piece for the key quality first and then the convention. Mark the paper as they point out places it could be improved. Some teachers find it useful to make changes for revision in one color and editing in another, visually separating revision from editing for the students.

During the revision and editing of the paper, think aloud—a lot. Explain your thinking at every turn. Read your piece aloud and then begin to comment about the key quality of the week—in this example, action verbs. *"Hmm, I think the verb* walk *could be more powerful. There are better words to describe what I'm trying to say. Class, can you help me think of another word for* walk? *I want a word that explains that as I come in from the parking lot, I'm eager for today's field trip to the art museum."*

List the words they suggest and encourage them to look for others in resources such as a Google synonym search: *stroll, saunter, amble, trudge, plod, dawdle, hike, tramp, tromp, slog, stomp, trek, march, stride, sashay, glide, troop, patrol, wander, ramble, tread, prowl, promenade, roam, traipse.* Don't be surprised if students are unfamiliar with some of these words—what a great opportunity, though, to stretch their vocabulary and add new words to your word wall or other vocabulary-building resources. (You might consider vocabulary development as a different wrinkle of another key quality of the word choice trait, such as selecting striking words and phrases or using specific and accurate words, but never miss a chance to double-team.)

Go through the verbs they find and talk about their meanings. Ask them which ones match the connotation of what you are trying to express in your writing. Consider having students act out their favorites—you should do it, too. Eliminate those that don't work in your piece, and have them help you choose the best one among those that are left. Cross out *walk* and replace it with *sashay* or *traipse*, for instance. Read the sentence aloud before and after the revision, and ask students which works better to help the reader understand. Note aloud whether you agree or not, and move on to another example in the text where you talk through a writer's decision on active verbs. Then repeat this process for the specific convention you're working on that relates to a grade-specific skill in spelling, capitalization, punctuation, or grammar.

When you have spent five to ten minutes working on your piece, put it in your Writing Wallet. You might want to note aloud that changing the verbs also added to the voice of the writing—now you are triple-teaming the benefits of the lesson! Then ask students to get out their Writing Wallets and follow your lead working with the key quality for revision and the convention for editing. They know what to do because you've modeled it for them. Working with your own writing is a technique you can return to over and over again.

This is modeling. It doesn't mean creating a piece that is ready for publication. It means showing students what writers do as they go through the writing process. Talk through all the writing decisions you make: how you select your topic, what details you choose for making that topic clear, the places where you think the piece is working and the places where it isn't. Remember, you've deliberately created a piece that has flaws so it should be easy for students to point them out and for you to respond. Validate their observations by letting them know what you think about each one. And keep talking! You can't talk aloud too much when you model. How else are student writers going to understand what goes on inside a writer's mind during revision?

Modeling with examples of authors' drafts

Even though modeling your own writing and revision process is paramount, you can also show students how some of their favorite published authors work through their drafts.

Figure 6.2 provides links to well-known children's book authors who have shared their drafts and thinking about familiar works. Check out the revision of the beloved text *Because of Winn-Dixie* by Kate DiCamillo, and note how her thinking changed as she reworked the opening paragraph.

Or how about the notes from Dr. Seuss as he played with the form and rhythm of *All Sorts of Sports*, a book that was never completed? Notice how J. K. Rowling planned the organization of her series of Harry Potter books; her thinking about order and transition from one book to the next is clear in her notebook chart, but there is much more to be fleshed out through writing. And finally, look at a page from E. B. White's classic *Charlotte's Web*. What a treasure to have an example of how his thinking changed in the second draft of his first page—and how fascinating that the final book starts with very different lines! It's clear that one thing all of these extraordinary writers have in common is the amount of thinking and reflecting that goes into their planning, writing, and revising.

Figure 6.2 *Examples of author drafts and revisions*

Kate DiCamillo	http://teacher.scholastic.com/activities/flashlightreaders/pdfs/WinnDixie_story.pdf	Revision of the first page of *Because of Winn-Dixie*
Dr. Seuss	http://natedsanders.com/blog/2016/10/dr-seuss-autograph/	Draft-in-process of unpublished story
J. K. Rowling	https://www.buzzfeed.com/ailbhemalone/read-jk-rowlings-hand-written-plan-for-harry-potter-and-the?utm_term=.pmMM1OyNe#.ux7GPxNEl	Planning chart for Harry Potter series
E. B. White	https://www.brainpickings.org/2013/10/15/e-b-white-on-charlottes-web/	Revision of the first page of *Charlotte's Web*

TEACH WRITING WELL

Use the Internet as a resource for more examples of authors' works in draft form. Maybe students will have a favorite author whose works they can explore in more depth. A delightful group project might ask students to study how authors write and revise, make a chart or tips page, and then connect to how they can do the same with their own writing.

Model with students' writing

You can also model and apply the traits to an anonymous piece of writing. (Appendix A contains anonymous pieces you could use as examples.) This modeling and mentoring happens over time as you work on writing, one trait and key quality at a time. The example below uses a flawed third-grade informational paper as a draft to revise as a class. The teacher made it clear that the paper didn't come from anyone in her class, so no one was uncomfortable.

First, they read the paper and assessed it together, using their student-friendly scoring guides.

PENGUINS

Penguins are black and white. Thay come in diferent sizes and are realy cute. The mothers dont do as much as the fathers to get redy for the penguins to be born. Penguin Fathers kepe babys warm on there feet penguins liv in groups and they make alot of noic. It would be fun to have a penguin as a pet but I think thay have to liv in realy cold places and zoos ar places you can find penguins.

The assessment turned out as follows:

Ideas: 2

Organization: 2

Voice: 2

Word Choice: 2

Sentence Fluency: 2

Conventions: 1

The final assessment was discussed and agreed on by the class. Then, the students and teacher began the work of revising—one writing skill at a time, with a new landing point each week—beginning with developing the idea. The teacher made changes to the text using a digital projector so all students could see, think, and discuss.

The teacher showed the class the three parts of the paper and started a discussion about how they might add additional, relevant information. She said, *"Good for this writer for sticking with one idea: penguins. It's the start of a strong piece that contains lots of intriguing information about them. Let's think about what he's already mentioned about penguins, do a little reading, and add specific facts that will develop the idea. Where shall we start?"* As students responded, she wrote a list of questions that encompassed the information already provided:

- What do penguins look like?

- What are the differences between mother and father penguins?

- Where do penguins live?

Then she asked, *"Where could we look for this information?"* The class brainstormed a variety of sources such as picture books, Internet resources, articles on penguins, and so on.

On her own, the teacher collected various resources about penguins for the students to read and use to create notes. She divided the class into three groups to align with the three questions they pulled out of the original text. Each group recorded their information on one of three large poster charts labeled with their group's question for everyone to see. Students shared what they found and, based on the discussion, circled the most important facts or anecdotes they thought should be included in the revised penguin text.

One by one, the groups wrote a new paragraph, folding in the information they found from their research and conversations. After each group revised their paragraphs with more information, the piece was reassembled. Now the work to smooth the writing and work with the other traits began in earnest. As you'll see from the final piece, they dove into introductions (organization), accurate and specific words (word choice), taking risks to create voice (voice), varying sentence length (sentence fluency), and spelling (conventions), along with other key qualities of the traits—one at a time, one week at a time. Each time the class worked on a new key quality of a trait, they returned to the penguin piece to apply what they learned. This served as a good model for how students should revise the pieces in their own Writing Wallets, key quality by key quality.

It took several months of work, but here is how the piece turned out. It's no longer a solo attempt; now it's a third-grade group-write with the teacher's assistance. For students who doubt the power of revision, there can be no denying how much better the revised piece sounds. Once they see and feel that writing power, they yearn for it again and again.

Penguins: Revised by Class and Teacher

Penguins don't have to rent a tuxedo; they are born with one. But this colorful outfit is more than cute. It camouflages them from predators like seals, whales, and skua. Most penguins live on the frozen ice of Antarctica—brrr. Penguins are shaped like torpedoes so when they walk, they wobble. Most penguins are about three to four feet tall and about two feet wide. Some are fatter than others, just like people. Here is something maybe you didn't know about penguins. When a penguin egg is ready to hatch, the father, not the mother, keeps it warm in a special pouch on his feet while the mom goes away to eat as much as she wants. The father doesn't get to eat a meal until the mom comes back right before the egg hatches—about three to four months! Poor dad. He must get very hungry waiting for the penguin chick to be born.

Penguins don't have Twitter but they have busy social lives. They hang out all day together talking in their special penguin language, flapping flippers and chatting about, well, we just don't know. When penguin colonies get together, however, it can be as loud as a rock concert. It's too bad you can't have a penguin for a pet, but who'd want to keep the house cold as a freezer anyway?

Ideas: 6

Organization: 6

Voice: 6

Word Choice: 6

Sentence Fluency: 6

Conventions: 6

This kind of revision doesn't happen overnight, or by one student in isolation. There was excellent modeling, conversation, and lots of trial and error. The teacher weighed in and steered the revision process. Students had their own scoring guides and learned what they were trying to achieve in the revised version, trait by trait.

After a lesson on creating a lead in the organization trait, for instance, the teacher had students try to write a better one than *"Penguins are black and white."* That's all they did that day. Squeeze it once and let it go. Another day they worked on similes and found a good place to add one: *"When penguin colonies get together, however, it can be as loud as a rock concert."* Yet another day they worked on transitions and sequencing; when you read their final copy, it's worth noting they didn't use *first*, *second*, *third*, and *last*. Sweet! And so on and so on.

Months of work paid off beautifully. Now these students knew how to revise for one trait and key quality at a time and got to see the difference revision makes. They all contributed, and their collective work is astonishing. Students can use the pieces in their Writing Wallets and revise them each time, too. Next, they'll tackle a narrative or opinion piece that they can revise as a class over several months.

Even if you don't consider yourself the best writer in the world (and who does?), you can model. You can teach. You can show students the writing decisions they need to make as they work, and why it's perfectly fine that their first draft isn't the greatest. It's a start. Over time, as a piece grows and develops, students will come to understand how important revision and editing are to the writing process. You've shown them how your writing is improving—they will see theirs do the same. And, as a bonus, you may find that you are becoming a strong writer too.

Pause and Consider

Make a list of reasons that teachers shy away from the practice of modeling writing for students. Create a plan for how to help teachers conquer their fears in this area.

Flexibility and Room for Adjustment

Every lesson must be designed with your student writers in mind. Because no one lesson can accomplish every goal, think about how to adjust the lesson up or down in real time, and plan how to follow up to reinforce skills so they really stick. Learn to read your students. You want to challenge them but not overwhelm or underwhelm them. Body language and what happens naturally says a lot: Are they sitting up straighter, bright eyes full of interest? Are they interacting with peers, offering comments, and asking questions?

Lean to read your students.

Sometimes I am asked to visit a school and model a writing lesson with students for teachers. These opportunities are nothing but fun for me. I get all the benefits of grandparenting: upbeat interactions with kids and none of the long-term responsibility. I get a "kid fix"—a chance to be with children and try out new ideas—and then I go home, armed with feedback and ideas about how to revise the lesson for next time.

Before I arrive, however, the teacher and I discuss what the students are studying and what landing point he or she would like to see demonstrated in the writing lesson. Interestingly, more than half the time, the teacher asks for help with sentence fluency. It turns out there are many resources to teach about writing complete and grammatically correct sentences, but there is not much readily available to help with the fluency side of this trait—the way the sentences sound when put together so they flow smoothly across the page. This is the key quality of capturing smooth and rhythmic flow. In the best possible world, we want students' writing to sound like rolling thunder. We want to experience a sense of awe, majesty, and wonder that the words and phrases go together so beautifully.

In preparation for one elementary-grade lesson, I created a game that I thought would demonstrate how this key quality works as well as how it is tied to other elements of sentence fluency and conventions. I call it "Sentences Alive." Since I didn't know the students I'd be working with, or their abilities, I had to create something that was flexible and would allow all students to learn something about capturing smooth and rhythmic flow. The lesson needed to be structured so it could be altered on the fly as students reacted to it.

We want students' writing to sound like rolling thunder.

In "Sentences Alive," the point is to create a grammatically correct sentence that expands by adding words one by one, and then to deconstruct the sentence word by word until it is back to bare bones. I wanted to design a lesson that got kids engaged and out of their seats. I wanted talking. I wanted the lesson to have an element of fun and a clear learning goal. I wanted it to work at some level for all students. Not all writing lessons are done with paper and pencil; this is an interactive game that spotlights sentence fluency and its key qualities. Here is how it turned out. Feel free to try it as is, or modify it to fit the needs of your students.

Sentences Alive

A. Directions for creating cards: Write one word on each card, with the uppercase version of the word on the front and the lowercase version on the back. (I use 8.5-by-11-inch sheets of heavyweight paper for the cards so they are large enough to read from a distance.)

B. Optional: Write punctuation marks on different cards in a different color for the lesson extension.

C. Laminate the cards and store them when finished for long-term use.

Words for your first "Sentences Alive" game:

the	and
cat	gives
is	sweet
soft	rough
furry	scratchy
orangey-white	kisses
green-eyed	

Directions for play:

1. Review the sentence fluency trait and highlight the key qualities:
   - crafting well-built sentences
   - varying sentence types
   - capturing smooth and rhythmic flow
   - breaking the "rules" to create fluency

2. Tell students they are going to play a game in which they will listen for the sound of complete, grammatically correct sentences and make sound decisions about how the sentences are formed.

3. Ask for four volunteers to start the game.

4. Give each student one of these cards: *the, cat, is, soft*

5. Ask the four students to come to the front of the room, huddle, and create a correct sentence with their cards. (There are several ways this can turn out: *The cat is soft. Is the cat soft? Soft is the cat.*)

6. While students are determining the order of the words for the sentence, pass out the other word cards to groups of students at their tables. Explain that they will add their words to the sentence until all cards are used and the sentence is complete.

7. Once the four students decide on the sentence, have them stand together, in order, and hold up their cards for all to read.

8. Have the class read the sentence aloud with you. Ask them to indicate whether they believe the sentence is grammatically correct. If you wish, you can identify the type of sentence: simple, compound, or compound/complex. (I don't usually go down that road, because my focus for this lesson is capturing a smooth and rhythmic flow. However, traits and their key qualities merge and support one another, so this is your call.)

9. Now ask the class if anyone has a word card that could be added to the sentence. Pick one student and ask him or her to read the word aloud. This way, everyone will be thinking about where the word might fit, not just the student about to physically enter the sentence. We want everyone as involved as possible during this activity.

10. Rule: The student entering the sentence has all the power. He or she can move any of the words around to make a new sentence that includes the new word. If the student struggles to figure out where to put his or her word, other students can call out helpful ideas.

11. Ask the student who has just gone up to give you a thumbs-up sign when he or she is satisfied with the new word's position in the sentence. Check for capitalization: each card has an upper- and lowercase option.

12. Have the class read the sentence aloud with you. Ask them to decide whether the sentence is correct or not. If it isn't, kindly let the student know that the placement didn't work, and invite him or her to try again.

13. Continue adding one word at a time to the sentence, using the same procedure. Be sure to read the sentence aloud with the class after each word is added.

14. At some point, multiple adjectives will be strung together in the sentence. You may wish to introduce the cards with punctuation marks on them, or you may prefer to simply acknowledge where they are needed and continue building the sentence.

15. As new words are introduced that change the order of the existing words in the sentence, have students check that upper- and lowercase words are still correct. (See how we work conventions into the lesson on sentence fluency?)

16. After all the words are used, read the sentence aloud one last time. By the way, I have done this activity with students and teachers more than twenty-five times, and I don't believe the sentence has been created the same way twice. Be prepared to witness creative thinking!

17. Now begin the second half of the activity: deconstructing the sentence. The goal here is to end with a three- to four-word sentence that is different from the original. One word at a time, ask students who are not part of the sentence to call out a word that can be removed. Thank the person with that word card for participating, close the sentence up, and read it with students to make sure it still works.

18. Rule: Students can remove only one word at a time, and they cannot change the order of the words in the sentence. They must end with a different sentence than they started with: *The cat gives kisses,* for example, instead of *Is the cat soft?* (Allow students to remove two or more words at a time only if they show signs of complete frustration. Or you can let them move the words around—but again, if possible, make them figure it out.)

19. If the class asks for a word to be removed and the new sentence doesn't work without it, ask the student holding that word card to return to the sentence and have students make a different selection. Remember that this is being done orally, with your direction. Reading the sentences aloud is repetitive, but it's how students begin to "develop their ears" for how sentences should sound.

20. Once they've created a final sentence of three or four words that is different from the original sentence, the activity is complete. Collect the cards, thank students for their participation, and debrief what they learned about capturing a smooth and rhythmic flow from "Sentences Alive."

The Debrief: From "Sentences Alive" to the Writing Wallet

1. On the board or chart paper, record student observations about what mattered in the sentence to complete the activity correctly. Point out that the sentence got trickier when a second verb was introduced, creating a compound sentence from a simple one. Also note that one of the words, *kisses*, could be used as a noun or a verb.

2. Invite students to work with a partner and call out compound sentences they create on their own, such as *My dog is chocolate brown and he loves to roll around in the mud.*

3. Ask students which of the four key qualities of the sentence fluency trait they were working on during the "Sentences Alive" game. Note: This game touches on all of them in one way or another, but the emphasis is on capturing smooth and rhythmic flow.

4. Have a conversation with students about how they learned to "hear" which way the words went together to form the sentence. Discuss the importance of reading their own writing aloud to hear sentence fluency.

5. Invite students to look through their Writing Wallets to find a compound sentence, revise one or two simple sentences to become a compound sentence, or add a new compound sentence to their writing. Have them read the result to a partner.

6. Ask them to comment on the smooth and rhythmic flow of their drafts so far and note where they might make further revisions.

Creating additional sentences

As you try this lesson using your own lists of words, you'll notice that adding words to the sentence is the pivotal point where students really have to think about what to do next. The sample word list I've used works well because it includes two verbs and one word that can be used as either a noun or a verb. If you want to create more sentences like this for additional practice, make sure that your word list includes at least two verbs and a word that is flexible as a part of speech. And, if you want to step this lesson up a level, try adding a prepositional phrase.

Deconstruct this lesson and discuss the four elements of successful writing lessons examined in this chapter.

- A landing point and going deeper

- An element of energy and interest

- Modeling and resources

- Flexibility and room for adjustment

If possible, play a round of "Sentences Alive" with your colleagues so you can experience it firsthand. Make adjustments to the lesson to fit the needs of your students.

Wrap-Up

Goldilocks had it right: we are looking for "just right," whether it's a meal or a bed or anything else important. Designing "just right" writing lessons requires putting elements of the lesson together so students learn—regardless of their current level of writing skill—in a way that helps them own the skill at a more complex level. This thinking will enable students to retain the skill and use it effectively, over time and in different situations.

This we know: Reminding is not a teaching point. Correcting isn't either. Students learn best when they do the following:

1. *Clearly understand the point of the lesson.* Every lesson needs a landing place.

2. *Notice and wonder.* Plan carefully and build in places that invite imagination and creativity.

3. *Understand what writers think and do.* Model for students how writers approach writing and all the different resources they draw on to be successful.

4. *Immerse themselves in learning.* Not all lessons that teach important key qualities of the writing traits rely on paper and pencil. Make your lessons interactive when possible.

In the next chapter, we'll take this thinking a step further by looking closely at how to use mentor texts to inspire writing instruction and to link the reading and writing processes. I'll share both picture books and chapter books along with starter ideas to help students find their own "just right" landing spot for writing.

7 Reading Like a Writer

You cannot hope to sweep someone else away by the force of your writing until it has been done to you. ~ author Stephen King (2010, 146)

It happens to me regularly: I am overwhelmed with wonder, amazement, joy, and awe as I read.

Here is how I've always gone about introducing students of all ages to reading like a writer: I try to blow them away with the sheer force of exquisitely written books. We start slowly by pulling excerpts from favorite books, picture books, magazine articles, or everyday texts that clearly demonstrate each of the traits. I introduce the term *mentor text* as students discover powerful passages by favorite and new authors. We begin to look at mentor texts through a writer's eye—noting the writer's choices and techniques. We read. We talk. We laugh. We question. We are humbled by what we discover. We share titles; we share insights; we learn about one another and the world. And all the while, students improve their reading and writing. Even more important, they discover the joy of literacy that I dearly hope stays with them all their lives.

Researcher Frank Smith explains it this way:

> The only source of knowledge sufficiently right and reliable for learning about written language is the writing already done by others. In other words, one learns to write by reading. (1983, 28)

Let me share a story with you about a time I learned an important lesson about kids and reading, and how to find the best books to use as mentor texts.

I fretted and lost a lot of sleep the summer before I began teaching ninth grade for the first time. I had no idea what to expect from ninth graders—would they accept me, the recent sixth-grade teacher, into their midst? What if they knew more than I did about reading and writing? It seemed likely; they acted as though they ruled the world.

I quickly discovered, however, that most of my students were simply taller versions of my sixth graders—still struggling with writing, often making the same mistakes and challenged by the same parts of the writing process. This was a good news/bad news situation: good because my skills as an English language arts teacher were aligned with what the students needed, yet bad because ninth graders had not advanced much after three additional years of learning.

That first week—well, you know how it goes: getting used to a new schedule, learning names, setting up classroom procedures, conducting baseline work to understand the range of skills in each class, and so on. I had six classes of smart kids, interesting and polite (mostly) kids, but kids who really didn't enjoy reading and writing. They could read (sort of)—but didn't. They could write (sort of)—but didn't. I pledged to myself that I'd turn them on to literacy that year. Surely it wasn't too late; after all, you can fall in love with reading and writing at any point in your life, right?

One of my classroom rules was that everyone should have something of their own choosing to read every day. On about day three of that first week, I took my first-period class to the library to check out books and magazines. I had no classroom library at that time; I was the new teacher, after all, and I was lucky to have a pencil sharpener when I arrived. My room had been stripped bare.

The students went willingly to the library, but once they arrived they just stood there, looking around anxiously. Mistake #1: I assumed they'd know how to browse for what they wanted. They didn't. In fact, a large group of students huddled together, cast mystified looks in my direction, and then sent an emissary from the group to inquire, "Mrs. Culham, are we going to be doing a report?" I answered brightly, "Oh yes, of course. But not now. Today I only want you to find a book to read independently . . . on your own . . . as you have time." He nodded and reported back to the group. I heard more muttering, and then another student came over to me. "Mrs. Culham, are we doing a book report?" "Oh yes, we'll have many opportunities to work with the books we're reading, but not today. Today I only want you to find a book to read independently . . . on your own . . . as you have time." She nodded and went back to her group of peers, who were looking rather distressed at this point. So, I joined them and asked what was going on. Was I not explaining clearly what was needed?

We spend too much time teaching students "stuff" and not enough time helping them learn.

It was one of the saddest days of my teaching life, one I'll never forget, as the problem came into focus and the students 'fessed up: they didn't know how to browse for books on their own unless there was a specific assignment. I was stunned. Flabbergasted. Astonished. And deflated. How could these students reach ninth grade without knowing how to find a book or magazine to read just for pleasure? I sat down at one of the tables, put my head down on my crossed arms, and—Mistake #2—cried.

!!

Of course, the sight of their new English teacher crying in the library was shocking to these kids, and they moved away—far, far away—while I composed myself. I wiped away my tears, smiled reassuringly, and gathered everyone around the fiction section. I showed them how to browse for books—how to take a book off the shelf, read the jacket, and talk to others about the author and anything they knew about the book. I read a little from the first page of a book and dipped into the middle as well. They were spellbound. Then we moved to the nonfiction section and did the same. We spent several class periods in a row browsing for books until I was convinced they could find something they wanted to read on their own, at any time.

I'm fairly certain that on that first library day, several students ran to the counselor and asked for a transfer from the crazy English teacher's classroom. But my love of reading and books rubbed off on them eventually. At the end of the year, when students wrote evaluations about their year with me, several mentioned the impact of my reaction when they didn't know how to read for pleasure.

I share this story because I think we spend too much time teaching students "stuff" and not enough time helping them learn. Every book or magazine my students chose had valuable content, which they learned simply by reading it. The students had, for nine years, been shut off from this valuable way to become wiser, smarter, and more engaged in the world around them. They were "successful" at school but not at learning. Wouldn't it be great if those two things were one and the same?

I took away several lessons from this experience myself: don't assume that students know how to find the good stuff, the good authors, the good books that get them thinking. It's our job to teach them what to look for and how to make choices that lead to reading for pleasure. Readers like different texts—from fiction to nonfiction and all the genres in between. I was no lover of science fiction myself, but as I saw how many students in my class were devoted to that genre, I became an avid sci-fi reader just so I could talk with them about their favorites—and consequently, I fell in love with dystopian and speculative fiction. Likewise, for my students who found nonfiction their reading zone, I jumped in there too. I wanted to understand and be able to talk about what captivated them about information-based writing and what mattered to my students in their reading—and, therefore, writing—choices.

I had a method to my madness. If I could broaden my taste in reading, I could begin to teach writing through all the fine literature my students were learning to love. If I focused on their choices, their favorites, their "heart books," students would want to dig into books in new ways to learn about writing craft, not just to process the story lines in fiction and the facts of informative texts.

I used their burgeoning love of reading—in whatever form it took—as a big part of my writing curriculum. I let them take the lead by deciding on the texts that excited them as a jumping-off place.

This turned out to be an instructional gold mine. Using mentor texts to teach writing was some of the best teaching I ever did. It was fascinating, scholarly, and motivational. It made me read and improve my own game with books and ideas that students found interesting—which was a pleasure. It worked for all my students, regardless of their skills and abilities. When books and print and digital texts are added to the writing teacher's tool kit, the results are extraordinary. Many of my students went from *"I can't. I don't want to write"* to *"I kinda like this. I want to write something like it."* It's powerful to be in the room with them and watch this transformation with your own eyes.

I am not teaching students full-time anymore, but I still have the bug. I read books—picture books, chapter books, young adult books—like a writer. I can't stop. I collect books, mark passages, and think about what could be done with them to help students of all ages understand how writing works as they're enjoying what they are reading. I invite you to read my recent books *The Writing Thief: Using Mentor Texts to Teach the Craft of Writing* (Culham 2016b) and *Dream Wakers: Mentor Texts That Celebrate Latino Culture* (Culham 2016a) for a thorough discussion of why reading like a writer is one of the most successful practices to create confident, capable writers.

This chapter's purpose is to take the foundation established in *The Writing Thief* and *Dream Waker*s and show you how to tease out specific lessons about writing from your choice of books and resource materials. I'll model two lessons from beginning to end using the same book, *The Water Princess* by Susan Verde. One lesson is intended for early elementary students, and the other for students in upper elementary grades. I want to demonstrate how flexible a good book can be.

Moving from beige to technicolor writing requires reading and talking.

Since you read the books to students, reading level is not an issue. It's the quality of the writing that matters most. I chose *The Water Princess* because I admire everything about the book—from the powerful main idea and the elegant use of language to the lyrical sentences and fragments that are modeled from beginning to end. It's based on facts and information but told in narrative form, so you feel the full impact of the message.

I'll also provide you with a chart of picture and chapter books I've discovered recently that you can use to teach writing. The chart notes which traits and key qualities each book demonstrates so you have a ready reference for amazing mentor texts. This chart is just a starting point, though. The books you share with your students should be your choices. Don't let anyone else hand you the "perfect" book list. Your passion for a book, an author, a genre, or a mode needs to shine through so students will catch the joy you put out there about reading and writing.

Talking the Talk

I firmly believe that moving from beige to technicolor writing requires reading and talking. Talk matters in a writing classroom. One of our goals is to give students the opportunity to express their opinions and ideas about what works well in a text, and to use consistent vocabulary to back up their opinions. This is where traits and key qualities again come in handy. In most cases, there are ten steps to a successful mentor text lesson, which requires reading and talking before the writing flows.

1. Read the book aloud—don't stop.

2. Preview the trait and its key qualities.

3. Focus on the key quality for the lesson.

4. Review the student-friendly scoring guide.

5. Introduce the activity.

6. Reread the book or the portion in focus.

7. Conduct the activity with the "Work Together" sheet.

8. Wrap up the lesson activity and discuss.

9. Apply what was learned to a piece in the Writing Wallet.

10. Invite new mode-specific writing inspired by the mentor text.

Of course, this list is flexible, depending on what students ask, where your conversations take you, what they find fascinating about the book, and how it is written. In the lessons that follow, see if you can pinpoint each of these steps and discuss where you'd diverge and change the lesson to meet the needs of students in your own classroom.

Here is a mentor text to warm you up, a powerful poem by Nikki Grimes (2017) to begin the discussion of how writers use language to communicate meaning:

Pen in hand,

I tend a garden of language,

weed out words of hate and division,

plant healing nouns, verbs,

adjectives bursting with color,

and water them all with my tears.

Before you know it,

metaphors bloom

with meaning

Read the poem aloud and discuss it. What is its central message? How does the author use word choice to make her ideas clear? Read the poem again with your colleagues and look for evidence of the traits and their key qualities—word choice and ideas, in particular. Discuss how Grimes conveys meaning that goes below the surface through her careful choice of "just right" words and their placement. If you have a Writing Wallet, which you should at this point, try revising a piece of your own writing using something you notice about Grimes's mastery of one of the key qualities of word choice.

A Quick Tip for Organizing Mentor Texts

Choosing a mentor text is one of the most enjoyable parts of teaching writing. Look for books that students love—books they enjoy coming back to over and over, and that give clear examples of different key qualities of the traits. Look for books that represent the diversity of backgrounds in your classroom and books that may expand students' worldviews. Look for good stories, but also for books that are informative and provide well-grounded opinions so students see models of strong writing in the modes, too.

As you find mentor texts, mark them so you have an at-a-glance record of the traits and key qualities within. I buy multicolored, round adhesive stickers at a local office supply store. I've assigned a color to each trait: blue for ideas, orange for organization, green for voice, red for word choice, purple for sentence fluency, and yellow for conventions. There's no reason for these particular colors; they were simply the colors available. Make your own decision about colors and traits—but remember, color-coding works only if it is applied consistently. If you use this method, plan to stick with your colors forever.

When I find a book or a passage in a book, I put the sticker on the spine that matches the trait I've spotted in the text. I also write why I selected the book on its front pages to remind myself later. When you surround yourself with great literature, it's easy to forget the details of what you spotted during an earlier read. So, a note might read "Ideas: Great details on pages 9–11" or "Organization: Excellent use of an ending that wraps up loose ends." The book can have one or more colored stickers on its spine and be shelved in the classroom library for later use, when work on that trait and one of its key qualities comes into focus. You don't have to search or take the book out of circulation to locate it quickly. Because it's already labeled, it's right at your fingertips.

One Book: Two Ways In

What follows are two mentor text lessons using the same picture book, *The Water Princess* by Susan Verde. This is an extraordinary text to study for many reasons, but certainly its sentence fluency is flawless. The first lesson is aimed at early elementary students who are learning about sentences and how to make them flow using different lengths, and the second at upper elementary students who are ready for more sophisticated interaction with the sentences and fragments in the text. For both lessons, you'll want to have copies of the student-friendly scoring guide for sentence fluency (see Appendix B or download these from sten. pub/tww).

Based on the childhood experience of Georgie Badiel, *The Water Princess*, lusciously illustrated by Peter H. Reynolds, chronicles the daily journey of a mother and her daughter to find clean water in a small village in Burkina Faso, a landlocked country in West Africa, as told through the voice of "Princess" Gie Gie. Readers learn that every single day is a struggle to rise early, make the long trek to collect water, and return home to share the precious resource with the family. Gie Gie dreams of a time when water is abundant, available, and clean. The book's language is powerful, the phrasing and sentence structure varied and musical. As a bonus, readers will appreciate the voice-filled end pages that explore the work being done by the Georgie Badiel Foundation to bring clean water to this town and others—fulfilling Gie Gie's dream.

Lesson 1: The Long and the Short of It

Early Elementary Grades

This lesson is designed to help young writers understand how the fluency of the piece is directly affected by the differing lengths of the sentences.

1. *Read the book aloud.*

   If possible, read the book aloud while projecting it on a document camera. It is extremely helpful for students to see the words—and to admire the illustrations—while they are read aloud. Discuss what students learned from the text, answer questions, and point out the final pages of the book that share information on organizations dedicated to bringing fresh water to landlocked locations like Burkina Faso. Locate Burkina Faso on the map and show students.

2. *Preview the trait and its key qualities.*

   Discuss the sentence fluency trait with students. Ask them to share their understanding of what a sentence is and why it is an important part of writing. Jot down their ideas on chart paper or the whiteboard to return to later.

   Share the definition: sentence fluency is the way words and phrases flow through the piece. It is the auditory trait because it's "read" by the ear as much as the eye. Explain that there are four key qualities to the sentence fluency trait because there is a great deal to learn and know about sentences that you are eager to help them understand:

   - Crafting well-built sentences

   - Varying sentence types

   - Capturing smooth and rhythmic flow

   - Breaking the "rules" to create fluency

   Explain that you are going to help them look again at *The Water Princess* to see how the author handled the second key quality: varying sentence types.

3. *Focus on the key quality for the lesson.*

   Ask students to tell you what they think "varying sentence types" means. Add these comments to the notes about sentences you recorded earlier on chart paper or the whiteboard. Express the following or something similar to help students zero in on one key quality of sentence fluency: *"Do you want to know a secret to making your writing sound rhythmic and musical? Include sentences of all kinds—short ones, long ones, and medium-size ones. Include statements, questions, commands, and exclamations. Mix it up! Varying sentence types gives your writing color and flavor."* Ask students to comment on how important writing color and flavor are to the reader and if they recall any places in *The Water Princess* that stand out in this area.

4. *Review the student-friendly scoring guide.*

Hand out copies of the sentence fluency student-friendly scoring guide (see Figure 7.1; a full-size reproducible can be found in Appendix B and online) and review it with students. You can all use it during discussions about the sentences in the mentor text. Ask students which bullet under "I've Got It!" corresponds most closely to varying sentence types. (Hint: "I've varied the length and structure of my sentences.")

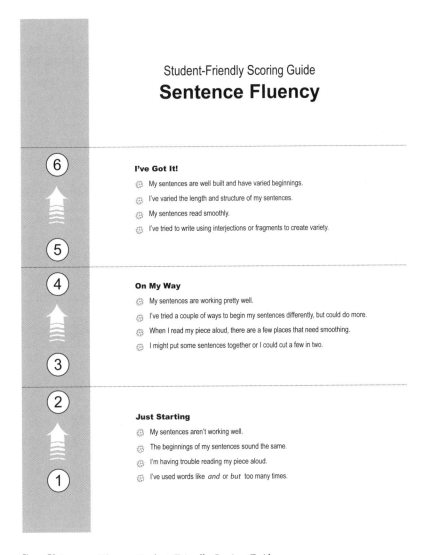

Figure 7.1 *Sentence Fluency Student-Friendly Scoring Guide*

5. *Set up the activity.*

    Explain to students that they will be rereading part of *The Water Princess* and examining it closely for how the sentences vary in length. Although there are many, many wonderful writing qualities in this book, remind them that you want to focus on sentences and their lengths.

6. *Reread the book.*

    The Water Princess is long, and reading the whole text is not necessary to make the point of the lesson clear. Focus on pages 12–14:

    > The thirst comes quick—dry lips, dry throat. I squeeze my eyes shut. I see it. Clear. I dip my toes in it. Cool. I scoop it up and bring it to my lips. Slowly, I open my eyes. Nothing. I kick the dust.

    Ask students to close their eyes as you reread these pages. Tell them to concentrate on how the sentences sound. When you are finished, invite their comments about the way the sentences resonated in the passage. Remind students that sentence fluency is something we hear as much as see in writing. Ask them to discuss what sentence fluency means to them as they write.

7. *Conduct the activity using the "Work Together" chart (see Figure 7.2).*

    Pass out the "Work Together" sheet and ask students to choose a partner and fill in the chart as you read the passage from pages 12–14 one more time. Be sure to project the pages so students can see the words on the pages this time.

    Read aloud the first sentence and show it to students. "The thirst comes quick—dry lips, dry throat." Count aloud how many words there are (eight) and show them where to record the number on

From *The Water Princess*: Sentence Length	From My Writing Wallet: Sentence Length for one piece of writing
1. 8	
2. 3	
3. 1	
4. 6	
5. 1	
6. 10	
7. 5	
8. 1	
9. 5	

Figure 7.2 *Work Together:* The Water Princess

their sheets. If you wish, discuss the use of the dash in the sentence as a link to conventions. Ask them how the dash adds to the fluency of the writing.

Project the rest of the sentences and give students time to fill in their charts. Circulate through the room and help any students who need it.

8. *Wrap up the lesson activity and discuss.*

When students have finished filling in their "Work Together" sheets, ask them to talk with their partners about what they notice about the lengths of sentences. Do they vary a lot? A little? How does the length of sentences affect the fluency of the passage? Ask partners to share with the class what they have concluded. Add these observations to the chart paper or whiteboard from the beginning of the lesson, and review what students have learned about sentences and their lengths.

Now, do a quick group activity to wrap up. Tell students to stand up. As you read each of the sentences from the passage, tell them to consult their "Work Together" sheets and stay standing if they think the sentence is long, crouch down if they think it is mid-length, and sit down if it is short. Talk about the variety of sentences in the passage when the activity is finished.

9. *Apply what was learned to a piece in the Writing Wallet.*

Tell students to get out their Writing Wallets (see Chapter 5) and choose a piece to examine for varying sentence length. Tell them to list the number of words in their sentences in the second column of the "Work Together" chart. Invite students to rewrite one of their sentences so it is longer, add a one-word sentence to a passage to break up the tempo, or do something with a sentence that makes it different from the others they've written. Remind them to aim for the "I've Got It!" level of sentence fluency on their student-friendly guides. When they finish, have them answer the following questions at the bottom of their "Work Together" sheets: *What is your favorite sentence from* The Water Princess? *What is your favorite sentence from your own piece?* Share their choices.

10. *Invite new mode-specific writing inspired by the mentor text.*

If time allows, encourage students to write a new piece based on information or an idea from *The Water Princess* that expresses their own thinking. You can discuss possible ideas with them, but don't give a specific writing prompt. Encourage the writers to come up with their own ideas. You might begin the conversation with ideas such as these:

- Tell a new story about Gie Gie's walk for water in which she makes a friend who is also bringing water back to her family every day. Write about something fun that happens when they meet at the place where the water flows. (Narrative)

- Do a walk-about around the school; make a list and draw pictures of all the places students are able to get fresh, clean water without any problem. (Informative)

- Why can't children go to school in *The Water Princess*? What is your opinion about how this will help or hurt them over time? (Opinion)

Lesson 2: Taming the Wild Fragment

Upper Elementary Grades

This lesson is designed to help young writers understand how sentence fluency can be created by using fragments and nontraditional sentence beginnings.

1. **Read the book aloud.**

   If possible, read the book aloud while projecting it on a document camera. It is extremely helpful for students to see the words—and to admire the illustrations—while they are read aloud. Discuss what they learned from the text, answer questions, and be sure to reference the last pages of the book that share additional information about the resources available from Ryan's Well and the Georgie Badiel Foundation.

2. **Preview the trait and its key qualities.**

   Discuss the sentence fluency trait with students. Ask them to share their understanding of what a sentence is and why it is an important part of writing. Jot down their ideas on chart paper or the whiteboard to return to later.

   Share the definition: *Sentence fluency* is the way words and phrases flow through the piece. It is the auditory trait because it's "read" by the ear as much as the eye. Explain that there are four key qualities to the sentence fluency trait because there is a great deal to learn and know about sentences that you are eager to help them understand:

- Crafting well-built sentences

- Varying sentence types

- Capturing smooth and rhythmic flow

- Breaking the "rules" to create fluency

Explain that you are going to help them look again at *The Water Princess* to see how the author handled the fourth key quality: breaking the "rules" to create fluency.

3. *Focus on the key quality for the lesson.*

Ask students what they think breaking the "rules" to create fluency means to a writer and how it might contribute to sentence fluency. Gather their thinking on the rules they've learned about sentences, and record their ideas on chart paper or the whiteboard. Expand students' thinking by sharing something like this:

You have learned many rules for writing sentences correctly: Always include a subject and verb. Don't use fragments. Never use one word as a sentence. But wait! To bring rhythm to your writing, you might need to break rules sometimes. Interjections can highlight points. Sentence fragments can add style. Shake it up. Break it up. Keep it flowing. Yes!

Ask students to react to this idea of "breaking" rules to create fluency, and jot down their thoughts.

4. *Review the student-friendly scoring guide.*

Make sure all students have a copy of the sentence fluency student-friendly scoring guide (Figure 7.1). Students can refer to the guide to stay on track during discussions about the sentences in the mentor text. Ask them which bullet under "I've Got It!" corresponds most closely to breaking the rules to create fluency. (Hint: "I've tried to write using interjections or fragments to create variety.")

You can find more complex versions of the student-friendly scoring guides for the traits that are intended for more experienced writers at www.culhamwriting.com. There are also simpler ones. Feel free to download and use the ones that best match your students' skills and knowledge. For this lesson, we'll stick with the grade 3–5 guides we've been using.

5. *Set up the activity.*

Explain to students that they will be rereading *The Water Princess* and examining it closely for how the sentences vary in length. Although there are many, many wonderful writing qualities in this book, remind them that you want to focus on sentences and how traditional "rules" may have been broken in order to create fluency.

6. *Reread the book.*

    Reread the first six pages: *"I am Princess Gie Gie. My Kingdom . . . the African sky, so wide and so close . . ."* to *"I cannot make the water run clearer. No matter what I command."*

    Ask students to note any techniques Susan Verde used to make the piece sound fluent by breaking "rules." Record on chart paper or the whiteboard anything students point out. Here are some examples to mention if they get stuck:

    - *The use of an ellipsis in the first sentence instead of words to draw out the sound of the description.* If she were following the rules, the sentence might read: "I am Princess Gie Gie. My Kingdom is the African sky, so wide and so close." Ask students how the ellipsis affects the sound of the sentence.

    - *Repetition of sentence beginnings to create a poetic passage:* "I can almost touch . . . I can tame . . . I can make . . . I can make . . ." Typically, we caution students not to repeat sentence beginnings over and over. Ask students why this technique works or doesn't work to create fluency at this point in the text.

    - *The use of a conjunction to begin a sentence:* "But I cannot make the water come closer." Although this rule is frequently broken in contemporary texts, ask students to explain how *But* changes the sound from the previous repetitive sentence patterns and makes the reader hear the emphasis on what she can't do versus what she can.

    - *The use of a fragment*: "No matter what I command." Discuss its use to make the author's point clear. Read the sentence before it and show students how you can combine the two. Ask them which version better maintains the rhythm of the passage—the original one or "No matter what I command, I cannot make the water run clearer"?

7. *Conduct the activity using the "Work Together" chart.*

    Using the "Work Together" sheet in Figure 7.3, continue reading from page 7 to the end of the book. Have students work in groups of three or four to discuss and mark the columns with hash marks for places where the author "breaks" sentence rules. The first pages are already filled in.

From *The Water Princess*	From My Writing Wallet	List examples of punctuation marks used to create fluency.
"Breaking" a Rule Use a hash mark to show how many examples you spot (pages 1–6 are already filled in; start from page 7).	"Breaking" a Rule Try two of the following sentence fluency techniques.	
Fragments: |||		
Starting a sentence with a conjunction: |		
Sentence structure repetition: ||		

Fragments: ℍℍ ℍℍ ℍℍ ||

Starting a sentence with a conjunction: |||

Sentence structure repetition: ℍℍ |||

Figure 7.3 *Work Together:* The Water Princess

8. *Wrap up the lesson activity and discuss.*

After students have combed through the book looking for examples of breaking the rules in sentence fluency, ask them to look at how the artful use of punctuation marks also adds to the flow of the writing. Make a list of the different marks—ellipses, semicolons, hyphens, dashes, and so on—used within sentences that give it the intended fluency. Review how many times they found fragments, sentences that started with conjunctions, and passages that repeated sentence patterns. Their numbers may not completely agree with yours, but the purpose of the exercise is simply to find some examples of each type.

Return to the notes and ideas students contributed to the chart paper or whiteboard at the beginning of the lesson; add new thoughts as students reflect on what they learned in the lesson.

9. *Apply what was learned to a piece in the Writing Wallet.*

Ask students to select a piece from their Writing Wallets (see Chapter 5) and zero in on at least two of the techniques they noted in *The Water Princess* that are examples of breaking the "rules" to create fluency.

Have them revise a few of their own sentences so they look and sound like those in the mentor text. Remind writers to aim for the "I Got It!" level of sentence fluency on their student-friendly guides.

10. *Invite new mode-specific writing inspired by the mentor text.*

This book is rich with opportunities for discussion and further writing. Ask students to consider what it would be like to live without easy access to water. Reread the last two pages to students; challenge their thinking about everyday life in Burkina Faso and ask them to compare it with life in their city or town. If time allows, ask students to write more about the ideas that spring from *The Water Princess*. For example:

- Write the story of a day in your life if you suddenly found there was no running water at home or at school—or anyplace nearby. Describe what happens and any possible solutions. (Narrative)

- Call an expert from your city or town, or use the Internet to learn about the process of obtaining water, purifying it, and testing it to make sure it's safe for drinking. Discuss the steps needed to make drinking water safe and available for all. (Informative)

- Voice your opinion about the benefits of clean water versus the problems caused by contaminated water. Should everyone in the world have access to clean water? If so, who should be responsible for making sure it happens? (Opinion)

Books to Consider as Mentor Texts

I'm a self-professed bookaholic, so knowing when to finish a recommended book list is not easy for me. I am in perpetual book-hunting mode, haunting local bookstores for new titles, checking lists of recommendations from literacy groups, and, of course, spending hours surfing on Amazon—and trying not to hit the "Buy with 1-Click" button too often. Stunning new books, especially picture books, are written and published all the time. As this book goes to print, I'll be begging my editor to include "just one more" and she'll counsel me to breathe and let it go.

So, I've included a chart here that lists picture books and chapter books that I've discovered since I completed *The Writing Thief* and *Dream Wakers*. I hope you'll find some keepers in here—and pay special attention to the diversity of the texts you share with students. Remember that the writing trait and key quality recommendations are just that: recommendations. Many of these books could be used for a wide variety of teaching purposes; I've just tried to focus on one each to get you started.

Picture Books That Mentor Traits and Key Qualities of Writing

Picture Book Title	Author	Illustrator	Publisher & Date	Book Audience	Genre
Ideas					
Finding a Topic					
Sarabella's Thinking Cap	Schachner, Judy	Schachner, Judy	Dial Books, 2017	All	Fiction: Realistic
A Squiggly Story	Larsen, Andrew	Lowery, Mike	Kids Can, 2016	Early Elementary	Fiction: Realistic
Thunder Boy Jr.	Alexie, Sherman	Morales, Yuyi	Hachette Book Group, 2016	All	Fiction: Realistic
The Tragic Tale of the Great Auk	Thornhill, Jan	Thornhill, Jan	Groundwood Books, 2016	Upper Elementary	Nonfiction
Focusing the Topic					
Penguin Day	Bishop, Nic	Bishop, Nic	Scholastic, 2017	Early Elementary	Nonfiction
They Say Blue	Tamaki, Jillian	Tamaki, Jillian	Abrams Books for Young Readers, 2018	All	Fiction: Realistic
Windows	Denos, Julia	Goodale, E. B.	Candlewick, 2017	All	Fiction: Realistic

Developing the Topic

Freedom in Congo Square	Weatherford, Carole Boston	Christie, R. Gregory	Little Bee Books, 2016	All	Fiction: Historical
Grand Canyon	Chin, Jason	Chin, Jason	Roaring Brook, 2017	Upper Elementary	Nonfiction
How This Book Was Made	Barnett, Mac	Rex, Adam	Disney Book Group, 2016	All	Fiction: Humor
One Day	Dotlich, Rebecca Kai	Koehler, Fred	Boyds Mills, 2015	Early Elementary	Fiction: Realistic

Using Details

A Different Pond	Phi, Bao	Bui, Thi	Capstone Young Readers, 2017	All	Fiction: Realistic
How to Be an Elephant	Roy, Katherine	Roy, Katherine	David Macaulay Studio, 2017	All	Nonfiction
In Plain Sight	Jackson, Richard	Pinkney, Jerry	Roaring Brook, 2016	All	Fiction: Realistic
The Whisper	Zagarenski, Pamela	Zagarenski, Pamela	Houghton Mifflin Harcourt, 2015	All	Fiction: Fantasy

TEACH WRITING WELL

Organization

Title	Author	Illustrator	Publisher	Level	Genre
Four Feet, Two Sandals	Williams, Karen Lynn, and Khadra Mohammed	Chayka, Doug	Eerdmans, 2016	All	Fiction: Realistic
The Journey	Sanna, Francesca	Sanna, Francesca	Flying Eye Books, 2016	All	Fiction: Historical
Radiant Child	Steptoe, Javaka	Steptoe, Javaka	Hachette Book Group, 2016	All	Biography

Using Sequence Words and Transition Words

Title	Author	Illustrator	Publisher	Level	Genre
Because of an Acorn	Schaefer, Lola M., and Adam Schaefer	Preston-Gannon, Frann	Chronicle Books, 2016	Early Elementary	Nonfiction
Before Morning	Sidman, Joyce	Krommes, Beth	Houghton Mifflin Harcourt, 2016	Early Elementary	Fiction: Realistic
Imagine That! How Dr. Seuss Wrote "The Cat in the Hat"	Sierra, Judy	Hawkes, Kevin	Random House, 2017	All	Nonfiction: Biography

Structuring the Body

Title	Author	Illustrator	Publisher	Level	Genre
How to Code a Sandcastle	Funk, Josh	Palacios, Sara	Viking Books for Young Readers, 2018	Upper Elementary	Fiction: Realistic

Title	Author	Illustrator	Publisher	Grade	Genre
Little Fox in the Forest	Graegin, Stephanie	Graegin, Stephanie	Schwartz and Wade, 2017	Early Elementary	Fiction: Wordless
This House, Once	Freedman, Deborah	Freedman, Deborah	Atheneum Books for Young Readers, 2017	Early Elementary	Fiction: Realistic
This Is How We Do It	Lamothe, Matt	Lamothe, Matt	Chronicle Books, 2017	All	Nonfiction

Ending with a Sense of Resolution

Title	Author	Illustrator	Publisher	Grade	Genre
Far Apart, Close in Heart	Birtha, Becky	Kastelic, Maja	Albert Whitman and Company, 2017	All	Fiction: Realistic
Goodnight Already!	John, Jory	Davies, Benji	HarperCollins, 2016	All	Fiction: Fantasy
Perfect	Davies, Nicola	Fisher, Cathy	Graffeg, 2016	Upper Elementary	Fiction: Realistic

Voice

Establishing a Tone

Title	Author	Illustrator	Publisher	Grade	Genre
The Legend of Rock Paper Scissors	Daywalt, Drew	Rex, Adam	Balzer + Bray, 2017	All	Fiction: Fantasy

Title	Author	Illustrator	Publisher	Audience	Genre
Let the Children March	Clark-Robinson, Monica	Morrison, Frank	HMH Books for Young Readers, 2018	Upper Elementary	Nonfiction
Pride: The Story of Harvey Milk and the Rainbow Flag	Sanders, Rob	Salerno, Steven	Random House, 2018	Upper Elementary	Nonfiction: Biography
Snappsy the Alligator	Falatko, Julie	Miller, Tim	Penguin Random House, 2016	All	Fiction: Humor
Conveying the Purpose					
Malala's Magic Pencil	Yousafzai, Malala	Kerascoët	Little, Brown, 2017	Upper Elementary	Nonfiction
A Perfect Day	Smith, Lane	Smith, Lane	Roaring Brook, 2017	Early Elementary	Fiction: Realistic
Stepping Stones	Ruurs, Margriet	Ali Badr, Nizar	Orca, 2016	All	Biography
Creating a Connection to the Audience					
The Flying Girl	Engle, Margarita	Palacios, Sara	Atheneum Books for Young Readers, 2018	All	Nonfiction: Biography
Nerdy Bird Tweets	Reynolds, Aaron	Davies, Matt	Roaring Brook, 2017	All	Fiction: Humor

Title	Author	Illustrator	Publisher, Year	Grade Level	Genre
Walk with Me	Buitrago, Jairo	Yockteng, Rafael	Groundwood Books, 2017	All	Fiction: Realistic
Taking Risks to Create Voice					
Bigfoot Is Missing	Lewis, J. Patrick, and Kenn Nesbitt	MinaLima	Chronicle Books, 2015	Upper Elementary	Fiction: Legends
The Blue Hour	Simler, Isabelle	Simler, Isabelle	Eerdmans, 2017	Early Elementary	Fiction: Realistic
Rudas: Niño's Horrendous Hermanitas	Morales, Yuyi	Morales, Yuyi	Roaring Brook, 2016	All	Fiction: Humor
This Is a Serious Book	Parachini, Jodie	Rieley, Daniel	HarperCollins, 2016	All	Fiction: Humor
Word Choice					
Applying Strong Verbs					
Giant Squid	Fleming, Candace	Rohmann, Eric	Roaring Brook, 2016	All	Nonfiction
Joan Procter, Dragon Doctor	Valdez, Patricia	Sala, Felicita	Knopf Books for Young Readers, 2018	Upper Elementary	Nonfiction: Biography

Title	Author(s)	Illustrator	Publisher, Year	Grade Level	Genre
Lost and Found Cat	Kuntz, Doug, and Amy Shrodes	Cornelison, Sue	Crown Books for Young Readers, 2017	Upper Elementary	Fiction: Realistic
TEK	McDonnell, Patrick	McDonnell, Patrick	Hachette Book Group, 2016	All	Fiction: Fantasy
Selecting Striking Words and Phrases					
An Ambush of Tigers	Rosenthal, Betsy	Jago	Millbrook, 2015	All	Fiction: Realistic
Crown: An Ode to the Fresh Cut	Barnes, Derrick	James, Gordon C.	Agate Bolden, 2017	All	Fiction: Realistic
The Great Dictionary Caper	Sierra, Judy	Comstock, Eric	Simon and Schuster, 2018	All	Fiction: Fantasy
Lesser Spotted Animals	Brown, Martin	Brown, Martin	David Fickling Books, 2016	All	Nonfiction
Using Specific and Accurate Words					
Big Words for Little Geniuses	Patterson, Susan, and James Patterson	Pan, Hsinping	Jimmy Patterson Books, 2017	Early Elementary	Nonfiction
Esquivel!	Wood, Susan	Tonatiuh, Duncan	Charlesbridge, 2016	Upper Elementary	Biography

Title	Author	Illustrator	Publisher	Level	Genre
Her Right Foot	Eggers, Dave	Harris, Shawn	Chronicle Books, 2017	All	Nonfiction
She Persisted Around the World	Clinton, Chelsea	Boiger, Alexandra	Philomel Books, 2018	Upper Elementary	Nonfiction: Biography
Choosing Words That Deepen Meaning					
Little Leaders: Bold Women in Black History	Harrison, Vashti	Harrison, Vashti	Little, Brown, 2017	All	Nonfiction
Love	de la Peña, Matt	Long, Loren	G. P. Putnam's Sons Books for Young Readers, 2018	All	Fiction
The Word Collector	Reynolds, Peter	Reynolds, Peter	Orchard Books, 2018	All	Fiction: Realistic
Sentence Fluency					
Capturing Smooth and Rhythmic Flow					
Miguel's Brave Knight	Engle, Margarita	Colón, Raúl	Peachtree, 2017	Upper Elementary	Biography
Muddy: The Story of Blues Legend Muddy Waters	Mahin, Michael	Turk, Evan	Atheneum Books for Young Readers, 2017	All	Nonfiction: Biography

Title	Author	Illustrator	Publisher, Year	Level	Genre
Shh! We Have a Plan	Haughton, Chris	Haughton, Chris	Candlewick, 2014	Early Elementary	Fiction: Humor
Voice of Freedom	Weatherford, Carole Boston	Holmes, Ekua	Candlewick, 2015	Upper Elementary	Nonfiction: Biography
Crafting Well-Built Sentences					
Danza! Amalia Hernández and El Ballet Folklórico de México	Tonatiuh, Duncan	Tonatiuh, Duncan	Abrams, 2017	Upper Elementary	Biography
Freedom Over Me	Bryan, Ashley	Bryan, Ashley	Simon and Schuster, 2016	Upper Elementary	Biography
Juna's Jar	Bahk, Jane	Hoshino, Felicia	Lee and Low Books, 2015	All	Fiction: Realistic
Varying Sentence Patterns					
Ada Twist, Scientist	Beaty, Andrea	Roberts, David	Abrams, 2016	Upper Elementary	Fiction: Realistic
Henry & Leo	Zagarenski, Pamela	Zagarenski, Pamela	Houghton Mifflin, 2016 Harcourt, 2016	All	Fiction: Fantasy
Six Dots	Bryant, Jen	Kulikov, Boris	Penguin Random House, 2016	Upper Elementary	Biography

Breaking the "Rules" to Create Fluency

Title	Author	Illustrator	Publisher	Grade	Genre
Are We There Yet?	Santat, Dan	Santat, Dan	Little, Brown, 2016	All	Fiction: Realistic
Dragon Loves Tacos 2: The Sequel	Rubin, Adam	Salmieri, Daniel	Dial Books for Young Readers, 2017	All	Fiction: Fantasy
The Water Princess	Verde, Susan	Reynolds, Peter H.	G. P. Putnam's Sons, 2016	All	Fiction: Realistic

Conventions

Capitalization

Title	Author	Illustrator	Publisher	Grade	Genre
The Duckster Ducklings Go to Mars	Loewen, Nancy	Sinkovec, Igor	Capstone, 2016	All	Fiction: Fantasy

Punctuation

Title	Author	Illustrator	Publisher	Grade	Genre
The Punctuation Station	Cleary, Brian P.	Lew-Vriethoff, Joanne	Millbrook, 2018	All	Fiction: Fantasy

Three Fun and Informative Books on Modes

Narrative					
Stella Tells Her Story	Wagstaff, Janiel	Regan, Dana	SDE, 2015	All	Fiction: Realistic
Informative					
Stella and Class: Information Experts	Wagstaff, Janiel	Regan, Dana	SDE, 2015	All	Fiction: Realistic
Opinion					
Stella Writes an Opinion	Wagstaff, Janiel	Regan, Dana	SDE, 2015	All	Fiction: Realistic

Wrap-Up: Doing More with Less

Writing is a big deal in today's classrooms for all the right reasons. There is renewed interest in writing because writing is thinking, and clear thinking is required for everything a student does—and will do—throughout his or her life. Given that we have this collective goal, and that resources to teach writing well are not likely to come flooding in anytime soon, it behooves us to look at what is already present in every classroom (and outside the classroom as well): print and non-print materials. One of the best teaching strategies I know is to learn to examine high-quality books and resources for more than their original purpose—to see them as writing models, too.

Figure 7.4 *A young writer shares his work.*

If you doubt the power and energy that mentor texts bring to the writing process, look at the pure joy on this student's face as he proudly displays his first book inspired by a text his teacher read and then used to motivate and teach. During summer school, after first announcing he hated to write and was terrible at it, he's singing a different tune now.

Here is your charge: find a book, a passage from a book, a brochure, a sign, or whatever format provides a model of good writing, and share it with students. With their student-friendly versions of the traits scoring guides in hand, they can pinpoint what the author has done well and discuss it using the shared vocabulary essential to understanding how writing works. Then challenge your writers to try the same technique on a piece from their Writing Wallets and share the results. Be prepared to be amazed.

Wrapping It Up

This book, its contents, and its intent have been on my mind and in my heart for a long time. As I've traveled conducting professional development, I've learned from teachers across the country and the world. I've listened to the challenges you face and the questions you have about teaching writing in today's classroom, and they are many and varied. I truly believe the traits of writing are at the center of what we should be doing, from learning how to assess to invigorating instruction and rethinking revision.

I also believe that if you can see it, you can do it. This book shows you how to organize your writing curriculum around best practices but keep time and management firmly under control. It's about how to use formative assessment to teach revision. It's about finding the joy in teaching writing by believing in your students and their ability to succeed.

No one can teach everything about writing in one year—this is a team sport. You can, however, make sure students gain knowledge and skill that builds successfully, one year upon the next, until what they know and can do will dazzle you. Truly. I've seen it, and it's within your grasp to teach writing well.

W hat follows are sample papers on which you can practice your formative assessment skills using the traits of writing scoring guides. Dive in—the more you use and apply the scoring guides, the easier assessing becomes. You'll begin to internalize the criteria, name what is working and to what degree, and think of ways you can nudge each writer forward in his or her writing.

This appendix is set up similarly to Chapter 2. Two of the papers are scored on one trait at a time using the scoring guides to home in on key qualities. The other six papers are scored for all the traits holistically, with trait-by-trait comments included. The writers of these samples range from grade two to grade six, to give you a sense of how broad students' writing skills are during these years. These samples also represent all of the modes: narrative, expository, and persuasive.

Appendix A
Sample Writing Papers for Practice

A special note about students in grade two: Many second graders can create multiple sentences—a paragraph—on the same topic. Some second graders may not be at this point yet, so they would benefit more from the application of the developmental scoring guide, which will match their needs as beginning writers. Regardless of age, other writers might also appreciate the feedback from the beginning scoring guide if they are not yet at the stage where they can write a paragraph. The scoring guide for grades 1–2 can be downloaded from my website, www. culhamwriting.com, along with student versions that will support learning.

As you read these sample papers, be sure to have your scoring guides handy and work with a partner or two if you can. The conversation that takes place as you practice on these papers will be rich and constructive—and on the other side, you'll know how to assess with confidence and reliability. If the scores provided are no more than one point different from those you assign, that is considered agreement; we assess the writing in the same zone of performance. Remember that formative assessment is not really about the score as much as it is about learning how to read the writing for strengths and areas that need development.

Grade 2: "Unicorn"—Traits and Key Qualities

Who wouldn't want a flying unicorn as a pet? This young writer has a vivid imagination and ideas to share. She's at that turning point where she's no longer a beginning writer—she's a developing writer with something to say that can be expressed in multiple sentences that stay on the topic.

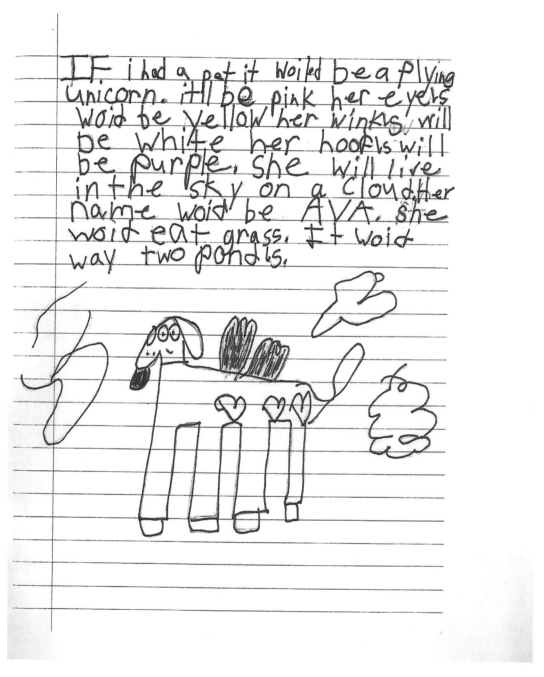

Teach Writing Well by Ruth Culham. Copyright © 2018. Stenhouse Publishers.

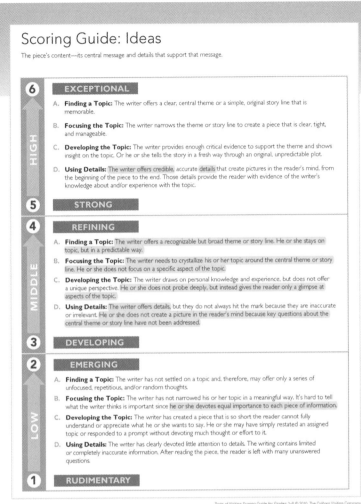

Scoring Guide: Ideas

The piece's content—its central message and details that support that message.

HIGH

6 EXCEPTIONAL

A. **Finding a Topic:** The writer offers a clear, central theme or a simple, original story line that is memorable.

B. **Focusing the Topic:** The writer narrows the theme or story line to create a piece that is clear, tight, and manageable.

C. **Developing the Topic:** The writer provides enough critical evidence to support the theme and shows insight on the topic. Or he or she tells the story in a fresh way through an original, unpredictable plot.

D. **Using Details:** The writer offers credible, accurate details that create pictures in the reader's mind, from the beginning of the piece to the end. Those details provide the reader with evidence of the writer's knowledge about and/or experience with the topic.

5 STRONG

MIDDLE

4 REFINING

A. **Finding a Topic:** The writer offers a recognizable but broad theme or story line. He or she stays on topic, but in a predictable way.

B. **Focusing the Topic:** The writer needs to crystallize his or her topic around the central theme or story line. He or she does not focus on a specific aspect of the topic.

C. **Developing the Topic:** The writer draws on personal knowledge and experience, but does not offer a unique perspective. He or she does not probe deeply, but instead gives the reader only a glimpse at aspects of the topic.

D. **Using Details:** The writer offers details, but they do not always hit the mark because they are inaccurate or irrelevant. He or she does not create a picture in the reader's mind because key questions about the central theme or story line have not been addressed.

3 DEVELOPING

LOW

2 EMERGING

A. **Finding a Topic:** The writer has not settled on a topic and, therefore, may offer only a series of unfocused, repetitive, and/or random thoughts.

B. **Focusing the Topic:** The writer has not narrowed his or her topic in a meaningful way. It's hard to tell what the writer thinks is important since he or she devotes equal importance to each piece of information.

C. **Developing the Topic:** The writer has created a piece that is so short the reader cannot fully understand or appreciate what he or she wants to say. He or she may have simply restated an assigned topic or responded to a prompt without devoting much thought or effort to it.

D. **Using Details:** The writer has clearly devoted little attention to details. The writing contains limited or completely inaccurate information. After reading the piece, the reader is left with many unanswered questions.

1 RUDIMENTARY

Traits of Writing Scoring Guide for Grades 3–8 © 2010. The Culham Writing Company.

Key Quality Scores

Finding a Topic: 3

Focusing the Topic: 3

Developing the Topic: 3

Using Details: 3

Overall Ideas score: 3

Sentence Fluency: 5

Conventions: 6

The choice of a flying unicorn as a pet shows imagination and creativity. The writer explains what it would look like and where it would live. The writer does not, however, provide any insight on the topic, which keeps this piece from scoring higher in the ideas trait. The picture is a nice complement, but it lacks significant detail to build onto the text. This writer is definitely on her way to having a strong piece. Next steps might include asking the writer to develop additional details that make the piece memorable and original, taking a dive into what life with a flying unicorn might be like.

Worth Mentioning

Notice that the score has an up arrow after it. That's because there is no one, perfect, precise, mathematically provable score. This piece scores in the middle for ideas, but it leans upward. Some readers might assign a 3.5, a 3/4 split, or a 3+. I prefer to use arrows so students can see visually where they are on the continuum with a piece. I don't use down arrows, though—that's too negative. Remember, we're assessing the writing at this point in its development and looking for clues about where it can improve.

Grade 2: *"Unicorn" Organization Summary*

Though the piece begins with a statement of the intended topic, it then devolves into a series of descriptive statements about the unicorn that could appear in any order and make perfect sense. There is no inherent sense of order in the piece as it stands. Nor does it have an ending—it just stops. Next steps for this writer would be to think about grouping statements regarding appearance, where the unicorn lives, why she is named as she is, and so on, using transition words and phrases. As the piece develops in the ideas trait, the logic of the organization will become more clear. Finally, the writer can come up with an ending that reflects the new direction of the piece.

Worth Mentioning

Notice that there's no arrow after this piece's overall score. That's because it is a solid 2, not leaning upward. There is no formula for how many of the key qualities need to be met before a piece moves between points. I look at how the piece scores for each key quality, after I have worked through all of them, and make my assessment based on that. It helps to use a highlighter on the scoring guide, as I have done, for visual impact.

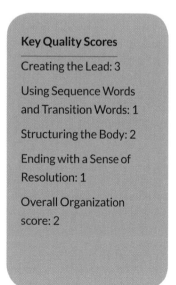

Key Quality Scores

Creating the Lead: 3

Using Sequence Words and Transition Words: 1

Structuring the Body: 2

Ending with a Sense of Resolution: 1

Overall Organization score: 2

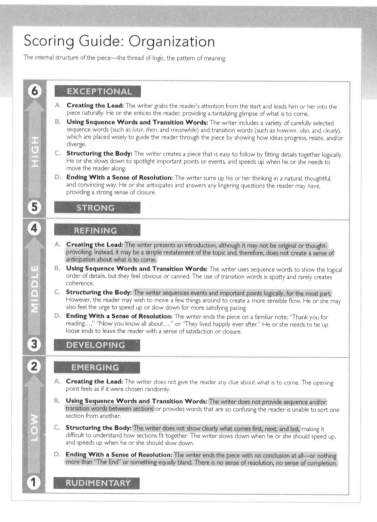

Scoring Guide: Organization

The internal structure of the piece—the thread of logic, the pattern of meaning.

6 — EXCEPTIONAL

A. **Creating the Lead:** The writer grabs the reader's attention from the start and leads him or her into the piece naturally. He or she entices the reader, providing a tantalizing glimpse of what is to come.

B. **Using Sequence Words and Transition Words:** The writer includes a variety of carefully selected sequence words (such as *later, then,* and *meanwhile*) and transition words (such as *however, also,* and *clearly*), which are placed wisely to guide the reader through the piece by showing how ideas progress, relate, and/or diverge.

C. **Structuring the Body:** The writer creates a piece that is easy to follow by fitting details together logically. He or she slows down to spotlight important points or events, and speeds up when he or she needs to move the reader along.

D. **Ending With a Sense of Resolution:** The writer sums up his or her thinking in a natural, thoughtful, and convincing way. He or she anticipates and answers any lingering questions the reader may have, providing a strong sense of closure.

5 — STRONG

4 — REFINING

A. **Creating the Lead:** The writer presents an introduction, although it may not be original or thought-provoking. Instead, it may be a simple restatement of the topic and, therefore, does not create a sense of anticipation about what is to come.

B. **Using Sequence Words and Transition Words:** The writer uses sequence words to show the logical order of details, but they feel obvious or canned. The use of transition words is spotty and rarely creates coherence.

C. **Structuring the Body:** The writer sequences events and important points logically, for the most part. However, the reader may wish to move a few things around to create a more sensible flow. He or she may also feel the urge to speed up or slow down for more satisfying pacing.

D. **Ending With a Sense of Resolution:** The writer ends the piece on a familiar note: "Thank you for reading...," "Now you know all about...," or "They lived happily ever after." He or she needs to tie up loose ends to leave the reader with a sense of satisfaction or closure.

3 — DEVELOPING

2 — EMERGING

A. **Creating the Lead:** The writer does not give the reader any clue about what is to come. The opening point feels as if it were chosen randomly.

B. **Using Sequence Words and Transition Words:** The writer does not provide sequence and/or transition words between sections or provides words that are so confusing the reader is unable to sort one section from another.

C. **Structuring the Body:** The writer does not show clearly what comes first, next, and last, making it difficult to understand how sections fit together. The writer slows down when he or she should speed up, and speeds up when he or she should slow down.

D. **Ending With a Sense of Resolution:** The writer ends the piece with no conclusion at all—or nothing more than "The End" or something equally bland. There is no sense of resolution, no sense of completion.

1 — RUDIMENTARY

HIGH · MIDDLE · LOW

Grade 2: "Unicorn" Voice Summary

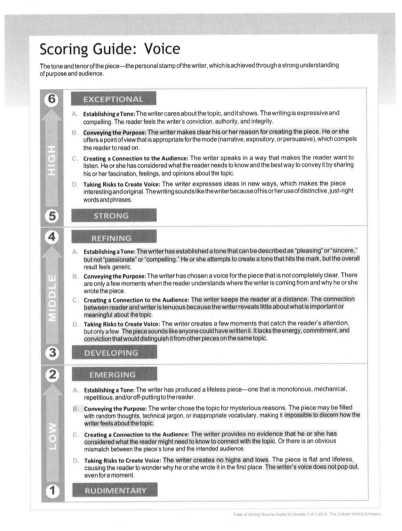

Scoring Guide: Voice

The tone and tenor of the piece—the personal stamp of the writer, which is achieved through a strong understanding of purpose and audience.

HIGH

6 EXCEPTIONAL

A. **Establishing a Tone:** The writer cares about the topic, and it shows. The writing is expressive and compelling. The reader feels the writer's conviction, authority, and integrity.

B. **Conveying the Purpose:** The writer makes clear his or her reason for creating the piece. He or she offers a point of view that is appropriate for the mode (narrative, expository, or persuasive), which compels the reader to read on.

C. **Creating a Connection to the Audience:** The writer speaks in a way that makes the reader want to listen. He or she has considered what the reader needs to know and the best way to convey it by sharing his or her fascination, feelings, and opinions about the topic.

D. **Taking Risks to Create Voice:** The writer expresses ideas in new ways, which makes the piece interesting and original. The writing sounds like the writer because of his or her use of distinctive, just-right words and phrases.

5 STRONG

MIDDLE

4 REFINING

A. **Establishing a Tone:** The writer has established a tone that can be described as "pleasing" or "sincere," but not "passionate" or "compelling." He or she attempts to create a tone that hits the mark, but the overall result feels generic.

B. **Conveying the Purpose:** The writer has chosen a voice for the piece that is not completely clear. There are only a few moments when the reader understands where the writer is coming from and why he or she wrote the piece.

C. **Creating a Connection to the Audience:** The writer keeps the reader at a distance. The connection between reader and writer is tenuous because the writer reveals little about what is important or meaningful about the topic.

D. **Taking Risks to Create Voice:** The writer creates a few moments that catch the reader's attention, but only a few. The piece sounds like anyone could have written it. It lacks the energy, commitment, and conviction that would distinguish it from other pieces on the same topic.

3 DEVELOPING

LOW

2 EMERGING

A. **Establishing a Tone:** The writer has produced a lifeless piece—one that is monotonous, mechanical, repetitious, and/or off-putting to the reader.

B. **Conveying the Purpose:** The writer chose the topic for mysterious reasons. The piece may be filled with random thoughts, technical jargon, or inappropriate vocabulary, making it impossible to discern how the writer feels about the topic.

C. **Creating a Connection to the Audience:** The writer provides no evidence that he or she has considered what the reader might need to know to connect with the topic. Or there is an obvious mismatch between the piece's tone and the intended audience.

D. **Taking Risks to Create Voice:** The writer creates no highs and lows. The piece is flat and lifeless, causing the reader to wonder why he or she wrote it in the first place. The writer's voice does not pop out, even for a moment.

1 RUDIMENTARY

Traits of Writing Scoring Guide for Grades 3–8 © 2010. The Culham Writing Company

Key Quality Scores

Establishing a Tone: 2

Conveying the Purpose: 1

Creating a Connection to the Audience: 2

Taking Risks to Create Voice: 2

Overall Voice score: 2

It wouldn't surprise me if you assessed this paper a little higher than I did. It is a charming topic, and it's easy to understand why readers have a positive reaction to it. Here's the issue: if you scored it higher, were you responding to actual moments of voice in the writing or to the potential of the idea? Unicorns are fun to read about, but in this work I see little evidence of the writer's engagement with the topic other than the details about how it looks and where it lives.

That's not enough. Next steps for this writer would be to weave in some wording that catches our attention in new ways, original reasons why unicorns would be great pets, and reaching out to the reader with original thinking.

Worth Mentioning

No one enjoys reading writing without voice, whether it's narrative, expository, or persuasive. Voice is not just a narrative trait; it's critical to make connections to the reader in the other modes as well. Narrative writing draws upon emotion, whereas informational writing should be reliable, credible, and believable. Both are within the voice domain, however. Great models in all modes help students understand this.

Grade 2: "Unicorn" Word Choice Summary

The use of color words works okay in this piece but doesn't nail the word choice criteria. Why the writer chose certain colors to describe different parts of the unicorn feels random—for example, what's the reason for yellow eyes or pink wings? This writer has also relied on passive voice throughout, which keeps the energy level low (contributing to voice). The piece overall is ordinary in the word choice trait. Next steps for this writer would be to brainstorm action verbs to spice up the sentences. Then we'd work in some precision with the color words to create a visual and imaginative image.

Worth Mentioning

Sometimes, when assessing writing, it is useful to first read it carefully and then ask yourself, *Is this piece weaker or stronger in this trait?* If your gut tells you stronger, you can focus on the high and medium key quality zones. If, as is the case with this piece, your reaction is weaker, then you can dial in on the middle and low areas of the scoring guide. Remember, this is not an exact science. Look at the message your score sends. To this writer it says, "You've communicated your message, but I bet we can make it clearer with some revision in word choice." That's a fair assessment.

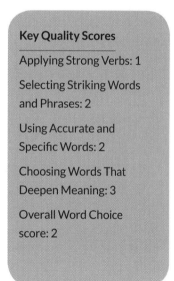

Key Quality Scores

Applying Strong Verbs: 1

Selecting Striking Words and Phrases: 2

Using Accurate and Specific Words: 2

Choosing Words That Deepen Meaning: 3

Overall Word Choice score: 2

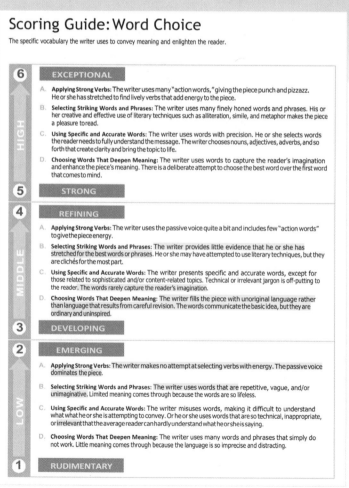

Scoring Guide: Word Choice

The specific vocabulary the writer uses to convey meaning and enlighten the reader.

6 EXCEPTIONAL — HIGH

A. **Applying Strong Verbs:** The writer uses many "action words," giving the piece punch and pizzazz. He or she has stretched to find lively verbs that add energy to the piece.

B. **Selecting Striking Words and Phrases:** The writer uses many finely honed words and phrases. His or her creative and effective use of literary techniques such as alliteration, simile, and metaphor makes the piece a pleasure to read.

C. **Using Specific and Accurate Words:** The writer uses words with precision. He or she selects words the reader needs to fully understand the message. The writer chooses nouns, adjectives, adverbs, and so forth that create clarity and bring the topic to life.

D. **Choosing Words That Deepen Meaning:** The writer uses words to capture the reader's imagination and enhance the piece's meaning. There is a deliberate attempt to choose the best word over the first word that comes to mind.

5 STRONG

4 REFINING — MIDDLE

A. **Applying Strong Verbs:** The writer uses the passive voice quite a bit and includes few "action words" to give the piece energy.

B. **Selecting Striking Words and Phrases:** The writer provides little evidence that he or she has stretched for the best words or phrases. He or she may have attempted to use literary techniques, but they are clichés for the most part.

C. **Using Specific and Accurate Words:** The writer presents specific and accurate words, except for those related to sophisticated and/or content-related topics. Technical or irrelevant jargon is off-putting to the reader. The words rarely capture the reader's imagination.

D. **Choosing Words That Deepen Meaning:** The writer fills the piece with unoriginal language rather than language that results from careful revision. The words communicate the basic idea, but they are ordinary and uninspired.

3 DEVELOPING

2 EMERGING — LOW

A. **Applying Strong Verbs:** The writer makes no attempt at selecting verbs with energy. The passive voice dominates the piece.

B. **Selecting Striking Words and Phrases:** The writer uses words that are repetitive, vague, and/or unimaginative. Limited meaning comes through because the words are so lifeless.

C. **Using Specific and Accurate Words:** The writer misuses words, making it difficult to understand what what he or she is attempting to convey. Or he or she uses words that are so technical, inappropriate, or irrelevant that the average reader can hardly understand what he or she is saying.

D. **Choosing Words That Deepen Meaning:** The writer uses many words and phrases that simply do not work. Little meaning comes through because the language is so imprecise and distracting.

1 RUDIMENTARY

Traits of Writing Scoring Guide for Grades 3-5 © 2010, The Culham Writing Company

Teach Writing Well by Ruth Culham. Copyright © 2018. Stenhouse Publishers.

Grade 2: "Unicorn" Sentence Fluency Summary

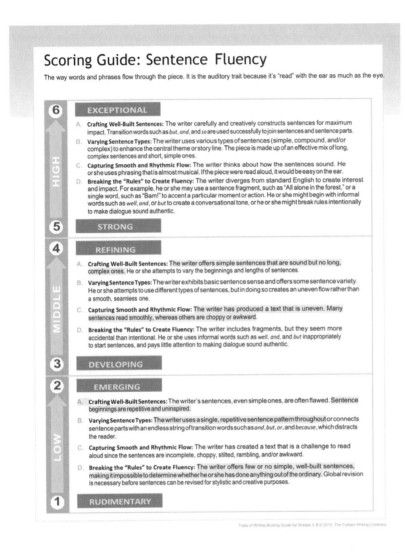

Scoring Guide: Sentence Fluency

The way words and phrases flow through the piece. It is the auditory trait because it's "read" with the ear as much as the eye.

6 · EXCEPTIONAL

HIGH

A. **Crafting Well-Built Sentences:** The writer carefully and creatively constructs sentences for maximum impact. Transition words such as *but*, *and*, and *so* are used successfully to join sentences and sentence parts.

B. **Varying Sentence Types:** The writer uses various types of sentences (simple, compound, and/or complex) to enhance the central theme or story line. The piece is made up of an effective mix of long, complex sentences and short, simple ones.

C. **Capturing Smooth and Rhythmic Flow:** The writer thinks about how the sentences sound. He or she uses phrasing that is almost musical. If the piece were read aloud, it would be easy on the ear.

D. **Breaking the "Rules" to Create Fluency:** The writer diverges from standard English to create interest and impact. For example, he or she may use a sentence fragment, such as "All alone in the forest," or a single word, such as "Bam!" to accent a particular moment or action. He or she might begin with informal words such as *well*, *and*, or *but* to create a conversational tone, or he or she might break rules intentionally to make dialogue sound authentic.

5 · STRONG

4 · REFINING

MIDDLE

A. **Crafting Well-Built Sentences:** The writer offers simple sentences that are sound but no long, complex ones. He or she attempts to vary the beginnings and lengths of sentences.

B. **Varying Sentence Types:** The writer exhibits basic sentence sense and offers some sentence variety. He or she attempts to use different types of sentences, but in doing so creates an uneven flow rather than a smooth, seamless one.

C. **Capturing Smooth and Rhythmic Flow:** The writer has produced a text that is uneven. Many sentences read smoothly, whereas others are choppy or awkward.

D. **Breaking the "Rules" to Create Fluency:** The writer includes fragments, but they seem more accidental than intentional. He or she uses informal words such as *well*, *and*, and *but* inappropriately to start sentences, and pays little attention to making dialogue sound authentic.

3 · DEVELOPING

2 · EMERGING

LOW

A. **Crafting Well-Built Sentences:** The writer's sentences, even simple ones, are often flawed. Sentence beginnings are repetitive and uninspired.

B. **Varying Sentence Types:** The writer uses a single, repetitive sentence pattern throughout or connects sentence parts with an endless string of transition words such as *and*, *but*, *or*, and *because*, which distracts the reader.

C. **Capturing Smooth and Rhythmic Flow:** The writer has created a text that is a challenge to read aloud since the sentences are incomplete, choppy, stilted, rambling, and/or awkward.

D. **Breaking the "Rules" to Create Fluency:** The writer offers few or no simple, well-built sentences, making it impossible to determine whether he or she has done anything out of the ordinary. Global revision is necessary before sentences can be revised for stylistic and creative purposes.

1 · RUDIMENTARY

Traits of Writing Scoring Guide for Grades 3–8 © 2010, The Culham Writing Company

Key Quality Scores

Crafting Well-Built Sentences: 2

Varying Sentence Types: 1

Capturing Smooth and Rhythmic Flow: 3

Breaking the "Rules" to Create Fluency: 1

Overall Sentence Fluency score: 2

This young writer uses simple, grammatically correct sentences. Yippee! This is a milestone and definitely worth celebrating. However, since the writer is capable of writing multiple sentences on the same topic (a paragraph), we begin to expect more variety, different constructions, and a smoother overall sound to the piece when read aloud. This piece is correct but choppy. The next step for this writer is to begin working with coordinating conjunctions such as *and*, *but*, and *or*. *"It would be pink but her eyes would be yellow,"* for example. Working hand in hand with word choice and ideas, the sentences will expand and become more varied and therefore more fluent.

Worth Mentioning

Teacher–readers are able to read past the conventions and see the other traits. They have magic eyes that mere mortals don't possess. In this case, it's a bit of a challenge to see where the sentences start and stop because the conventions aren't in place to help us. If you read a piece that is highly flawed in conventions, you may want to score that area first and then reread for the other traits that may be partially obscured.

Grade 2: "Unicorn" Word Conventions Summary

Oh my goodness. You have probably been itching to get to this trait all along. With the exception of grammar and usage, this piece needs a thorough edit in every area: spelling, capitalization, and punctuation. It doesn't show control of basic issues such as capitalization at the beginning of sentences, punctuation at the end, and spelling of high-frequency words such as *would*. Next steps for this piece would be to focus on one area, perhaps capitalization, and ask the student to edit her writing for that one key quality. Then move on to the next area of concern. An interesting punctuation issue to notice is that this writer uses an apostrophe when the noun is plural—*hoof's, wink's, and pond's*, for instance. This may be easy to clear up with a one-on-one conference or chat, now that you see the thinking behind the error.

Worth Mentioning

It's difficult to assess conventions as one unit. You would be wise to think about each of the four key qualities separately as you assess. Don't lump everything together here or you may miss the fact that the grammar and usage are under control, given the basic sentences this student has written. This is an example of why holistic scores are not as useful as analytical ones: when you assign one score for conventions, you don't see the strengths and weaknesses in as much definition to know where to help the student work to improve.

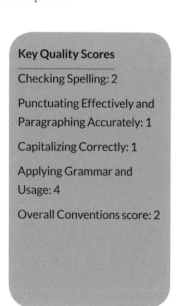

Key Quality Scores

Checking Spelling: 2

Punctuating Effectively and Paragraphing Accurately: 1

Capitalizing Correctly: 1

Applying Grammar and Usage: 4

Overall Conventions score: 2

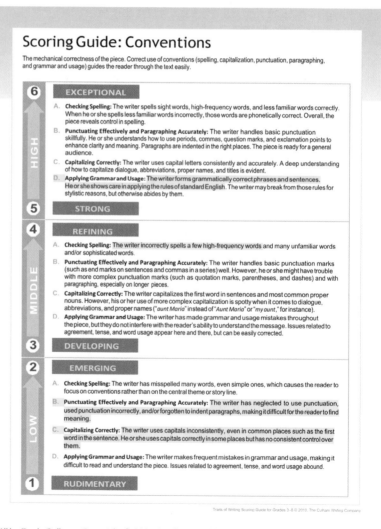

Scoring Guide: Conventions

The mechanical correctness of the piece. Correct use of conventions (spelling, capitalization, punctuation, paragraphing, and grammar and usage) guides the reader through the text easily.

6 — HIGH — EXCEPTIONAL

A. **Checking Spelling:** The writer spells sight words, high-frequency words, and less familiar words correctly. When he or she spells less familiar words incorrectly, those words are phonetically correct. Overall, the piece reveals control in spelling.

B. **Punctuating Effectively and Paragraphing Accurately:** The writer handles basic punctuation skillfully. He or she understands how to use periods, commas, question marks, and exclamation points to enhance clarity and meaning. Paragraphs are indented in the right places. The piece is ready for a general audience.

C. **Capitalizing Correctly:** The writer uses capital letters consistently and accurately. A deep understanding of how to capitalize dialogue, abbreviations, proper names, and titles is evident.

D. **Applying Grammar and Usage:** The writer forms grammatically correct phrases and sentences. He or she shows care in applying the rules of standard English. The writer may break from those rules for stylistic reasons, but otherwise abides by them.

5 — STRONG

4 — MIDDLE — REFINING

A. **Checking Spelling:** The writer incorrectly spells a few high-frequency words and many unfamiliar words and/or sophisticated words.

B. **Punctuating Effectively and Paragraphing Accurately:** The writer handles basic punctuation marks (such as end marks on sentences and commas in a series) well. However, he or she might have trouble with more complex punctuation marks (such as quotation marks, parentheses, and dashes) and with paragraphing, especially on longer pieces.

C. **Capitalizing Correctly:** The writer capitalizes the first word in sentences and most common proper nouns. However, his or her use of more complex capitalization is spotty when it comes to dialogue, abbreviations, and proper names ("aunt Maria" instead of "Aunt Maria" or "my aunt," for instance).

D. **Applying Grammar and Usage:** The writer has made grammar and usage mistakes throughout the piece, but they do not interfere with the reader's ability to understand the message. Issues related to agreement, tense, and word usage appear here and there, but can be easily corrected.

3 — DEVELOPING

2 — LOW — EMERGING

A. **Checking Spelling:** The writer has misspelled many words, even simple ones, which causes the reader to focus on conventions rather than on the central theme or story line.

B. **Punctuating Effectively and Paragraphing Accurately:** The writer has neglected to use punctuation, used punctuation incorrectly, and/or forgotten to indent paragraphs, making it difficult for the reader to find meaning.

C. **Capitalizing Correctly:** The writer uses capitals inconsistently, even in common places such as the first word in the sentence. He or she uses capitals correctly in some places but has no consistent control over them.

D. **Applying Grammar and Usage:** The writer makes frequent mistakes in grammar and usage, making it difficult to read and understand the piece. Issues related to agreement, tense, and word usage abound.

1 — RUDIMENTARY

Traits of Writing Scoring Guide for Grades 3–8 © 2010. The Culham Writing Company

Grade 2: "Unicorn" Presentation Summary

Score: 3. This piece is in the middle for presentation.

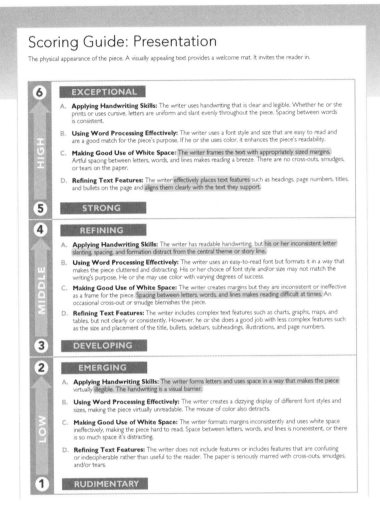

Scoring Guide: Presentation

The physical appearance of the piece. A visually appealing text provides a welcome mat. It invites the reader in.

6 — EXCEPTIONAL (HIGH)

A. **Applying Handwriting Skills:** The writer uses handwriting that is clear and legible. Whether he or she prints or uses cursive, letters are uniform and slant evenly throughout the piece. Spacing between words is consistent.

B. **Using Word Processing Effectively:** The writer uses a font style and size that are easy to read and are a good match for the piece's purpose. If he or she uses color, it enhances the piece's readability.

C. **Making Good Use of White Space:** The writer frames the text with appropriately sized margins. Artful spacing between letters, words, and lines makes reading a breeze. There are no cross-outs, smudges, or tears on the paper.

D. **Refining Text Features:** The writer effectively places text features such as headings, page numbers, titles, and bullets on the page and aligns them clearly with the text they support.

5 — STRONG

4 — REFINING (MIDDLE)

A. **Applying Handwriting Skills:** The writer has readable handwriting, but his or her inconsistent letter slanting, spacing, and formation distract from the central theme or story line.

B. **Using Word Processing Effectively:** The writer uses an easy-to-read font but formats it in a way that makes the piece cluttered and distracting. His or her choice of font style and/or size may not match the writing's purpose. He or she may use color with varying degrees of success.

C. **Making Good Use of White Space:** The writer creates margins but they are inconsistent or ineffective as a frame for the piece. Spacing between letters, words, and lines makes reading difficult at times. An occasional cross-out or smudge blemishes the piece.

D. **Refining Text Features:** The writer includes complex text features such as charts, graphs, maps, and tables, but not clearly or consistently. However, he or she does a good job with less complex features such as the size and placement of the title, bullets, sidebars, subheadings, illustrations, and page numbers.

3 — DEVELOPING

2 — EMERGING (LOW)

A. **Applying Handwriting Skills:** The writer forms letters and uses space in a way that makes the piece virtually illegible. The handwriting is a visual barrier.

B. **Using Word Processing Effectively:** The writer creates a dizzying display of different font styles and sizes, making the piece virtually unreadable. The misuse of color also detracts.

C. **Making Good Use of White Space:** The writer formats margins inconsistently and uses white space ineffectively, making the piece hard to read. Space between letters, words, and lines is nonexistent, or there is so much space it's distracting.

D. **Refining Text Features:** The writer does not include features or includes features that are confusing or indecipherable rather than useful to the reader. The paper is seriously marred with cross-outs, smudges, and/or tears.

1 — RUDIMENTARY

We notice right away that the handwriting is not easy to read. Partly because the letter formation and the use of white space between words are inconsistent, the eye sees a mass of letters, not individual words. What works well is the layout of the page. The writing respects the left and right margins, and the picture (text feature) fits nicely underneath. The next step for this student is to try writing on every other line in order to visually separate the words from one another vertically. Once that's done, we can help the student work on letter formation and adding the appropriate amount of space (finger spacing) between words horizontally. It might be helpful for the writer to use dotted writing paper, the type that clearly defines the size of the letter shapes, until this becomes more natural and varied, and therefore more fluent.

Grade 2: "Unicorn" Paper Wrap-Up
Percentage: 70% Using the six-point grading chart (16 points earned out of 42)

Ideas	Organization	Voice	Word Choice	Sentence Fluency	Conventions	Presentation
3	2	2	2	2	2	3

Grade 4: "Garibaldi"—Traits and Key Qualities

As writers develop and are able to write more about specific topics, their ability to handle the traits grows in tandem. We look for elements of sophistication with language when writers arrive at the upper elementary grades, and applaud their attempts to create more text that demonstrates smart thinking.

Garibaldi

Giuseppe Garibaldi was one of Ital's famous soldier. Giuseppe born in Nizza, Italy in 1807. He became the captain of a big garrison. Giuseppe and his garrison wore a red shirt and blue pants. Giuseppe also conected Italy to be a whole big comunity. Giuseppe won a lot of wars, never gived up, and even in a war Gisepppe hurted his leg and never stoped giving up! Giuseppe died but not in war, indeed he lived a happy life until he got a bronchitis and died i Caprera, Italy on June 2nd, 1882. We call him Garibaldi from his family name. People still remember him and see him as a herow.

Grade 4: "Garibaldi" Ideas Summary

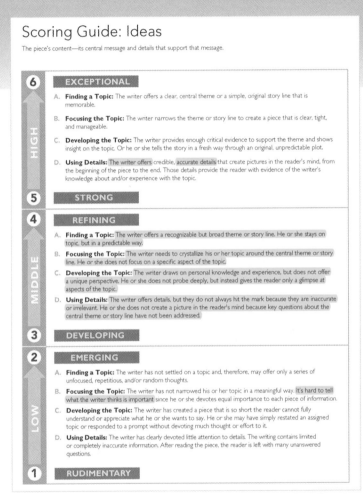

Scoring Guide: Ideas

The piece's content—its central message and details that support that message.

6 EXCEPTIONAL

A. **Finding a Topic:** The writer offers a clear, central theme or a simple, original story line that is memorable.

B. **Focusing the Topic:** The writer narrows the theme or story line to create a piece that is clear, tight, and manageable.

C. **Developing the Topic:** The writer provides enough critical evidence to support the theme and shows insight on the topic. Or he or she tells the story in a fresh way through an original, unpredictable plot.

D. **Using Details:** The writer offers credible, accurate details that create pictures in the reader's mind, from the beginning of the piece to the end. Those details provide the reader with evidence of the writer's knowledge about and/or experience with the topic.

5 STRONG

4 REFINING

A. **Finding a Topic:** The writer offers a recognizable but broad theme or story line. He or she stays on topic, but in a predictable way.

B. **Focusing the Topic:** The writer needs to crystallize his or her topic around the central theme or story line. He or she does not focus on a specific aspect of the topic.

C. **Developing the Topic:** The writer draws on personal knowledge and experience, but does not offer a unique perspective. He or she does not probe deeply, but instead gives the reader only a glimpse at aspects of the topic.

D. **Using Details:** The writer offers details, but they do not always hit the mark because they are inaccurate or irrelevant. He or she does not create a picture in the reader's mind because key questions about the central theme or story line have not been addressed.

3 DEVELOPING

2 EMERGING

A. **Finding a Topic:** The writer has not settled on a topic and, therefore, may offer only a series of unfocused, repetitious, and/or random thoughts.

B. **Focusing the Topic:** The writer has not narrowed his or her topic in a meaningful way. It's hard to tell what the writer thinks is important since he or she devotes equal importance to each piece of information.

C. **Developing the Topic:** The writer has created a piece that is so short the reader cannot fully understand or appreciate what he or she wants to say. He or she may have simply restated an assigned topic or responded to a prompt without devoting much thought or effort to it.

D. **Using Details:** The writer has clearly devoted little attention to details. The writing contains limited or completely inaccurate information. After reading the piece, the reader is left with many unanswered questions.

1 RUDIMENTARY

HIGH · MIDDLE · LOW

Traits of Writing Scoring Guide for Grades 3–8 © 2010 The Culham Writing Company

There is a lot of information in this piece, but some of it matters and some of it doesn't. It's an interesting fact, for example, that Garibaldi was the captain of a big garrison; I'd like to hear more about his leadership skills rather than the color of their uniforms. The writer emphasizes that Garibaldi never gave up, but we don't get a clear understanding about what he did that was so notable. However, the writer nails the criteria at the middle level and is clearly moving in the right direction. Next steps for this writer would be diving into what really matters about the life of Giuseppe Garibaldi and developing that part with interesting details that really show the kind of person he was.

Worth Mentioning

If this writer chose Garibaldi as a fascinating historical person, I would expect to see more specific information in the text about what made him interesting enough to research. The writer is struggling to move from notes to running text in order to capture important information, which is a very difficult skill for all writers. After students research, they must take some time to prioritize and think, *What will the reader want to know about this topic?* Then they can develop their idea around the answer, feeling free to drop details that just don't matter.

Grade 4: "Garibaldi" Organization Summary

This piece is an example of how organization and ideas work hand in hand. It's difficult to show control over organization when the information is not solid throughout. However, there are some obvious places where the writer needs to make transitions and connect the thinking so the idea doesn't jump around from detail to detail. For example, *"We call him Garibaldi from his family name"* appears to be tossed in randomly. The beginning and ending are there, but they don't shine. A next step would be to group the information (personal information, major accomplishments, impact on history, etc.) and link it using sequence and transition words. Doing this might reveal where the information is lacking as well, and these two traits could improve simultaneously.

Worth Mentioning

Organization is a relatively easy trait to score but difficult for a writer to implement. Writers struggle with organization at every age. Knowing you need a lead, transitions, an internal structure, and a conclusion is quite different from being able to pull them off. Be patient—show great models. Work on organization, key quality by key quality. It will help to demystify this challenging trait.

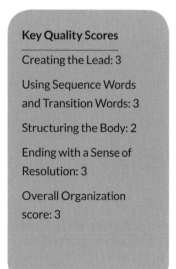

Key Quality Scores

Creating the Lead: 3

Using Sequence Words and Transition Words: 3

Structuring the Body: 2

Ending with a Sense of Resolution: 3

Overall Organization score: 3

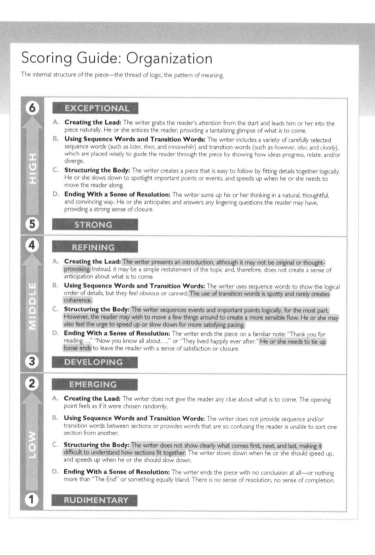

Scoring Guide: Organization

The internal structure of the piece—the thread of logic, the pattern of meaning.

6 EXCEPTIONAL HIGH

A. **Creating the Lead:** The writer grabs the reader's attention from the start and leads him or her into the piece naturally. He or she entices the reader, providing a tantalizing glimpse of what is to come.

B. **Using Sequence Words and Transition Words:** The writer includes a variety of carefully selected sequence words (such as *later*, *then*, and *meanwhile*) and transition words (such as *however*, *also*, and *clearly*), which are placed wisely to guide the reader through the piece by showing how ideas progress, relate, and/or diverge.

C. **Structuring the Body:** The writer creates a piece that is easy to follow by fitting details together logically. He or she slows down to spotlight important points or events, and speeds up when he or she needs to move the reader along.

D. **Ending With a Sense of Resolution:** The writer sums up his or her thinking in a natural, thoughtful, and convincing way. He or she anticipates and answers any lingering questions the reader may have, providing a strong sense of closure.

5 STRONG

4 REFINING MIDDLE

A. **Creating the Lead:** The writer presents an introduction, although it may not be original or thought-provoking. Instead, it may be a simple restatement of the topic and, therefore, does not create a sense of anticipation about what is to come.

B. **Using Sequence Words and Transition Words:** The writer uses sequence words to show the logical order of details, but they feel obvious or canned. The use of transition words is spotty and rarely creates coherence.

C. **Structuring the Body:** The writer sequences events and important points logically, for the most part. However, the reader may wish to move a few things around to create a more sensible flow. He or she may also feel the urge to speed up or slow down for more satisfying pacing.

D. **Ending With a Sense of Resolution:** The writer ends the piece on a familiar note: "Thank you for reading…," "Now you know all about…," or "They lived happily ever after." He or she needs to tie up loose ends to leave the reader with a sense of satisfaction or closure.

3 DEVELOPING

2 EMERGING LOW

A. **Creating the Lead:** The writer does not give the reader any clue about what is to come. The opening point feels as if it were chosen randomly.

B. **Using Sequence Words and Transition Words:** The writer does not provide sequence and/or transition words between sections or provides words that are so confusing the reader is unable to sort one section from another.

C. **Structuring the Body:** The writer does not show clearly what comes first, next, and last, making it difficult to understand how sections fit together. The writer slows down when he or she should speed up, and speeds up when he or she should slow down.

D. **Ending With a Sense of Resolution:** The writer ends the piece with no conclusion at all—or nothing more than "The End" or something equally bland. There is no sense of resolution, no sense of completion.

1 RUDIMENTARY

Grade 4: "Garibaldi" Voice Summary

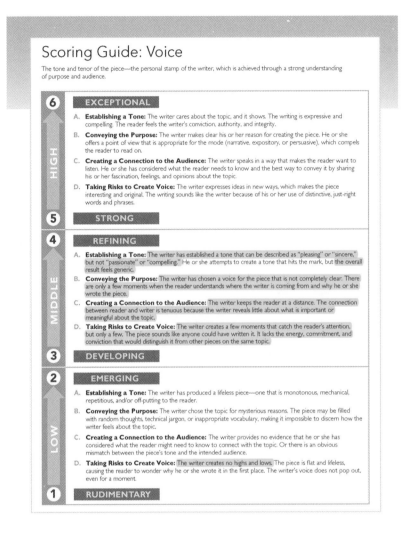

Scoring Guide: Voice

The tone and tenor of the piece—the personal stamp of the writer, which is achieved through a strong understanding of purpose and audience.

6 EXCEPTIONAL

A. **Establishing a Tone:** The writer cares about the topic, and it shows. The writing is expressive and compelling. The reader feels the writer's conviction, authority, and integrity.

B. **Conveying the Purpose:** The writer makes clear his or her reason for creating the piece. He or she offers a point of view that is appropriate for the mode (narrative, expository, or persuasive), which compels the reader to read on.

C. **Creating a Connection to the Audience:** The writer speaks in a way that makes the reader want to listen. He or she has considered what the reader needs to know and the best way to convey it by sharing his or her fascination, feelings, and opinions about the topic.

D. **Taking Risks to Create Voice:** The writer expresses ideas in new ways, which makes the piece interesting and original. The writing sounds like the writer because of his or her use of distinctive, just-right words and phrases.

5 STRONG

4 REFINING

A. **Establishing a Tone:** The writer has established a tone that can be described as "pleasing" or "sincere," but not "passionate" or "compelling." He or she attempts to create a tone that hits the mark, but the overall result feels generic.

B. **Conveying the Purpose:** The writer has chosen a voice for the piece that is not completely clear. There are only a few moments when the reader understands where the writer is coming from and why he or she wrote the piece.

C. **Creating a Connection to the Audience:** The writer keeps the reader at a distance. The connection between reader and writer is tenuous because the writer reveals little about what is important or meaningful about the topic.

D. **Taking Risks to Create Voice:** The writer creates a few moments that catch the reader's attention, but only a few. The piece sounds like anyone could have written it. It lacks the energy, commitment, and conviction that would distinguish it from other pieces on the same topic.

3 DEVELOPING

2 EMERGING

A. **Establishing a Tone:** The writer has produced a lifeless piece—one that is monotonous, mechanical, repetitious, and/or off-putting to the reader.

B. **Conveying the Purpose:** The writer chose the topic for mysterious reasons. The piece may be filled with random thoughts, technical jargon, or inappropriate vocabulary, making it impossible to discern how the writer feels about the topic.

C. **Creating a Connection to the Audience:** The writer provides no evidence that he or she has considered what the reader might need to know to connect with the topic. Or there is an obvious mismatch between the piece's tone and the intended audience.

D. **Taking Risks to Create Voice:** The writer creates no highs and lows. The piece is flat and lifeless, causing the reader to wonder why he or she wrote it in the first place. The writer's voice does not pop out, even for a moment.

1 RUDIMENTARY

Key Quality Scores

Establishing a Tone: 3

Conveying the Purpose: 3

Creating a Connection to the Audience: 3

Taking Risks to Create Voice: 3

Overall Voice score: 3

What is important to the writer about the life of Garibaldi? We don't know. That's as much a voice issue as an ideas one. We see a glimpse of voice in the middle—*"Giuseppe hurted his leg and never stoped giving up!"*—but then it fades away. It's a safe piece, but it lacks the voice that would make it more compelling and memorable. A next step for this writer would be to identify where the voice begins to pop out, such as *"indeed he lived a happy life,"* and to ask him to develop that point more, emphasizing why the audience would find the information as fascinating as the writer does.

Worth Mentioning

We don't teach students how to trait, we teach them how to write. Using the traits gives us a way to dig into the writing and examine it, much like a scientist. However, we know that one trait can highly influence the others, as we see in this piece. Because the idea isn't nailed yet, the other traits can't flourish. Voice is often the successful outcome of all the traits working well together; when the other traits improve, we'll see confidence and energy emerge in the voice, too.

Grade 4: "Garibaldi" Word Choice Summary

Unfortunately, there is a sense of word-choice ordinariness in this piece. Words like *garrison* and *community* stand out because they are specific, unlike many of the other words and phrases. *"Won a lot of wars"* could be described much more clearly, for example. My favorite line in this piece is *"Giuseppe died but not in war, indeed he lived a happy life until he got a bronchitis and died i Caprera, Italy on June 2nd, 1882."* We'll deal with the sentence construction issue in the next trait, but I enjoyed the smooth and natural word choice at the beginning of the sentence. A next step for this writer is to pluck out a sentence such as *"He became the captain of a big garrison"*; here, he can rework the verb and add specific, more-accurate words to explain Garibaldi's rank in the military and how many men he commanded in a garrison.

Worth Mentioning

Perhaps you noticed how I cherry-picked my way through the scoring guide on this piece. Not every criterion will match the writing you are assessing. This writer didn't attempt literary techniques, for example, so I didn't highlight that part. Unless I see evidence of an attempt, I can't respond to it in the writing. That means you can highlight parts of the criteria and look for a pattern of what's been done and what hasn't. This piece is a 3, for instance, because of what it does, but the parts of the scoring guide that aren't highlighted are a good place to note what the writer could try next.

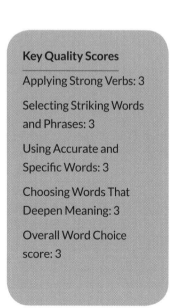

Key Quality Scores

Applying Strong Verbs: 3

Selecting Striking Words and Phrases: 3

Using Accurate and Specific Words: 3

Choosing Words That Deepen Meaning: 3

Overall Word Choice score: 3

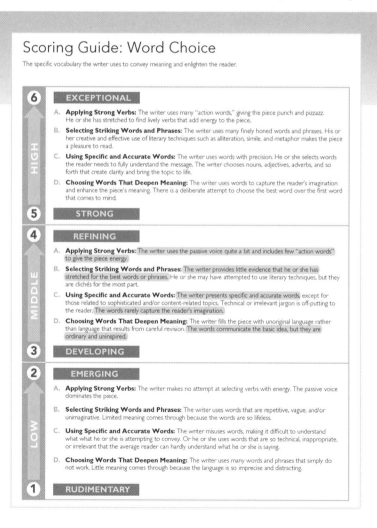

Scoring Guide: Word Choice

The specific vocabulary the writer uses to convey meaning and enlighten the reader.

6 EXCEPTIONAL — HIGH

A. **Applying Strong Verbs:** The writer uses many "action words," giving the piece punch and pizzazz. He or she has stretched to find lively verbs that add energy to the piece.

B. **Selecting Striking Words and Phrases:** The writer uses many finely honed words and phrases. His or her creative and effective use of literary techniques such as alliteration, simile, and metaphor makes the piece a pleasure to read.

C. **Using Specific and Accurate Words:** The writer uses words with precision. He or she selects words the reader needs to fully understand the message. The writer chooses nouns, adjectives, adverbs, and so forth that create clarity and bring the topic to life.

D. **Choosing Words That Deepen Meaning:** The writer uses words to capture the reader's imagination and enhance the piece's meaning. There is a deliberate attempt to choose the best word over the first word that comes to mind.

5 STRONG

4 REFINING — MIDDLE

A. **Applying Strong Verbs:** The writer uses the passive voice quite a bit and includes few "action words" to give the piece energy.

B. **Selecting Striking Words and Phrases:** The writer provides little evidence that he or she has stretched for the best words or phrases. He or she may have attempted to use literary techniques, but they are clichés for the most part.

C. **Using Specific and Accurate Words:** The writer presents specific and accurate words, except for those related to sophisticated and/or content-related topics. Technical or irrelevant jargon is off-putting to the reader. The words rarely capture the reader's imagination.

D. **Choosing Words That Deepen Meaning:** The writer fills the piece with unoriginal language rather than language that results from careful revision. The words communicate the basic idea, but they are ordinary and uninspired.

3 DEVELOPING

2 EMERGING — LOW

A. **Applying Strong Verbs:** The writer makes no attempt at selecting verbs with energy. The passive voice dominates the piece.

B. **Selecting Striking Words and Phrases:** The writer uses words that are repetitive, vague, and/or unimaginative. Limited meaning comes through because the words are so lifeless.

C. **Using Specific and Accurate Words:** The writer misuses words, making it difficult to understand what what he or she is attempting to convey. Or he or she uses words that are so technical, inappropriate, or irrelevant that the average reader can hardly understand what he or she is saying.

D. **Choosing Words That Deepen Meaning:** The writer uses many words and phrases that simply do not work. Little meaning comes through because the language is so imprecise and distracting.

1 RUDIMENTARY

Grade 4: *"Garibaldi" Sentence Fluency Summary*

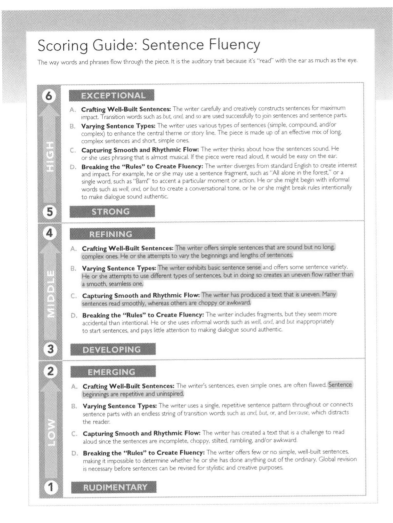

Scoring Guide: Sentence Fluency

The way words and phrases flow through the piece. It is the auditory trait because it's "read" with the ear as much as the eye.

6 — EXCEPTIONAL

A. **Crafting Well-Built Sentences:** The writer carefully and creatively constructs sentences for maximum impact. Transition words such as *but, and,* and *so* are used successfully to join sentences and sentence parts.

B. **Varying Sentence Types:** The writer uses various types of sentences (simple, compound, and/or complex) to enhance the central theme or story line. The piece is made up of an effective mix of long, complex sentences and short, simple ones.

C. **Capturing Smooth and Rhythmic Flow:** The writer thinks about how the sentences sound. He or she uses phrasing that is almost musical. If the piece were read aloud, it would be easy on the ear.

D. **Breaking the "Rules" to Create Fluency:** The writer diverges from standard English to create interest and impact. For example, he or she may use a sentence fragment, such as "All alone in the forest," or a single word, such as "Bam!" to accent a particular moment or action. He or she might begin with informal words such as *well, and,* or *but* to create a conversational tone, or he or she might break rules intentionally to make dialogue sound authentic.

5 — STRONG

4 — REFINING

A. **Crafting Well-Built Sentences:** The writer offers simple sentences that are sound but no long, complex ones. He or she attempts to vary the beginnings and lengths of sentences.

B. **Varying Sentence Types:** The writer exhibits basic sentence sense and offers some sentence variety. He or she attempts to use different types of sentences, but in doing so creates an uneven flow rather than a smooth, seamless one.

C. **Capturing Smooth and Rhythmic Flow:** The writer has produced a text that is uneven. Many sentences read smoothly, whereas others are choppy or awkward.

D. **Breaking the "Rules" to Create Fluency:** The writer includes fragments, but they seem more accidental than intentional. He or she uses informal words such as *well, and,* and *but* inappropriately to start sentences, and pays little attention to making dialogue sound authentic.

3 — DEVELOPING

2 — EMERGING

A. **Crafting Well-Built Sentences:** The writer's sentences, even simple ones, are often flawed. Sentence beginnings are repetitive and uninspired.

B. **Varying Sentence Types:** The writer uses a single, repetitive sentence pattern throughout or connects sentence parts with an endless string of transition words such as *and, but, or,* and *because,* which distracts the reader.

C. **Capturing Smooth and Rhythmic Flow:** The writer has created a text that is a challenge to read aloud since the sentences are incomplete, choppy, stilted, rambling, and/or awkward.

D. **Breaking the "Rules" to Create Fluency:** The writer offers few or no simple, well-built sentences, making it impossible to determine whether he or she has done anything out of the ordinary. Global revision is necessary before sentences can be revised for stylistic and creative purposes.

1 — RUDIMENTARY

Key Quality Scores

Crafting Well-Built Sentences: 2

Varying Sentence Types: 3

Capturing Smooth and Rhythmic Flow: 3

Breaking the "Rules" to Create Fluency: N/A

Overall Sentence Fluency score: 3

The unevenness of this writer's skill with sentences really shows up in this piece. On one hand, we can applaud his effort to create one or two differently constructed sentences, but they don't work. The sentences begin much the same way throughout—"Giuseppe . . ."—creating a singsong sound to the text when read aloud. A suggestion for this writer might be to take one of the flawed sentences that shows an attempt to do something more complex—such as *"Giuseppe died but not in war, indeed he lived a happy life until he got a bronchitis and died i Caprera, Italy on June 2nd, 1882,"*—and help him construct it correctly or break it into at least two interesting-sounding, grammatically correct sentences.

Worth Mentioning

Sometimes, as in this piece, a key quality will not apply. The writer didn't attempt anything that applies to "Breaking the 'Rules' to Create Fluency," so it's not marked at all. The other key qualities reveal that this writer needs work in sentences; perhaps during that process, the "Breaking the 'Rules'" technique can be introduced. In other words, this particular writer needs to work on learning the rules and using them consistently before we worry about breaking the rules to create fluency. Certainly, this writer needs support with sentence beginnings as well.

Grade 4: "Garibaldi" Conventions Summary

Reading this piece for conventions is an exercise in using the full range of scores. This writer shows strength in some conventions and needs to improve in others. We need to be sure the writer's strengths, such as punctuation and capitalization, are pointed out and celebrated; then we can pick an area, such as grammar and usage (*give*, not *gived*; *hurt*, not *hurted*), to work on further. These are editing points that matter in the final draft of the writing. Of course this piece has some revision to go through before editing, but there will be plenty of work to do on conventions to clean it up for the reader.

Worth Mentioning

When scoring conventions, it's fair to consider the degree of difficulty of the attempt. We want to reward more complex use of conventions—more difficult words spelled well and more advanced use of punctuation than a period, for instance. If we jump on every error, then writers stop trying to do more with conventions, and that's not the goal. Ask yourself this as you assess: *How much editing must be done to get this piece ready for a public audience?* A lot (score 1–2)? Some (score 3–4)? Very little (score 5-6)?

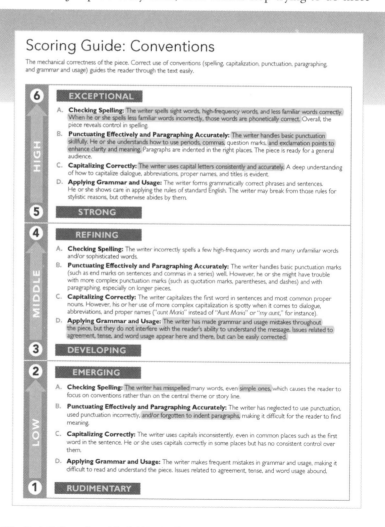

Scoring Guide: Conventions

The mechanical correctness of the piece. Correct use of conventions (spelling, capitalization, punctuation, paragraphing, and grammar and usage) guides the reader through the text easily.

6 EXCEPTIONAL

A. **Checking Spelling:** The writer spells sight words, high-frequency words, and less familiar words correctly. When he or she spells less familiar words incorrectly, those words are phonetically correct. Overall, the piece reveals control in spelling.

B. **Punctuating Effectively and Paragraphing Accurately:** The writer handles basic punctuation skillfully. He or she understands how to use periods, commas, question marks, and exclamation points to enhance clarity and meaning. Paragraphs are indented in the right places. The piece is ready for a general audience.

C. **Capitalizing Correctly:** The writer uses capital letters consistently and accurately. A deep understanding of how to capitalize dialogue, abbreviations, proper names, and titles is evident.

D. **Applying Grammar and Usage:** The writer forms grammatically correct phrases and sentences. He or she shows care in applying the rules of standard English. The writer may break from those rules for stylistic reasons, but otherwise abides by them.

5 STRONG

4 REFINING

A. **Checking Spelling:** The writer incorrectly spells a few high-frequency words and many unfamiliar words and/or sophisticated words.

B. **Punctuating Effectively and Paragraphing Accurately:** The writer handles basic punctuation marks (such as end marks on sentences and commas in a series) well. However, he or she might have trouble with more complex punctuation marks (such as quotation marks, parentheses, and dashes) and with paragraphing, especially on longer pieces.

C. **Capitalizing Correctly:** The writer capitalizes the first word in sentences and most common proper nouns. However, his or her use of more complex capitalization is spotty when it comes to dialogue, abbreviations, and proper names ("*aunt Maria*" instead of "*Aunt Maria*" or "*my aunt*," for instance).

D. **Applying Grammar and Usage:** The writer has made grammar and usage mistakes throughout the piece, but they do not interfere with the reader's ability to understand the message. Issues related to agreement, tense, and word usage appear here and there, but can be easily corrected.

3 DEVELOPING

2 EMERGING

A. **Checking Spelling:** The writer has misspelled many words, even simple ones, which causes the reader to focus on conventions rather than on the central theme or story line.

B. **Punctuating Effectively and Paragraphing Accurately:** The writer has neglected to use punctuation, used punctuation incorrectly, and/or forgotten to indent paragraphs, making it difficult for the reader to find meaning.

C. **Capitalizing Correctly:** The writer uses capitals inconsistently, even in common places such as the first word in the sentence. He or she uses capitals correctly in some places but has no consistent control over them.

D. **Applying Grammar and Usage:** The writer makes frequent mistakes in grammar and usage, making it difficult to read and understand the piece. Issues related to agreement, tense, and word usage abound.

1 RUDIMENTARY

Key Quality Scores

Checking Spelling: 4 ↑

Punctuating Effectively and Paragraphing Accurately: 5

Capitalizing Correctly: 5

Applying Grammar and Usage: 3

Overall Conventions score: 4

Grade 4: "Garibaldi" Presentation Summary

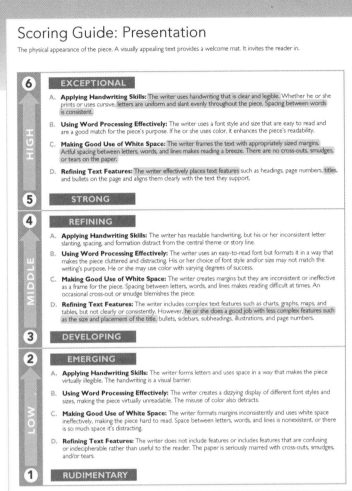

Scoring Guide: Presentation

The physical appearance of the piece. A visually appealing text provides a welcome mat. It invites the reader in.

6 EXCEPTIONAL

HIGH

A. **Applying Handwriting Skills:** The writer uses handwriting that is clear and legible. Whether he or she prints or uses cursive, letters are uniform and slant evenly throughout the piece. Spacing between words is consistent.

B. **Using Word Processing Effectively:** The writer uses a font style and size that are easy to read and are a good match for the piece's purpose. If he or she uses color, it enhances the piece's readability.

C. **Making Good Use of White Space:** The writer frames the text with appropriately sized margins. Artful spacing between letters, words, and lines makes reading a breeze. There are no cross-outs, smudges, or tears on the paper.

D. **Refining Text Features:** The writer effectively places text features such as headings, page numbers, titles, and bullets on the page and aligns them clearly with the text they support.

5 STRONG

4 REFINING

MIDDLE

A. **Applying Handwriting Skills:** The writer has readable handwriting, but his or her inconsistent letter slanting, spacing, and formation distract from the central theme or story line.

B. **Using Word Processing Effectively:** The writer uses an easy-to-read font but formats it in a way that makes the piece cluttered and distracting. His or her choice of font style and/or size may not match the writing's purpose. He or she may use color with varying degrees of success.

C. **Making Good Use of White Space:** The writer creates margins but they are inconsistent or ineffective as a frame for the piece. Spacing between letters, words, and lines makes reading difficult at times. An occasional cross-out or smudge blemishes the piece.

D. **Refining Text Features:** The writer includes complex text features such as charts, graphs, maps, and tables, but not clearly or consistently. However, he or she does a good job with less complex features such as the size and placement of the title, bullets, sidebars, subheadings, illustrations, and page numbers.

3 DEVELOPING

2 EMERGING

LOW

A. **Applying Handwriting Skills:** The writer forms letters and uses space in a way that makes the piece virtually illegible. The handwriting is a visual barrier.

B. **Using Word Processing Effectively:** The writer creates a dizzying display of different font styles and sizes, making the piece virtually unreadable. The misuse of color also detracts.

C. **Making Good Use of White Space:** The writer formats margins inconsistently and uses white space ineffectively, making the piece hard to read. Space between letters, words, and lines is nonexistent, or there is so much space it's distracting.

D. **Refining Text Features:** The writer does not include features or includes features that are confusing or indecipherable rather than useful to the reader. The paper is seriously marred with cross-outs, smudges, and/or tears.

1 RUDIMENTARY

Traits of Writing Scoring Guide for Grades 3–6 © 2010. The Culham Writing Company.

Key Quality Scores

Crafting Well-Built Sentences: 2

Varying Sentence Types: 3

Capturing Smooth and Rhythmic Flow: 3

Breaking the "Rules" to Create Fluency: N/A

Overall Sentence Fluency score: 3

This piece is easy to read. Skipping a line helps the eye focus on the words. Since the letters are so small, it's nice to have uniform white space. The margins are neat and tidy, and the spacing between words and at the end of sentences also contributes to the readability.

Worth Mentioning

Score: 5. This piece is strong in presentation. It does not receive a 6, however, because the writer did not try anything advanced, such as bullets, subheads, graphs, charts, and so on.

Grade 4: "Garibaldi" Paper Wrap-Up

Percentage: 79%   Using the six-point grading chart (24 points earned out of 42)

Ideas	Organization	Voice	Word Choice	Sentence Fluency	Conventions	Presentation
3	3	3	3	3	4	5

Grade 2: "Chameleon!"—All Traits

This young writer has learned a lot about chameleons. She has written an informational piece with multiple sentences that stay on topic. The inclusion of an exclamation point in her title seems to indicate that this may be a topic of interest to her. However, the writing falls short of grabbing or keeping the attention of the reader—not unusual for a young, developing writer. There are many directions our comments can take to help this writer improve.

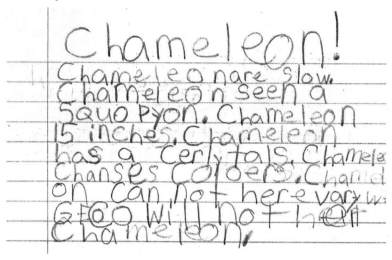

Comments by Trait

Ideas: 2

This writer can tell the reader a lot about chameleons. Sentences stay on topic, which is not always easy for a second grader to do. Although this paper includes some good information and credible details, it's difficult to know what the writer thinks is important. Refining the details will not only paint a better picture in the reader's mind, but will also help to clarify the topic.

Organization: 1

Though this piece gives much information about the topic, it is composed of a string of sentences that could be cut apart and put into any order. There's an old song from the 1960s group the Troggs that goes, "There's no beginning, there'll be no end." That line worked in the song, but it doesn't work when it comes to writing. Helping this writer create a lead that hooks the reader and an ending that ties things up will go a long way toward improving the organization of this piece.

Voice: 1

Sentences that are monotonous and repetitious result in writing that is flat and lifeless. The exclamation point in the title hints that this writer finds chameleons interesting, perhaps even fun. But the passion in this piece stops there. Why do chameleons change colors? Why won't geckos eat chameleons? Answering these questions might be a good way to begin bringing voice into this writing, establishing a tone that adds some of the passion that was hinted at in the title.

Word Choice: 2

Although this writer has used accurate words in describing chameleons, the piece lacks striking words and phrases and strong verbs. Swapping out passive verbs for action verbs will add energy to the piece. Strengthen the energy, and chances are she will also strengthen the voice.

Sentence Fluency: 1 ↑

The good news is, we have some simple sentences and this writer has basic sentence sense! But the beginnings are repetitive, and some sentences are incomplete and choppy. Sentence fluency is the auditory trait, so a good place to start for improvement would be to read this paper aloud to help this writer hear the repetition and choppiness. Starting even a couple of sentences differently and joining others with the word *and* will make this piece more musical to the ear.

Conventions: 2

This is a good example of a paper that's emerging for the trait of conventions. All sentences start with a capital letter and end with a period. That's cause for celebration, for sure, and goes a long way in guiding the reader through the text easily. There are several places to start with conventions, but let's tackle one at a time. Spelling risks have been taken with more-challenging words, but there are others that should be corrected, such as *very* instead of *vary*. Or you might choose to offer a reminder about indenting, the use of capitals where they aren't appropriate, or grammar and usage issues. Choose one. Remember: Writing is a process, and it takes time.

> One day I was sleeping in my room until Bandit came in got his leash, kissed me and woke me up. I wouldn't wake up, But he wanted me up, so he kept kissing me I got up and we went for a walk, we both ran and ran. It was a good day!

Grade 2: "Bandit"—All Traits

Dog owners and dog lovers will want this to receive a high score after reading the first sentence. After all, what dog owner can't relate to their pet smothering them with kisses to persuade them to go for a walk? There's much potential here. Getting this dog owner to really think about Bandit in detail will help him to add that personal stamp. With some revision, this will score well for all the traits.

Comments by Trait

Ideas: 4

This writer has written a short piece with a narrow theme that stays on topic. Adding details to describe Bandit, Bandit's kisses, more about the walk, or what made it a good day would go a long way to further the development of the topic and strengthen the ideas trait.

Organization: 4

A promising lead starts this paper off on a strong note. As the ideas trait is developed, it will also strengthen the body of the piece. The writer is beginning to use transition and sequence words. The piece ends on a familiar note, and exposure to different endings in mentor texts will help this writer go beyond *"It was a good day!"*

Voice: 3

Thinking about what the reader will want to know about Bandit can help this writer's voice emerge. There are hints of voice when the writer talks about Bandit's kisses. Readers who are dog lovers might be waiting for a little bit more that connects them to the writing and brings out a smile . . . but this isn't quite there yet. Letting the reader see more of Bandit's personality will create a connection and add voice to this piece.

Word Choice: 3

This is a classic example of word choice that communicates the basic idea, but the chosen words are rather ordinary and uninspiring. Adding some lively verbs and stretching for better words and phrases (*slathered me with kisses, sprinted around the block*) will not only strengthen the word choice trait but will also bring out the writer's voice.

Sentence Fluency: 4

Read aloud, this piece is easy on the ear. Some sentences are shorter; some are longer and joined by transition words such as *but* and *and*. This writer has moved beyond choppy sentences and is ready to try more complex sentence structure.

Conventions: 2 ↑

With only one spelling error (*wauldn't* for *wouldn't*), this writer has fairly good spelling control in this piece of writing. Some end punctuation and commas are missing, and there are capital letters in places they don't belong. Reading this aloud for the writer might help him focus on the punctuation errors and how to fix them. Once those have been edited, it will be easier for the writer to check for capitals at the beginning of sentences and make sure there are none in the middle (unless they're proper nouns).

Monday my class went on a trail trip. It was really really hot and I was really really really sweaty. There was a really really scary jumpy bridge. The bridge felt like the brige was going to snap. The trail trip was fun, but, sweaty and hot.

Grade 3: "Trail Trip"—All Traits

As is often the case, when you work on one trait or key quality, the others also improve. This paper is a great example of how the addition of details can provide a starting point that will carry revision through all of the traits. Add details, and there will be a way to add sequence and transition words. Those details will most likely add to the voice and word choice, too. More details will make it easier to combine sentences or vary the beginnings. The addition of sequence and transition words will add variety, as well. Some of the added details just might include stretching to use more striking words and phrases, adding to the voice, and providing the opportunity to try spelling more-challenging words and punctuating differently. See how that works?

Comments by Trait

Ideas: 1

Sometimes, if you use a word over and over, the reader might not notice that you really haven't said much. However, it seems there was a bridge on the trail trip that just might provide an opportunity to tell more. Adding details about the bridge will help create a picture for the reader, narrow the topic, and answer questions that the reader has about that "scary jumpy bridge."

Organization: 2

The lead and ending of this piece, while present, could use a boost. Adding details will provide a better opportunity to include sequence and transition words, and will strengthen not only the body but also the lead and ending of the piece. This is a perfect example of how strengthening one trait or key quality also strengthens others.

Voice: 1 ↑

The voice of this writer can be glimpsed when he or she talks about the *"scary jumpy bridge"* that *"felt like the bridge was going to snap."* Tell me more! Developing this part of the writing will add to the overall voice of the writing and create more of a connection to the reader.

Word Choice: 2

Specific words such as *scary*, *jumpy*, and *sweaty* begin to bring this piece to life. The feeling that the bridge might snap also adds energy. Yet these don't go far enough for us to say that this writing is developing where the word choice trait is concerned. The passive voice dominates this writing, and a good first step would be to replace passive verbs with lively verbs to add punch and pizzazz to the writing.

Sentence Fluency: 2

There isn't anything out of the ordinary when it comes to sentence fluency in this story. The text is uneven and would benefit from some carefully placed transition words; the writer could also vary sentence beginnings to change up the repetitive sentence pattern.

Conventions: 3

This writer has not taken risks to show what he or she might be able to do when it comes to conventions. The one spelling error (*brige*) is a word that was previously spelled correctly, indicating that it might have been a careless error. Other words are not stretches that would show what this writer is truly capable of when it comes to spelling. The one place the writer appears to take a risk is in the last sentence, using commas: "*The trail trip was fun, but, sweaty and hot.*" It doesn't quite work. Since this is the one "risk" the writer attempts, a logical next step might be to provide support and guidance in the use of commas by adding to and reworking some of the sentences.

Grade 4: "Trumpt"—All Traits

This piece starts with the potential for more. Voice makes an early appearance, and it certainly makes the reader smile, but things get off-track quickly. This is a good illustration of how important a focused, developed topic with good details is when it comes to creating a well-written piece.

Comments by Trait

Ideas: 2

This writer has something to say but has ended up with a short, undeveloped, confusing piece. Once the topic is more focused (for example, why I want to play the trumpet), then it will be easier to develop the topic using specific details.

Organization: 2

Here is a classic example of a piece with a little bit of this and a little bit of that when it comes to the organization trait. There's a start to this paper, but it doesn't give us much of a clue about what's to come. Some transition and sequence words are included. Then we have the end of the story, which feels like the writer ran out of steam. Once the topic is more developed, it will be easier to jump in and pick a key quality of organization to work on.

Yesersday I ask my mother if I could play the trumpt. But guess (class say what) MY MOTHER SAID "NO", because a trumpt A LOT OF MONEY "O-KAY KA-PES." What will you feel about your parent buying you a trumpt or any other type of insterment while I feel mmmmm mmm mm pretty kind of embrassing because my parent's thank that if I blow a trumpt it will take the air which is the oxygen that is inside your body.

But they changd their mind and got me a trumpt and I am still alive and can breathe.

Voice: 2 ↑

While there is definitely voice in this writing, the scoring guide helps us to see that it's not quite as strong as it might seem at first glance. There are a few moments that catch the reader's attention, but the piece doesn't go beyond that. The writer attempts to create a tone yet falls short. To truly connect with the reader, this writer will need to delve deeper into the topic so that we know what's important or meaningful about it.

Word Choice: 2

Just as with voice, there are a few signs of attempts at word choice, but they just aren't enough—and they're distracting. No matter how good the word choice attempts are, they don't really matter until the message begins to make more sense.

Sentence Fluency: 2

The sentence beginnings may be varied, but the sentences in this piece are flawed and awkward. Part of the problem can be fixed with editing, followed by work on sentence construction. Reading this aloud so that the writer can hear how it sounds is a good place to start.

Conventions: 2

There's a bit of work to be done before this writing is ready for an audience. The conventions are distracting and make scoring, in general, more difficult. Grammar, spelling, and punctuation need work. The use of quotation marks is something that should be celebrated. When used, they are done well!

Grade 5: "Sharks"—All Traits

This writer seems to know the importance of the traits and their role in writing well. This piece has a lot that's working. It's hard not to wonder if the five-paragraph essay format or the large scope of the topic is what made it score lower in ideas and organization.

Comments by Trait

Ideas: 3

This piece includes information about several different types of sharks, but it doesn't focus enough on any one type. Key qualities of the ideas trait will be strengthened if the writer chooses to focus on one type of shark and provides a lot of information about that type.

Organization: 2 ↑

Here's a classic example of the five-paragraph essay format. It starts with a "padded" version of "In this essay I will talk about . . ." includes three supporting paragraphs, and has a fairly predictable ending. Transition words are not used to guide the reader from paragraph to paragraph.

Voice: 3 ↑

> ### Sharks
>
> Sharks are amazing creatures that live under the sea. Some people are frightened by sharks but they really aren't that frightening they just want food. In this essay I will tell you about sharks habitat ,different types of sharks and some useful facts. If you want to know more about sharks you will have to read this essay!
>
> I'm sure you have been dying to know where shark habitats are. Well let me tell you where! Sharks love to hangout around the Great Barrier Reef which is down at the bottom of the deep sandy ocean. There is no doubt about it that the Whale shark loves the deep salty water, that is why they enjoy swimming around hunting for plankton in the deep dark water. Sand sharks are a tad bit shyer than the other sharks and that is why they burrow down under the sand at the bottom of the ocean.
>
> There are so many different types of sharks I can't even talk about t them all. The Great White shark is one of the fiercest sharks. This now takes us to the Whale shark. The whale shark is one of the friendliest sharks. I'll be the first to admit the Tiger shark doesn't kid around when hunting for food. The Sand shark is the calmest out of all sharks.

This writer has clearly tried to establish a tone that hits the mark. He or she knows that exclamation marks can be used to show voice, but overuse can be a distraction. Because the idea is not well developed, it feels like there is a lack of commitment to the writing. The voice isn't completely clear and leaves the reader wondering why this piece was written. My best guess is that it might be tied to an assignment to write a five-paragraph essay on a topic.

Word Choice: 5

Word choice is the strength of this piece. The writer has chosen words that bring the topic to life and paint a picture for the reader. The writing feels accurate and natural.

Sentence Fluency: 4

This is a piece that has some well-written sentences and others that need work. Sentence beginnings are varied, and there is a mix of long and short sentences throughout. This writer is ready to try a bit of rule breaking to create fluency.

Conventions: 4

Not much editing will be needed to get this ready for an audience. Spelling, punctuation, basic capitalization, and grammar show control. More-complex capitalization is inconsistent, however, when it comes to the names of various types of sharks.

The Night

I look out the sliding glass door. There watching the last bit if sunlight sink under the hills was my grandmother. Her familiar knit sweater is wrapped around her.

Quietly, I pull open the door and sit next to her on the cement bench covered with tiny rocks.

I look at the sky and see why my grandmother is out here.

The sky is streaked with bold shades of red, orange, and purple. My grandmother looks at me and smiles.

"Beautiful" she says. I could see that idea on her face before, but I say "yes" anyway.

Little by little, the colors fade until there is nothing left but but faint shadows in the dark sky.

Slowly, tiny stars flicker into view. I start to search for constellations hidden behind the horizon.

I make sure not to close my eyes.

I would much rather be out here with my grandmother than in bed or asleep.

I scan the sky over and over, pretending to be up there with the stars.

The moon appears from behind a cloud, big, smooth, and round. The shimmering light falls silkily across the hills around me.

In a way, this place is like my grandmother. Peaceful, calm, and beautiful in a way that is hard to find.

A light goes off in the house as my grandfather goes to bed. Gradually, two more lights flicker off.

Then it is just me, my grandmother, and the velvety sky dotted with stars.

I glance over at my grandmother's face filled with small lines, more glad to be there with her than anyone else.

I close my eyes and rest my head on the shoulder of her sweater, smelling the familiar smell of sage and juniper that always huvvers around her.

Then, late into the cool night, we sit there, my grandmother smiling at the sky.

Grade 6: "The Night"—All Traits

This writer has paid attention to the night sky! Detailed descriptions will make the reader look twice and spend some time noticing the night sky when evening comes. What a beautiful, touching piece that highlights writing done well. A good writer knows how to engage the reader from beginning to end, making a lasting impression.

Comments by Trait

Ideas: 6

This is a focused piece, capturing with great detail a night spent with the writer's grandmother. The story is memorable, and the writer's strong word choices combined with specific details paint the picture of this night in the reader's mind.

Organization: 6

From beginning to end, this writing flows. It brings the reader in, guides us through with the use of transition and sequence words, and wraps the night up in a satisfying way. The organization works beautifully.

Voice: 6

The tone of this piece is thoughtful and compelling. This writing can be described just as the writer describes the grandmother: peaceful, calm, and beautiful. The writer has made a connection to the reader by sharing her feelings about one night with her grandmother.

Word Choice: 6

Filled with finely honed words and phrases, this piece shows us writing from the heart. The writer has chosen strong verbs and precise words that capture the reader's imagination and deepen the meaning, from start to finish. You can almost smell the sage and juniper that "huvvers" around the grandmother's sweater.

Sentence Fluency: 5

This piece sounds beautiful when read aloud. It has a musical quality to it—a result of the use of longer and shorter sentences. This writer is ready to try her hand at using some sentence fragments to add even more to the fluency.

Conventions: 4 ↑

As might be expected, this writer has a good handle on most conventions. Spelling, capitalization, and grammar show good control. She needs to work on punctuation (mostly commas) and paragraphing, but the piece is easy to read.

Appendix B
Reproducible Tools

Scoring Guide: Ideas

The piece's content—its central message and details that support that message.

6 EXCEPTIONAL

HIGH

A. Finding a Topic: The writer offers a clear, central theme or a simple, original story line that is memorable.

B. Focusing the Topic: The writer narrows the theme or story line to create a piece that is clear, tight, and manageable.

C. Developing the Topic: The writer provides enough critical evidence to support the theme and shows insight on the topic. Or he or she tells the story in a fresh way through an original, unpredictable plot.

D. Using Details: The writer offers credible, accurate details that create pictures in the reader's mind, from the beginning of the piece to the end. Those details provide the reader with evidence of the writer's knowledge about and/or experience with the topic.

5 STRONG

4 REFINING

MIDDLE

A. Finding a Topic: The writer offers a recognizable but broad theme or story line. He or she stays on topic, but in a predictable way.

B. Focusing the Topic: The writer needs to crystallize his or her topic around the central theme or story line. He or she does not focus on a specific aspect of the topic.

C. Developing the Topic: The writer draws on personal knowledge and experience, but does not offer a unique perspective. He or she does not probe deeply, but instead gives the reader only a glimpse at aspects of the topic.

D. Using Details: The writer offers details, but they do not always hit the mark because they are inaccurate or irrelevant. He or she does not create a picture in the reader's mind because key questions about the central theme or story line have not been addressed.

3 DEVELOPING

2 EMERGING

LOW

A. Finding a Topic: The writer has not settled on a topic and, therefore, may offer only a series of unfocused, repetitious, and/or random thoughts.

B. Focusing the Topic: The writer has not narrowed his or her topic in a meaningful way. It's hard to tell what the writer thinks is important since he or she devotes equal importance to each piece of information.

C. Developing the Topic: The writer has created a piece that is so short the reader cannot fully understand or appreciate what he or she wants to say. He or she may have simply restated an assigned topic or responded to a prompt without devoting much thought or effort to it.

D. Using Details: The writer has clearly devoted little attention to details. The writing contains limited or completely inaccurate information. After reading the piece, the reader is left with many unanswered questions.

1 RUDIMENTARY

Scoring Guide: Organization

The internal structure of the piece—the thread of logic, the pattern of meaning.

6 **EXCEPTIONAL**

HIGH

A. Creating the Lead: The writer grabs the reader's attention from the start and leads him or her into the piece naturally. He or she entices the reader, providing a tantalizing glimpse of what is to come.

B. Using Sequence Words and Transition Words: The writer includes a variety of carefully selected sequence words (such as *later*, *then*, and *meanwhile*) and transition words (such as *however*, *also*, and *clearly*), which are placed wisely to guide the reader through the piece by showing how ideas progress, relate, and/or diverge.

C. Structuring the Body: The writer creates a piece that is easy to follow by fitting details together logically. He or she slows down to spotlight important points or events, and speeds up when he or she needs to move the reader along.

D. Ending With a Sense of Resolution: The writer sums up his or her thinking in a natural, thoughtful, and convincing way. He or she anticipates and answers any lingering questions the reader may have, providing a strong sense of closure.

5 **STRONG**

4 **REFINING**

MIDDLE

A. Creating the Lead: The writer presents an introduction, although it may not be original or thought-provoking. Instead, it may be a simple restatement of the topic and, therefore, does not create a sense of anticipation about what is to come.

B. Using Sequence Words and Transition Words: The writer uses sequence words to show the logical order of details, but they feel obvious or canned. The use of transition words is spotty and rarely creates coherence.

C. Structuring the Body: The writer sequences events and important points logically, for the most part. However, the reader may wish to move a few things around to create a more sensible flow. He or she may also feel the urge to speed up or slow down for more satisfying pacing.

D. Ending With a Sense of Resolution: The writer ends the piece on a familiar note: "Thank you for reading…," "Now you know all about…," or "They lived happily ever after." He or she needs to tie up loose ends to leave the reader with a sense of satisfaction or closure.

3 **DEVELOPING**

2 **EMERGING**

LOW

A. Creating the Lead: The writer does not give the reader any clue about what is to come. The opening point feels as if it were chosen randomly.

B. Using Sequence Words and Transition Words: The writer does not provide sequence and/or transition words between sections or provides words that are so confusing the reader is unable to sort one section from another.

C. Structuring the Body: The writer does not show clearly what comes first, next, and last, making it difficult to understand how sections fit together. The writer slows down when he or she should speed up, and speeds up when he or she should slow down.

D. Ending With a Sense of Resolution: The writer ends the piece with no conclusion at all—or nothing more than "The End" or something equally bland. There is no sense of resolution, no sense of completion.

1 **RUDIMENTARY**

Scoring Guide: Voice

The tone and tenor of the piece—the personal stamp of the writer, which is achieved through a strong understanding of purpose and audience.

6 **EXCEPTIONAL**

A. **Establishing a Tone:** The writer cares about the topic, and it shows. The writing is expressive and compelling. The reader feels the writer's conviction, authority, and integrity.

B. **Conveying the Purpose:** The writer makes clear his or her reason for creating the piece. He or she offers a point of view that is appropriate for the mode (narrative, expository, or persuasive), which compels the reader to read on.

C. **Creating a Connection to the Audience:** The writer speaks in a way that makes the reader want to listen. He or she has considered what the reader needs to know and the best way to convey it by sharing his or her fascination, feelings, and opinions about the topic.

D. **Taking Risks to Create Voice:** The writer expresses ideas in new ways, which makes the piece interesting and original. The writing sounds like the writer because of his or her use of distinctive, just-right words and phrases.

5 **STRONG**

4 **REFINING**

A. **Establishing a Tone:** The writer has established a tone that can be described as "pleasing" or "sincere," but not "passionate" or "compelling." He or she attempts to create a tone that hits the mark, but the overall result feels generic.

B. **Conveying the Purpose:** The writer has chosen a voice for the piece that is not completely clear. There are only a few moments when the reader understands where the writer is coming from and why he or she wrote the piece.

C. **Creating a Connection to the Audience:** The writer keeps the reader at a distance. The connection between reader and writer is tenuous because the writer reveals little about what is important or meaningful about the topic.

D. **Taking Risks to Create Voice:** The writer creates a few moments that catch the reader's attention, but only a few. The piece sounds like anyone could have written it. It lacks the energy, commitment, and conviction that would distinguish it from other pieces on the same topic.

3 **DEVELOPING**

2 **EMERGING**

A. **Establishing a Tone:** The writer has produced a lifeless piece—one that is monotonous, mechanical, repetitious, and/or off-putting to the reader.

B. **Conveying the Purpose:** The writer chose the topic for mysterious reasons. The piece may be filled with random thoughts, technical jargon, or inappropriate vocabulary, making it impossible to discern how the writer feels about the topic.

C. **Creating a Connection to the Audience:** The writer provides no evidence that he or she has considered what the reader might need to know to connect with the topic. Or there is an obvious mismatch between the piece's tone and the intended audience.

D. **Taking Risks to Create Voice:** The writer creates no highs and lows. The piece is flat and lifeless, causing the reader to wonder why he or she wrote it in the first place. The writer's voice does not pop out, even for a moment.

1 **RUDIMENTARY**

HIGH

MIDDLE

LOW

Scoring Guide: Word Choice

The specific vocabulary the writer uses to convey meaning and enlighten the reader.

6 **EXCEPTIONAL**

HIGH

A. **Applying Strong Verbs:** The writer uses many "action words," giving the piece punch and pizzazz. He or she has stretched to find lively verbs that add energy to the piece.

B. **Selecting Striking Words and Phrases:** The writer uses many finely honed words and phrases. His or her creative and effective use of literary techniques such as alliteration, simile, and metaphor makes the piece a pleasure to read.

C. **Using Specific and Accurate Words:** The writer uses words with precision. He or she selects words the reader needs to fully understand the message. The writer chooses nouns, adjectives, adverbs, and so forth that create clarity and bring the topic to life.

D. **Choosing Words That Deepen Meaning:** The writer uses words to capture the reader's imagination and enhance the piece's meaning. There is a deliberate attempt to choose the best word over the first word that comes to mind.

5 **STRONG**

4 **REFINING**

MIDDLE

A. **Applying Strong Verbs:** The writer uses the passive voice quite a bit and includes few "action words" to give the piece energy.

B. **Selecting Striking Words and Phrases:** The writer provides little evidence that he or she has stretched for the best words or phrases. He or she may have attempted to use literary techniques, but they are clichés for the most part.

C. **Using Specific and Accurate Words:** The writer presents specific and accurate words, except for those related to sophisticated and/or content-related topics. Technical or irrelevant jargon is off-putting to the reader. The words rarely capture the reader's imagination.

D. **Choosing Words That Deepen Meaning:** The writer fills the piece with unoriginal language rather than language that results from careful revision. The words communicate the basic idea, but they are ordinary and uninspired.

3 **DEVELOPING**

2 **EMERGING**

LOW

A. **Applying Strong Verbs:** The writer makes no attempt at selecting verbs with energy. The passive voice dominates the piece.

B. **Selecting Striking Words and Phrases:** The writer uses words that are repetitive, vague, and/or unimaginative. Limited meaning comes through because the words are so lifeless.

C. **Using Specific and Accurate Words:** The writer misuses words, making it difficult to understand what he or she is attempting to convey. Or he or she uses words that are so technical, inappropriate, or irrelevant that the average reader can hardly understand what he or she is saying.

D. **Choosing Words That Deepen Meaning:** The writer uses many words and phrases that simply do not work. Little meaning comes through because the language is so imprecise and distracting.

1 **RUDIMENTARY**

Scoring Guide: Sentence Fluency

The way words and phrases flow through the piece. It is the auditory trait because it's "read" with the ear as much as the eye.

6

EXCEPTIONAL

A. **Crafting Well-Built Sentences:** The writer carefully and creatively constructs sentences for maximum impact. Transition words such as *but*, *and*, and *so* are used successfully to join sentences and sentence parts.

B. **Varying Sentence Types:** The writer uses various types of sentences (simple, compound, and/or complex) to enhance the central theme or story line. The piece is made up of an effective mix of long, complex sentences and short, simple ones.

C. **Capturing Smooth and Rhythmic Flow:** The writer thinks about how the sentences sound. He or she uses phrasing that is almost musical. If the piece were read aloud, it would be easy on the ear.

D. **Breaking the "Rules" to Create Fluency:** The writer diverges from standard English to create interest and impact. For example, he or she may use a sentence fragment, such as "All alone in the forest," or a single word, such as "Bam!" to accent a particular moment or action. He or she might begin with informal words such as *well*, *and*, or *but* to create a conversational tone, or he or she might break rules intentionally to make dialogue sound authentic.

5

STRONG

4

REFINING

A. **Crafting Well-Built Sentences:** The writer offers simple sentences that are sound but no long, complex ones. He or she attempts to vary the beginnings and lengths of sentences.

B. **Varying Sentence Types:** The writer exhibits basic sentence sense and offers some sentence variety. He or she attempts to use different types of sentences, but in doing so creates an uneven flow rather than a smooth, seamless one.

C. **Capturing Smooth and Rhythmic Flow:** The writer has produced a text that is uneven. Many sentences read smoothly, whereas others are choppy or awkward.

D. **Breaking the "Rules" to Create Fluency:** The writer includes fragments, but they seem more accidental than intentional. He or she uses informal words such as *well*, *and*, and *but* inappropriately to start sentences, and pays little attention to making dialogue sound authentic.

3

DEVELOPING

2

EMERGING

A. **Crafting Well-Built Sentences:** The writer's sentences, even simple ones, are often flawed. Sentence beginnings are repetitive and uninspired.

B. **Varying Sentence Types:** The writer uses a single, repetitive sentence pattern throughout or connects sentence parts with an endless string of transition words such as *and*, *but*, *or*, and *because*, which distracts the reader.

C. **Capturing Smooth and Rhythmic Flow:** The writer has created a text that is a challenge to read aloud since the sentences are incomplete, choppy, stilted, rambling, and/or awkward.

D. **Breaking the "Rules" to Create Fluency:** The writer offers few or no simple, well-built sentences, making it impossible to determine whether he or she has done anything out of the ordinary. Global revision is necessary before sentences can be revised for stylistic and creative purposes.

1

RUDIMENTARY

HIGH · **MIDDLE** · **LOW**

Scoring Guide: Conventions

The mechanical correctness of the piece. Correct use of conventions (spelling, capitalization, punctuation, paragraphing, and grammar and usage) guides the reader through the text easily.

6 — EXCEPTIONAL (HIGH)

A. **Checking Spelling:** The writer spells sight words, high-frequency words, and less familiar words correctly. When he or she spells less familiar words incorrectly, those words are phonetically correct. Overall, the piece reveals control in spelling.

B. **Punctuating Effectively and Paragraphing Accurately:** The writer handles basic punctuation skillfully. He or she understands how to use periods, commas, question marks, and exclamation points to enhance clarity and meaning. Paragraphs are indented in the right places. The piece is ready for a general audience.

C. **Capitalizing Correctly:** The writer uses capital letters consistently and accurately. A deep understanding of how to capitalize dialogue, abbreviations, proper names, and titles is evident.

D. **Applying Grammar and Usage:** The writer forms grammatically correct phrases and sentences. He or she shows care in applying the rules of standard English. The writer may break from those rules for stylistic reasons, but otherwise abides by them.

5 — STRONG

4 — REFINING (MIDDLE)

A. **Checking Spelling:** The writer incorrectly spells a few high-frequency words and many unfamiliar words and/or sophisticated words.

B. **Punctuating Effectively and Paragraphing Accurately:** The writer handles basic punctuation marks (such as end marks on sentences and commas in a series) well. However, he or she might have trouble with more complex punctuation marks (such as quotation marks, parentheses, and dashes) and with paragraphing, especially on longer pieces.

C. **Capitalizing Correctly:** The writer capitalizes the first word in sentences and most common proper nouns. However, his or her use of more complex capitalization is spotty when it comes to dialogue, abbreviations, and proper names ("*aunt Maria*" instead of "*Aunt Maria*" or "*my aunt*," for instance).

D. **Applying Grammar and Usage:** The writer has made grammar and usage mistakes throughout the piece, but they do not interfere with the reader's ability to understand the message. Issues related to agreement, tense, and word usage appear here and there, but can be easily corrected.

3 — DEVELOPING

2 — EMERGING (LOW)

A. **Checking Spelling:** The writer has misspelled many words, even simple ones, which causes the reader to focus on conventions rather than on the central theme or story line.

B. **Punctuating Effectively and Paragraphing Accurately:** The writer has neglected to use punctuation, used punctuation incorrectly, and/or forgotten to indent paragraphs, making it difficult for the reader to find meaning.

C. **Capitalizing Correctly:** The writer uses capitals inconsistently, even in common places such as the first word in the sentence. He or she uses capitals correctly in some places but has no consistent control over them.

D. **Applying Grammar and Usage:** The writer makes frequent mistakes in grammar and usage, making it difficult to read and understand the piece. Issues related to agreement, tense, and word usage abound.

1 — RUDIMENTARY

Scoring Guide: Presentation

The physical appearance of the piece. A visually appealing text provides a welcome mat. It invites the reader in.

6 **EXCEPTIONAL**

HIGH

A. **Applying Handwriting Skills:** The writer uses handwriting that is clear and legible. Whether he or she prints or uses cursive, letters are uniform and slant evenly throughout the piece. Spacing between words is consistent.

B. **Using Word Processing Effectively:** The writer uses a font style and size that are easy to read and are a good match for the piece's purpose. If he or she uses color, it enhances the piece's readability.

C. **Making Good Use of White Space:** The writer frames the text with appropriately sized margins. Artful spacing between letters, words, and lines makes reading a breeze. There are no cross-outs, smudges, or tears on the paper.

D. **Refining Text Features:** The writer effectively places text features such as headings, page numbers, titles, and bullets on the page and aligns them clearly with the text they support.

5 **STRONG**

4 **REFINING**

MIDDLE

A. **Applying Handwriting Skills:** The writer has readable handwriting, but his or her inconsistent letter slanting, spacing, and formation distract from the central theme or story line.

B. **Using Word Processing Effectively:** The writer uses an easy-to-read font but formats it in a way that makes the piece cluttered and distracting. His or her choice of font style and/or size may not match the writing's purpose. He or she may use color with varying degrees of success.

C. **Making Good Use of White Space:** The writer creates margins but they are inconsistent or ineffective as a frame for the piece. Spacing between letters, words, and lines makes reading difficult at times. An occasional cross-out or smudge blemishes the piece.

D. **Refining Text Features:** The writer includes complex text features such as charts, graphs, maps, and tables, but not clearly or consistently. However, he or she does a good job with less complex features such as the size and placement of the title, bullets, sidebars, subheadings, illustrations, and page numbers.

3 **DEVELOPING**

2 **EMERGING**

LOW

A. **Applying Handwriting Skills:** The writer forms letters and uses space in a way that makes the piece virtually illegible. The handwriting is a visual barrier.

B. **Using Word Processing Effectively:** The writer creates a dizzying display of different font styles and sizes, making the piece virtually unreadable. The misuse of color also detracts.

C. **Making Good Use of White Space:** The writer formats margins inconsistently and uses white space ineffectively, making the piece hard to read. Space between letters, words, and lines is nonexistent, or there is so much space it's distracting.

D. **Refining Text Features:** The writer does not include features or includes features that are confusing or indecipherable rather than useful to the reader. The paper is seriously marred with cross-outs, smudges, and/or tears.

1 **RUDIMENTARY**

The 6pt. Grading Chart

Grading Chart: Points to Percentages

Number of Traits Scored

Grade	Total Points	7	6	5	4	3	2	1
	1							60.00%
	2						60.00%	68.00%
	3					60.00%	64.00%	76.00%
	4				60.00%	62.67%	68.00%	84.00%
	5			60.00%	62.00%	65.33%	72.00%	92.00%
Grade	6		60.00%	61.60%	64.00%	68.00%	76.00%	100.00%
	7	60.00%	61.33%	63.20%	66.00%	70.67%	80.00%	
	8	61.14%	62.67%	64.80%	68.00%	73.33%	84.00%	
	9	62.29%	64.00%	66.40%	70.00%	76.00%	88.00%	
F	10	63.43%	65.33%	68.00%	72.00%	78.67%	92.00%	
	11	64.57%	66.67%	69.60%	74.00%	81.33%	96.00%	
	12	65.71%	68.00%	71.20%	76.00%	84.00%	100.00%	
	13	66.86%	69.33%	72.80%	78.00%	86.67%		
	14	68.00%	70.67%	74.40%	80.00%	89.33%		
	15	69.14%	72.00%	76.00%	82.00%	92.00%		
	16	70.29%	73.33%	77.60%	84.00%	94.67%		
D	17	71.43%	74.67%	79.20%	86.00%	97.33%		
	18	72.57%	76.00%	80.80%	88.00%	100.00%		
	19	73.71%	77.33%	82.40%	90.00%			
	20	74.86%	78.67%	84.00%	92.00%			
	21	76.00%	80.00%	85.60%	94.00%			
	22	77.14%	81.33%	87.20%	96.00%			
	23	78.29%	82.67%	88.80%	98.00%			
C	24	79.43%	84.00%	90.40%	100.00%			
	25	80.57%	85.33%	92.00%				
	26	81.71%	86.67%	93.60%				
	27	82.86%	88.00%	95.20%				
	28	84.00%	89.33%	96.80%				
	29	85.14%	90.67%	98.40%				
	30	86.29%	92.00%	100.00%				
B	31	87.43%	93.33%					
	32	88.57%	94.67%					
	33	89.71%	96.00%					
	34	90.86%	97.33%					
	35	92.00%	98.67%					
	36	93.14%	100.00%					
	37	94.29%						
A	38	95.43%						
	39	96.57%						
	40	97.71%						
	41	98.86%						
A+	42	100.00%						

Scoring Guide: Narrative Writing

Narrative writing re-creates a real or imagined experience. It usually contains four elements: characters, a setting, a chronological sequence of events, and a conflict or problem to be solved. The writer typically builds in high points by putting characters into interesting situations, weaving in plot twists, incorporating vivid details, and creating a central conflict or problem that builds suspense and holds the piece together.

 6

Exceptional

- Starts with a lead that sets up the story and draws in the reader.
- Contains characters that are believable, fresh, and well described. The characters grow and learn.
- Describes a setting that is unique and rich.
- Features events that are logically sequenced and move the story forward. Time and place work in harmony.
- Is a complete story that has never been told or is an original twist on a familiar story. The plot is well developed. There is a key conflict or problem that is compelling and eventually solved.
- Features well-used literary techniques, such as foreshadowing and symbolism.
- Leaves the reader feeling intrigued, delighted, surprised, entertained, and/or informed.
- Ends satisfyingly because the key conflict or problem is solved thoughtfully and credibly.

HIGH

 5 ### Strong

 4

Refining

- Starts with a lead that sets the scene, but is predictable or unoriginal.
- Contains characters that are a bit too familiar. The characters show little change in their thinking or understanding as the story moves along.
- Offers a setting that is not described all that well.
- Features events that are given the same level of importance. Significant ones mingle with trivial ones, and sometimes stray from the main story line.
- Is a nearly complete story that may not contain new or original thinking. The plot moves forward, but then stumbles. Minor conflicts and problems distract from major ones.
- Contains examples of literary techniques such as foreshadowing and symbolism that are not all that effective.
- Leaves the reader engaged at some points, detached at others.
- Ends by providing the reader with a sense of resolution, but he or she may also feel unsatisfied or perplexed.

MIDDLE

 3 ### Developing

 2

Emerging

- Starts with a lead that is perfunctory: "I'm going to tell you about the time…"
- Contains characters that don't feel real. The unconvincing characters are stereotypes or cardboard cutouts.
- Offers a setting that is not at all described clearly and/or completely.
- Features simple, incomplete events that don't relate to one another and/or add up to anything much. There is a mismatch between the time and place.
- Is a story that jumps around illogically. There is no clear conflict or problem to be solved.
- Contains no examples of literary techniques—or, at most, poor, purposeless ones
- Leaves the reader frustrated and/or disappointed. He or she feels the story was not thought out before it was committed to paper.
- Finishes with no clear ending or, at most, a halfhearted attempt at an ending, leaving the reader wondering why he or she bothered to read the piece.

LOW

1 ### Rudimentary

Scoring Guide: Expository/Informational

The primary purpose for expository writing is to inform or explain, using reliable and accurate information. Although usually associated with the research report or traditional essay, expository writing needn't always contain "just the facts." The writer might include personal experiences, details from his or her life, to enliven the piece. Strong expository writing has an authoritative, knowledgeable, and confident voice that adds credibility.

6 **exceptional**

HIGH

- Delves into what really matters about the topic.
- Offers an insider's perspective.
- Provides unexpected or surprising details that go beyond the obvious.
- Is focused, coherent, and well organized.
- Invites the reader to analyze and synthesize details to draw his or her own conclusions.
- Is bursting with fascinating, original facts that are accurate and, when appropriate, linked to a primary source.
- Contains anecdotes that bring the topic to life.
- Anticipates and answers the reader's questions.
- Stays on point and contains a compelling voice until the end.

5 **Strong**

4 **refining**

MIDDLE

- Provides an overview of the topic and only a few key facts.
- Offers the perspective of an outsider looking in.
- Lacks fresh thinking or surprises. Relies too heavily on common knowledge. Provides mostly mundane, predictable details about the topic.
- Is relatively focused, coherent, and organized. Generally stays on topic.
- Contains focused descriptions, but also fuzzy ones. The writer doesn't consistently connect the dots.
- Includes facts that are somewhat suspicious and not linked to primary sources.
- Features few, if any, anecdotes to bring the topic to life
- Does not anticipate the reader's questions.
- Speaks in a spotty voice—commanding one moment, cautious the next.

3 **developing**

2 **emerging**

LOW

- Misses the main point completely. The writer's purpose is not clear.
- Offers a complete outsider's perspective.
- Contains details that are completely unrelated to the main topic.
- Is unfocused, incoherent, and poorly organized.
- Makes sweeping statements. Nothing new is shared.
- Lacks fascinating, original facts. Any facts the piece does contain are seemingly inaccurate or unsupported.
- Contains no anecdotes to bring the topic to life.
- Does not anticipate the reader's questions. In fact, the piece contains no evidence that the writer has thought about audience at all.
- Requires energy to read from beginning to end.

1 **rudimentary**

Scoring Guide: Persuasive—Opinion/Argument

Persuasive writing contains a strong argument based on solid information that convinces the reader to embrace the writer's point of view. Sometimes persuasive writing is a call to action, such as a donation solicitation from a charitable organization. Other times, it's an attempt to change attitudes, such as an op-ed piece in your local newspaper. Regardless of the format, the writing needs to be clear, compelling, and well supported. The writer should not waver in his or her position.

 exceptional

- Influences the reader's thinking through sound reasoning and a compelling argument.
- Contains opinions are that well supported by facts and personal experiences. Differences between opinion, facts, and personal experiences are clear.
- Takes a position that is defensible and logical.
- Exposes weaknesses of other positions.
- Avoids generalities and exaggerations.
- Includes many moments of sound reasoning and judgment.
- Reveals only the best evidence to make the strongest statement possible.
- Connects to a larger "truth."

HIGH

 Strong

 refining

- Raises questions for the reader, but may fail to persuade him or her because the thinking is superficial and only hints at something deep.
- Mixes opinions, facts, and personal experiences. The piece relies on emotion more than truth. Data may be present, but not used to full effect.
- Contains an argument that starts out strong, but fades. Offers few new insights into the topic.
- Attempts to expose holes in other opinions, with mixed results.
- Features generalities or exaggerations, but also concrete information and clear examples.
- Includes a few moments of sound reasoning and judgment.
- Contains some evidence that hits the mark and some that veers off course.
- Waffles. Many statements are plausible while others are far-fetched, leaving the reader unconvinced.

MIDDLE

 developing

emerging

- Does not influence the reader. The writer's thinking and reasoning is vulnerable to attack.
- Abounds with opinions that are not supported by facts or personal experiences.
- Takes a position that is not clear or not credible. The argument is illogical or implausible.
- Ignores the opposing side of the argument.
- Offers only generalities and exaggerations—no hard facts that could sway the reader.
- Includes no moments of sound reasoning and judgment.
- Lacks the evidence necessary for the reader to take a stand.
- Does not question or does not probe. The piece misses the target.

LOW

 rudimentary

Think About FOR WRITING PROCESS

Think About Prewriting:

- Did I think through my topic?
- Did I plan the best way to organize my ideas?
- Did I consider the right voice for my audience?
- Did I read and gather information from lots of sources?

Think About Drafting:

- Did I check my prewriting ideas as I started to write?
- Did I let my ideas flow, knowing I can revise and edit later?
- Did I consider what the reader needs to know?
- Did I attempt a beginning, middle, and end that make sense?

Think About Revising:

- Did I focus the topic and use accurate and original details?
- Did I fit all the parts together logically from beginning to end?
- Did I add energy by showing how I think and feel?
- Did I use words and sentences that are precise, fresh, and varied?

Think About Editing:

- Did I correct any misspelled words?
- Did I use punctuation and paragraphing to make my ideas flow?
- Did I capitalize the right words?
- Did I follow the rules of standard English grammar and usage?

Think About Finishing/Publishing:

- Did I apply handwriting skills?
- Did I use word processing effectively?
- Did I make good use of white space?
- Did I add text features that help the reader through the text?

Think About KEY QUALITY **IDEAS**

Think About Finding a Topic

- Have I chosen a topic that I really like?
- Do I have something new to say about this topic?
- Am I writing about what I know and care about?
- Have I gathered enough information about it so that I'm ready to write?

Think About Focusing the Topic

- Have I zeroed in on one small part of a bigger idea?
- Can I sum up my idea in a simple sentence?
- Have I chosen the information that best captures my idea?
- Have I thought deeply about what the reader will need to know?

Think About Developing the Topic

- Am I sure my information is right?
- Have I thought about what the reader needs to know to understand this idea?
- Do my ideas offer a new way of thinking about this topic?
- Have I included enough information to be credible?

Think About Using Details

- Did I create a picture in the reader's mind?
- Did I use details that draw upon the five senses? (sight, touch, taste, smell, hearing)
- Do my details stay on the main topic?
- Did I stretch for details beyond the obvious?

Think About KEY QUALITY ORGANIZATION

Think About Creating the Lead

- Did I give the reader something interesting to think about right from the start?
- Will the reader want to keep reading?
- Have I tried to get the reader's attention?
- Did I let the reader know what is coming?

Think About Using Sequence Words and Transition Words

- Have I used sequence words such as *later, then,* and *meanwhile*?
- Did I use a variety of transition words such as *however, because, also,* and *for instance*?
- Have I shown how ideas connect from sentence to sentence?
- Does my organization make sense from paragraph to paragraph?

Think About Structuring the Body

- Have I shown the reader where to slow down and where to speed up?
- Do all the details fit where they are placed?
- Will the reader find it easy to follow my ideas?
- Does the organization help the main idea stand out?

Think About Ending with a Sense of Resolution

- Have I wrapped up all the loose ends?
- Have I ended at the best place?
- Do I have an ending that makes my writing feel finished?
- Did I leave the reader with something important to think about?

Think About KEY QUALITY VOICE

Think About Establishing a Tone
- Can I name the primary feeling of my writing (e.g., happy, frustrated, knowledgeable, scared, convincing)?
- Have I varied the tone from the beginning to the end?
- Have I used expressive language?
- Did I show that I care about this topic?

Think About Conveying the Purpose
- Is the purpose of my writing clear?
- Does my point of view come through?
- Is this the right tone for this kind of writing?
- Have I used strong voice throughout this piece?

Think About Creating a Connection to the Audience
- Have I thought about the reader?
- Is this the right voice for the audience?
- Have I shown what matters most to me in this piece?
- Will the reader know how I think and feel about the topic?

Think About Taking Risks to Create Voice
- Have I used words that are not ordinary?
- Is my writing interesting, fresh, and original?
- Have I tried to make my writing sound like me?
- Have I tried something different from what I've done before?

Think About KEY QUALITY **WORD CHOICE**

Think About Applying Strong Verbs

- Have I used action words?
- Did I stretch to use a more specific word—for example, *scurry* rather than *run*?
- Do my verbs give my writing punch and pizzazz?
- Did I avoid *is, am, are, was, were, be, being,* and *been* wherever I could?

Think About Selecting Striking Words and Phrases

- Did I try to use words that sound just right?
- Did I try hyphenating several shorter words to make an interesting-sounding new word?
- Did I try putting words that have the same sound together?
- Did I read my piece aloud to find at least one or two moments I love?

Think About Using Specific and Accurate Words

- Have I used nouns and modifiers that help the reader see a picture?
- Do I avoid using words that might confuse the reader?
- Did I try a new word and, if so, check to make sure I used it correctly?
- Are these the best words that can be used?

Think About Choosing Words That Deepen Meaning

- Did I choose words that show I really thought about them?
- Have I tried to use words without repeating myself?
- Do my words capture the reader's imagination?
- Have I found the best way to express myself?

Think About KEY QUALITY SENTENCE FLUENCY

Think About Crafting Well-Built Sentences

- Do my sentences begin in different ways?
- Are my sentences different lengths?
- Are my sentences grammatically correct unless constructed creatively for impact?
- Have I used conjunctions such as *and, but*, and *or* to connect parts of sentences?

Think About Varying Sentence Types

- Do I use different kinds of sentences?
- Are some of my sentences complex?
- Are some of my sentences simple?
- Did I intermingle sentence types from one to the next?

Think About Capturing Smooth and Rhythmic Flow

- Is it easy to read the entire piece aloud?
- Do my sentences flow from one to the next?
- Do individual passages sound smooth when I read them aloud?
- Did I thoughtfully use different sentence types to enhance the main idea?

Think About Breaking the "Rules" to Create Fluency

- Did I use fragments with style and purpose?
- Did I begin a sentence informally to create a conversational tone?
- Does my dialogue sound authentic?
- Did I try weaving in exclamations and single words to add emphasis?

Think About KEY QUALITY CONVENTIONS

Think About Checking Spelling

- Have I used standard English spelling, unless I chose not to for a good reason?
- Have I checked words that don't look right to me?
- Have I used the resources in the room (e.g., charts, word walls, word lists) to help with spelling?
- Have I checked my work for words I have trouble spelling?

Think About Punctuating Effectively

- Did I place quotation marks around dialogue and direct quotes?
- Did I punctuate complex sentences correctly?
- Did I use apostrophes to show possessives and contractions?
- Did I begin new paragraphs in the appropriate places?

Think About Capitalizing Correctly

- Did I capitalize proper nouns for people, places, and things?
- Did I capitalize dialogue correctly?
- Did I capitalize abbreviations, acronyms, and people's titles correctly?
- Did I capitalize the title and/or other headings?

Think About Applying Grammar and Usage

- Did I use special words such as homophones, synonyms, and antonyms correctly?
- Did I check my sentences for subject-verb agreement?
- Did I use verb tense (past, present, future) consistently throughout my piece?
- Did I make sure pronouns and their antecedents (the word they stand for) agree?

Think About KEY QUALITY PRESENTATION

Think About Applying Handwriting Skills

- Is my handwriting neat and legible?
- Did I take time to form each letter clearly?
- Do my letters slant evenly throughout?
- Did I leave space between words to enhance readability?

Think About Using Word Processing Effectively

- Is my choice of font easy to read and appropriate for the audience?
- Is the font size appropriate?
- Did I use formatting such as boldfacing, underlining, and italicizing effectively?
- Does color enhance the look and feel of my piece, or does it weaken them?

Think About Making Good Use of White Space

- Do my margins frame the text evenly on all four sides?
- Did I leave enough white space between letters, words, and lines to make the piece easy to read?
- Did I avoid cross-outs, smudges, and tears?
- Did I create a nice balance of text, text features, illustrations, photographs, and white space?

Think About Refining Text Features

- Do my illustrations and photographs help to make the piece easy to understand?
- Did I include my name, date, title, page numbers, and other headers and footers?
- Are text features such as bulleted lists, sidebars, and time lines clear, well positioned, and effective in guiding the reader and enhancing meaning?
- Are charts, graphs, and tables easy to read and understand?

Student-Friendly Scoring Guide
Ideas

6

I've Got It!

❋ I picked a topic and stuck with it.

❋ My topic is small enough to handle.

❋ I know a lot about this topic.

❋ My topic is bursting with fascinating details.

5

4

On My Way

❋ I've wandered off my main topic in a few places.

❋ My topic might be a little too big to handle.

❋ I know enough about my topic to get started.

❋ Some of my details are too general.

3

2

Just Starting

❋ I have included several ideas that might make a good topic.

❋ No one idea stands out as most important.

❋ I'm still looking for a topic that will work well.

❋ My details are fuzzy or not clear.

1

Student-Friendly Scoring Guide
Organization

I've Got It!

❋ I included a bold beginning.

❋ I've shown how the ideas connect.

❋ My ideas are in an order that really works.

❋ My ending leaves you with something to think about.

On My Way

❋ There is a beginning, but it's not particularly special.

❋ Most of my details fit logically; I could move or get rid of others.

❋ Sections of my writing flow logically, but other parts seem out of place.

❋ My ending is not original, but it does clearly show where the piece stops.

Just Starting

❋ I forgot to write a clear introduction to this piece.

❋ I have the right "stuff" to work with, but it's not in order.

❋ The order of my details are jumbled and confusing.

❋ Oops! I forgot to end my piece with a wrap-up.

Student-Friendly Scoring Guide
Voice

⑥

⑤

I've Got It!

❈ I used a distinctive tone that works with the topic.

❈ I was clear about why I was writing, so my voice is believable.

❈ The audience will connect with what I wrote.

❈ I tried some new ways of expressing myself to add interest.

④

③

On My Way

❈ I played it safe. You only get a glimpse of me in this piece.

❈ I wasn't always clear about my purpose, so my voice fades in and out.

❈ I'm only mildly interested in this topic.

❈ I didn't try to express myself in new ways.

②

①

Just Starting

❈ I didn't share anything about what I think and feel in this piece.

❈ I'm not sure what or why I'm writing.

❈ This topic is not interesting to me at all.

❈ I'm bored and it shows.

Student-Friendly Scoring Guide
Word Choice

6

5

I've Got It!

❖ I used strong verbs to add energy.

❖ My words are specific and are colorful, fresh, and snappy.

❖ My words help my reader see my ideas.

❖ My words are accurate and used correctly.

4

3

On My Way

❖ Only one or two verbs stand out in this piece.

❖ I've used many ordinary words; there's no sparkle.

❖ My words give the reader the most general picture of the idea.

❖ I've misused some words or overused others.

2

1

Just Starting

❖ I haven't used any verbs that convey energy.

❖ I've left out key words.

❖ Many of my words are repetitive or just wrong.

❖ I'm confused about how to use words as I write.

Student-Friendly Scoring Guide
Sentence Fluency

6

I've Got It!

- My sentences are well built and have varied beginnings.
- I've varied the length and structure of my sentences.
- My sentences read smoothly.
- I've tried to write using interjections or fragments to create variety.

5

4

On My Way

- My sentences are working pretty well.
- I've tried a couple of ways to begin my sentences differently, but could do more.
- When I read my piece aloud, there are a few places that need smoothing.
- I might put some sentences together or I could cut a few in two.

3

2

Just Starting

- My sentences aren't working well.
- The beginnings of my sentences sound the same.
- I'm having trouble reading my piece aloud.
- I've used words like *and* or *but* too many times.

1

Student-Friendly Scoring Guide
Conventions

6

I've Got It!

✣ My spelling is magnificent.

✣ I put capital letters in all the right places.

✣ I used punctuation correctly to make my writing easy to read.

✣ I used correct grammar and indented paragraphs where necessary.

5

4

On My Way

✣ Only my simpler words are spelled correctly.

✣ I used capital letters in easy spots.

✣ I have correct punctuation in some places but not in others.

✣ There are a few places where the grammar isn't quite right, and I've forgotten to indicate paragraphs except at the beginning.

3

2

Just Starting

✣ My words are hard to read and understand because of the spelling.

✣ I've not followed the rules for capitalization.

✣ My punctuation is missing or in the wrong places.

✣ The grammar needs a lot of work. I forgot about using paragraphs.

1

Student-Friendly Scoring Guide
Presentation

6

I've Got It!

- I've used my very best handwriting.
- My font choices are very readable.
- The margins on my paper are even and frame the writing.
- I've used a heading and numbered pages or bulleted a list or fancy capital.

5

4

On My Way

- My handwriting is readable, but it's not my best.
- I picked one main font but then added too many fancy fonts.
- I started out with even margins but they didn't end up that way.
- I put my name and date on my paper but I didn't try anything else..

3

2

Just Starting

- Yikes! I'm having a hard time reading my own handwriting.
- My fonts are distracting.
- I didn't use margins and my writing doesn't have white space.
- I forgot all about adding my name, the date, page numbers, and more.

1

Grades 3–5

Mode: Narrative
Informational / Explanatory

Purpose: To tell a story

I've Got It !

6

5

- My story has a solid plot with a conflict that is resolved. Yes!
- I have come up with several fresh and original characters.
- There is a setting I can see in my mind.
- Each event moves the story forward logically.

On My Way

4

3

- My story has a predictable plot with a conflict, but not much of a resolution.
- My characters are not very fresh or original.
- My setting is pretty ho-hum. I can do better here.
- My story moves forward predictably.

Just Starting

2

1

- My plot is thin and there is no real conflict.
- I've only come up with one ordinary character.
- Oops! I forgot to include a setting.
- My story isn't finished, and the parts don't fit together well.

Grades 3–5

Mode: Expository
Informational / Explanatory

Purpose: To report or convey information

6

I've Got It !

5

- I've covered my topic well, using specific details and facts.
- My information is both accurate and fascinating.
- I've answered questions for the reader.
- I stayed focused on my topic and developed it.

4

On My Way

3

- I gave an overview of my topic.
- My information is pretty ordinary and maybe inaccurate. I better do a fact check.
- I don't think I've answered my readers' questions.
- I tried to stay focused on my topic, but wandered here and there.

2

Just Starting

1

- I don't know much about my topic at all.
- I don't provide much information and didn't check my facts.
- My reader will wonder what I am writing about.
- Yikes! I need to rethink my topic.

Grades 3–5

Mode: Persuasive
Opinion / Argument

Purpose: To construct an argument

I've Got It !

6

5

- I offer an opinion that is my own. It's something I care about.
- I give detailed reasons and evidence—facts and personal experiences—for my opinion.
- I thought seriously about readers who might not agree with me.
- I support my opinion with credible, logical evidence and examples.

On My Way

4

3

- I offer an opinion, but I don't feel all that strongly about it.
- I give not-too-convincing reasons and evidence for my opinion.
- I give only a passing thought to readers who might not agree.
- I relied heavily on personal reasons to back up my opinion. It's a start!

Just Starting

2

1

- I don't state my opinion clearly.
- I don't give specific information, reasons, or evidence for my opinion.
- I didn't consider readers who might not agree with me.
- I need to think more about my opinion before I revise.

Traits and the Writing Process

◆ **Prewrite:** Discover what you want to say (Ideas, Organization, Voice).

◆ **Draft:** Get it down (Word Choice, Sentence Fluency).

◆ **Share/Feedback:** Find out what worked and what needs work (for one or more traits or the piece as a whole).

◆ **Revise:** Rework the text to make it clear (Ideas, Organization, Voice, Word Choice, Sentence Fluency).

◆ **Edit:** Make the text readable (Conventions: spelling, capitalization, punctuation, grammar, and paragraphing).

◆ **Finish/Publish:** Polish the final appearance (Presentation).

The Spiraled Traits

IDEAS

Finding a topic
Creating the lead
Establishing a tone
Applying strong verbs
Crafting well-built sentences
CONVENTIONS
PRESENTATION

ORGANIZATION

Focusing the topic
Using sequence words and transition words
Conveying the purpose
Selecting striking words and phrases
Varying sentence types
CONVENTIONS
PRESENTATION

VOICE

Developing the topic
Structuring the body
Creating a connection to the audience
Using specific and accurate words
Capturing smooth and rhythmic flow
CONVENTIONS
PRESENTATION

WORD CHOICE

SENTENCE FLUENCY

Using details
Ending with a sense of resolution
Taking risks to create voice
Choosing words that deepen meaning
Breaking the "rules" to create fluency
CONVENTIONS
PRESENTATION

CONVENTIONS
Checking Spelling
Punctuating Effectively & Paragraphing
Capitalizing Correctly
Applying Grammar and Usage

PRESENTATION
Applying Handwriting Skills
Using Word Processing Effectively
Making Good Use of White Space
Refining Text Features

From *The Water Princess*: Sentence Length	From My Writing Wallet: Sentence Length for one piece of writing
1. 8	
2. 3	
3. 1	
4. 6	
5. 1	
6. 10	
7. 5	
8. 1	
9. 5	

From *The Water Princess*	From My Writing Wallet	List examples of punctuation marks used to create fluency.
"Breaking" a Rule	"Breaking" a Rule	
Use a hash mark to show how many examples you spot (pages 1–6 are already filled in; start from page 7).	Try two of the following sentence fluency techniques.	
Fragments: ///		
Starting a sentence with a conjunction: /		
Sentence structure repetition: //		

Teach Writing Well by Ruth Culham. Copyright © 2018. Stenhouse Publishers.

References

Anderson, C. 2000. *How's It Going? A Practical Guide to Conferring with Student Writers*. Portsmouth, NH: Heinemann.

———. 2008. *Strategic Writing Conferences: Smart Conversations That Move Young Writers Forward, Grades 3–6*. Portsmouth, NH: Heinemann.

Benjamin, W. 2009. *One-Way Street and Other Writings*. New York: Penguin Classics.

Culham, Ruth. 2016a. *Dream Wakers: Mentor Texts That Celebrate Latino Culture*. Portland, ME: Stenhouse.

———. 2016b. *The Writing Thief: Using Mentor Texts to Teach the Craft of Writing*. Portland, ME: Stenhouse.

DiCamillo, K. 2015. Facebook post, July 14. https://www.facebook.com/KateDiCamillo/posts/1137856796230265:0.

Diederich, P. B. 1974. *Measuring Growth in English*. Urbana, IL: National Council of Teachers of English.

Fleming, C. 2016. *Giant Squid*. New York: Roaring Brook Press.

Flores-Galbis, E. 2010. *90 Miles to Havana*. New York: Roaring Brook Press.

Fox, M. 1993. *Radical Reflections: Passionate Opinions on Teaching, Learning, and Living*. San Diego, CA: Harcourt Brace.

Graham, S., K. Harris, and M. A. Hebert. 2011. *Informing Writing: The Benefits of Formative Assessment*. A Carnegie Corporation Time to Act report. Washington, DC: Alliance for Excellent Education.

Graves. D. 1994. *A Fresh Look at Writing*. Portsmouth, NH: Heinemann.

———. [N.d.] "Answering Your Questions About Teaching Writing: A Talk with Donald H. Graves." Scholastic com. http://www.scholastic.com/teachers/article/answering-your-questions-about-teaching-writing-talk-donald-h-graves.

Grimes, N. 2017. "A Garden of Words." Facebook post, April 1.

Hillocks, G., Jr. 1995. *Teaching Writing as Reflective Practice*. New York: Teachers College.

———. 2011. Commentary of "Research in Secondary English, 1912–2011: Historical Continuities and Discontinuities in the NCTE Imprint." *Research in the Teaching of English* 46 (2): 187–192.

King, S. 2010. *On Writing: A Memoir of the Craft*. New York: Simon and Schuster.

Lamott. A. 1994. *Bird by Bird*. New York: Random House.

Mathers, B. [N.d.] "Formative vs Summative." https://bryanmmathers.com/formative-vs-summative/.

Murray, D. 2013. *The Craft of Revision*. 5th ed. New York: Harcourt Brace.

National Archives. 2016. "A Date Which Will Life in Infamy: The First Typed Draft of Franklin D. Roosevelt's War Address." https://www.archives.gov/education/lessons/day-of-infamy.

National Center for Educational Statistics. 2012. *The Nation's Report Card: Writing 2011.* Washington, DC: National Center for Educational Statistics, Institute of Education Sciences, U.S. Department of Education.

National Council of Teachers of English. 2016. "Professional Knowledge for the Teaching of Writing." Position statement. http://www.ncte.org/positions/statements/teaching-writing.

National Governors Association Center for Best Practices & Council of Chief State School Officers. 2010. *Common Core State Standards for English Language Arts and Literacy in History/Social Studies, Science, and Technical Subjects.* Washington, DC: Authors.

Ransom, M., and M. Manning. 2013. "Worksheets, Worksheets, Worksheets." *Childhood Education* 89 (3): 188–190.

Scholastic Flashlight Readers. [N.d.] "Because of Winn-Dixie: See This Story Grow." Scholastic Flashlight Readers/Kate DiCamillo activity. http://teacher.scholastic.com/activities/flashlightreaders/pdfs/WinnDixie_story.pdf.

Seuss, Dr. 2013. Excerpts from *All Sorts of Sports.* Nate D. Sanders Auctions. http://natedsanders.com/blog/2013/11/rare_book_auction/.

Smith, F. 1975. *Comprehension and Learning.* New York: Harcourt.

———. 1983. *Essays into Literacy.* Portsmouth, NH: Heinemann.

Tate, M. L. 2015. *Worksheets Don't Grow Dendrites.* Thousand Oaks, CA: Corwin.

Verde, Susan. 2016. *The Water Princess.* New York: Penguin.

Index

Page numbers followed by *f* indicate figures.

www.stenhouse.com